ON WHAT WE MEAN

Arnold J. Chien

University Press of America,® Inc.
Lanham · New York · Oxford

Copyright © 2002 by
University Press of America,® Inc.
4720 Boston Way
Lanham, Maryland 20706

PO Box 317
Oxford
OX2 9RU, UK

Library of Congress Cataloging-in-Publication Data

Chien, Arnold J.
On what we mean / Arnold J. Chien
p.   cm.
1. Meaning (Philosophy) 2. Language and languages—
Philosophy. I. Title.

B840 .C47 2002
121'.68—dc21   2002032035 CIP

ISBN 0-7618-2417-0 (paperback : alk. ppr.)

CONTENTS

PREFACE

When I left the University of Massachusetts' Amherst campus in the summer of 1987, philosophy doctorate in hand, I moved south to begin a career in computer software. But I didn't think I was quite done with philosophy. I had started thinking about some issues in my dissertation and figured that it would be worth a paper or two in my spare time to work them out a bit more.

I wasn't very happy to eventually realize that a paper or two wouldn't do it. Among the difficulties of working on this book has been the isolation from academia. I'm grateful to the American Philosophical Association for its recognition of an early version of Chapter 2, encouragement that was much needed at the time and afterward. At various times I've also received commentary, advice, and other help from Barbara Partee, Ted Sider, Bruce Aune, Stephanie Lewis, Stephen Schiffer, and Mark Aronszajn, as well as several anonymous referees. I thank them all.

Excerpts from *A World of Ideas* by Bill Moyers (Betty Sue Flowers, ed.) are reprinted with kind permission from Doubleday, a division of Random House, Inc.

This book is dedicated with love and gratitude to Margaret, Sonia, and Colette.

CHAPTER 1

INTRODUCTION

I once witnessed a conversation that went something like this.

Al: Scientology is the road to total freedom.
Bo: What does that mean?
Al: Is there some word you don't understand?
Bo: Well, I don't have the concept.

The evident point of Al's sarcastic response is that "Scientology is the road to total freedom" is a perfectly good sentence of English, and hence ought to be comprehensible to a competent speaker of English such as Bo. So Bo's professed lack of understanding is dishonest.

It seems to me that the issues involved here are important and far-reaching. Let me try to identify and elaborate them in a preliminary way.

1. *What the speaker means should be distinguished from what the sentence means.*

Al's sarcasm doesn't seem to be warranted. The sentence "Scientology is the road to total freedom" is, true enough, a perfectly good sentence of English, with some meaning which is a matter of common knowledge. So insofar as anyone who knows the meaning "understands" the sentence, Bo indeed must understand. But what the sentence means must be distinguished from what the speaker means, which is not a matter of common knowledge. One who knows the meaning need not know the speaker's meaning. So there is nothing unreasonable about Bo's query, since he doesn't understand in the sense of knowing what Al means.

It might be objected that Bo doesn't ask what Al means, but what "that," i.e. the sentence, means. But note that Al is right in supposing that the sentence has a meaning, and that Bo knows perfectly well what it is. Imagine if the conversation had been:

Al: Scientology deliquesces.
Bo: What does that mean?

Here Bo presumably would be asking for the meaning. So we must conclude for the first case either that Bo is speaking loosely, and incorrectly, or that "the meaning" of a sentence can mean either its conventional meaning or what the speaker means by it. The choice depends on one's attitude toward ordinary usage. I don't want to take a stand on this; either alternative is consistent with the distinction between meaning and speaker's meaning, which is the important thing. But to avoid confusion I will stipulate that "the meaning" of a sentence will henceforth denote its meaning, not the speaker's; and "meaning," without qualification, will denote sentence or word meaning when there is no chance of confusion with speaker's meaning, and "sentence," "word," "communal," "public" or "conventional" meaning otherwise.

That "Scientology is the road to total freedom" has a meaning I take to be a consequence of the fact that it is not deviant in any way. This implies at least that all of the words are meaningful, are structured as a sentence by derivation from syntactic rules, and violate no "selection restrictions" of any words.[1] "Scientology is the road to total freedom" thus contrasts with "All mimsy were the borogroves," whose words are not all meaningful; with "hour slowly," which is not a sentence; and with "Colorless green ideas sleep furiously," which involves among other things a violation of a restriction for the verb "sleep," such that the verb can be combined without deviance only with animate subjects. The point is not that an "interpretation" can't be given to a sentence which is deviant in some respect, as it can be in metaphor. Nor is it even that the interpretation in such cases is "pragmatic" as opposed to semantic, i.e. that it is a matter of contextual inference as well as sentence meaning. Arguably "The child seems sleeping" has a meaning, the same as "The child seems to be sleeping," even though it is not well-formed.[2] If so, then it is not just well-formed structures that can be assigned meaning: that is, syntactic deviance does not entail semantic deviance. Exactly how to categorize and explain particular cases of deviance is matter for linguistic theory. But whatever the theory, there are clear cases of non-deviance: for instance, "Scientology is the road to total freedom." In such cases we may suppose that a sentence has a meaning.

While "Scientology is the road to total freedom" has a meaning, what Al means by it is another story. He might for instance mean any of:

S1: Scientology teaches how to make one's life unconditionally absent of worry.

S2: With scientology it is possible to remove all one's desires for material things.

S3: Scientology is the road to a state of enlightenment such that one may consider all possibilities for living that were previously hidden from view.

S4: Scientology enables one to overcome socially-imposed limits upon the imagination.

S5: Scientology teaches one how to think independently.

It would seem that further possibilities can be imagined indefinitely. Note the contrast with ambiguity. "John needs a table" has not indefinitely many but several possible meanings, corresponding (at least) to the several meanings of "table": furniture, chart, etc. Knowing these possibilities is simply a matter of linguistic competence, i.e. of having acquired the word. But S1-S5 seem as much to be a matter of imagination.

This is not to say that "Scientology is the road to total freedom" is not ambiguous. It is, certainly. But disambiguation is not what Bo is seeking; on the contrary, he has already disambiguated. In particular, he has already determined that "road" has the (once-metaphorical) meaning of "way" or "means" rather than "highway," and that "freedom" has roughly the generic meaning "the absence of necessity, coercion, or constraint in choice or action" rather than "political franchise" (roughly the two main categories according to *Webster's New Collegiate Dictionary*), for Bo knows enough about scientology to know that it is not a political organization but purports to deal with more spiritual matters. In asking his question he presupposes both the possible meanings of the sentence, across occasions, and the particular meaning on this occasion. So if Al were to reply by indicating some meaning of "road," "freedom," or any other word of his sentence, he would not satisfy Bo's request for a "concept."

The distinction between meaning and speaker's meaning must be refined at this point, because speaker's meaning may have to do with a particular sentence meaning on an occasion, as in "By 'John needs a table', he meant that John needs a chart." In this sense the possible meanings of an ambiguous sentence might after all be regarded as possible speaker's meanings.[3] So I must distinguish between different kinds of speaker's meaning. There are other kinds as well: for example, when one recovers from misspeaking as in "Could you lend me ten ducks...I mean, ten bucks?" (notice in this case that one does not mean "bucks" *by* "ducks"), or when one "implicates" something as in "By 'Smith has been spending a lot of time in New York lately' he meant that Smith may have a girlfriend in New York." A desideratum for an account of speaker's meaning would be to explain the variety. But for the time being, I will simply acknowledge the variety and continue to use "speaker's meaning" for the kind that I take Bo to be requesting.

2. Speaker's meaning here involves the speaker's "fixing" the content of his belief.

What kind of speaker's meaning is this? C.S. Peirce once remarked that "...honest people, when not joking, intend to make the meaning of their words determinate, so that there shall be no latitude of interpretation at all. That is to say, the character of their meaning consists in the implications and non-implications of their words; and they intend to fix what is implied and what is not implied" (Hartshorne and Weiss 1934, 300). This is close to what I have in mind, but not quite. I suggest not that the speaker fixes his implications, but that he fixes a certain propositional content, though this in turn has an effect on his implications: more generally, his inferences.[4] The sense of "fixes" here is captured by the locution "in the sense that." Given his meaning that scientology teaches how to make one's life unconditionally absent of worry, what Al believes is that scientology is the road to total freedom *in the sense that* it teaches how to make one's life unconditionally absent of worry.

This kind of speaker's meaning sheds special light on some of what is involved in understanding the speaker, as opposed to understanding what he says. To see this, let's first take the latter as closely related to the meaning of the uttered sentence (following Grice 1989, 25): in particular, assume that it is determined by the meaning of his sentence plus sufficient contextual evaluation to enable an assignment of truth or falsehood. This entails among other things that all his words be disambiguated and references determined. We can take Al as having said that scientology is the road to total freedom, provided we take the content clause as disambiguating "road" and "freedom" as previously noted.

But understanding what is said does not in itself entail any attribution to the speaker of beliefs or other mental states by which we might predict his inferences or behavior, a vital purpose of language. For example, of one who utters "Boston Beer Works closes at midnight" we might expect an inference that he may not make it to Boston Beer Works before it closes, and quick steps. Such expectations would be based partly on a certain belief we attribute to the speaker. According to the "disquotational principle" (e.g. Kripke 1979, 248-249), an utterer of "p" can be attributed the belief that p, if he is a normal speaker of the language, is sincere and serious, and "p" contains no ambiguity or indexicals (so that one who utters "I'm sick" is not attributed the belief that I, the author of this book, am sick). On the basis of this principle we would likely take one who utters "Boston Beer Works closes at midnight" to believe that Boston Beer Works closes at midnight. But not solely on the basis of understanding what he has said, since for example he may not be sincere.

We likewise would attribute to Al the belief that scientology is the road to total freedom. Or so it seems. But consider the belief's associated "inferential role." For example, inferences from

S1: Scientology teaches how to make one's life unconditionally absent of worry

and

S2: With scientology it is possible to remove all one's desires for material things

have some degree of strength.[5] As premises to the conclusion that scientology is the road to total freedom, such items might constitute Al's evidence. But now suppose Al means, in the "fixing" sense, that scientology teaches how to make one's life unconditionally absent of worry. Then we should expect a different inferential role. Centrally, the inference from S1 would have maximal strength. The inference from S2 would have little strength, less than before, since indifference to material things is not particularly an indicator for absence of worry. The difference may also show up in Al's behavior. If Al means that scientology teaches how to make one's life unconditionally absent of worry, then he may be inclined to advocate scientology to those whom he thinks suffer from stress, and not to those he considers caught up in their material possessions. In contrast, he would be about equally inclined or disinclined in both cases if his belief had the first role.

Hence if Al means, say, that scientology teaches how to make one's life absent of worry, the disquotational principle as generally understood fails. It would have us attribute to the speaker the wrong belief, as indicated by the wrong inferences and behavior. So this elemental principle by which we infer a speaker's mental states from his utterances has yet to be properly formulated. Though Al has said that scientology is the road to total freedom, and he is sincere and serious (or as Peirce puts it, "honest" and "not joking"), this is not what he believes.

Is this odd? Consider that a belief is not there for the mind's eye to read off. Saying what one believes can be hard, and one might not quite get there despite good faith. Thus by "fixing" I have not meant a conscious act; indeed it is a familiar phenomenon for a speaker to not be aware of what he means. His recourse is the same as the hearer's: dialectic, i.e. a process of indefinite extent marked by question and answer at each stage.[6] This is what Bo tries to initiate. The sentence meaning does not obviate the process, but rather enables it by making possible an "initial" understanding. That may be all there is to be had; and even if not, it may well be adequate depending on our purposes or mood. But with effort "deeper" understanding may otherwise be pursued, one which might be as much the speaker's achievement as the hearer's.

3. *Speaker's meanings are subject to constraints, knowledge of which is partly a matter of linguistic competence.*

Speakers are not free to mean whatever they want. There is such a thing as stipulation, which is unconstrained, but this is not speaker's meaning in the current sense. Listing the likes of S1-S5 is a matter of exercising imagination freely, yet within constraints: thus

S6: Birds fly south for the winter

isn't included. Knowing the constraints seems to be a matter of linguistic competence. We would expect anyone who had learned the language to recognize S1-S5 as permissible, recognize that S6 is excluded, and think of other possibilities. But since one who has learned the language also has other capabilities, such as the ability to reason, it is possible that not just competence is involved.

Though S1-S5 are propositional, intuitively they "unpack" the word "freedom." This is problematic because, with lexical meanings having been ruled out as the source of possibilities, it is yet to be determined whether there is any lexical source. But following the intuition it seems natural to at least initially posit competence at the lexical level. This is not captured by notions of competence prevalent in philosophy and linguistics. It is not knowing a word's contribution to truth-conditions (Davidson and Harman 1972, Larson and Segal 1995) or to "conceptual role" (Block 1986), or knowing a function from context to content (Kaplan 1989). Nor is it knowing a stereotype (Putnam 1975), or having inferential and referential abilities of a certain sort (Marconi 1997). All of these notions can be taken as analyzing the meaning of an expression, or an aspect of the meaning. Since "Scientology is the road to total freedom" and "freedom" have meanings, I assume that one or another of these accounts applies. I assume that knowing the meaning of "freedom" has something to do with knowing what things in the world it applies to, under what conditions, or with knowing how to make inferences with the sentences in which it occurs. But in addition, there is the ability to recognize and invent novel senses. A novel sense has associated inferences and reference, but they do not directly relate to the aspect of competence I am concerned with. It's not what you can do once you're there but your ability to get there, and anywhere else within bounds.

4. *Conceptual indeterminacy is a pervasive phenomenon, and encompasses metaphor.*

Let us provisionally understand the "conceptual indeterminacy" of a sentence to be the potential for any number of constrained speaker's meanings. "Scientology is the road to total freedom" is conceptually indeterminate in that the speaker may mean any of S1 - S5, among many other possibilities. I take this to be a pervasive phenomenon.

I am not in a position to demonstrate, because the notion is not yet precisely delineated. But I can offer a heuristic. For a candidate word, take a sentence in which it occurs and try to imagine an idiosyncratic sense thereof which is not identifiable with any dictionary meaning. Consider a speaker who means by "The state cannot absorb any more immigrants" that any further jobs in the state taken by immigrants will come at the expense of currently resident job-seekers. Then the content fixed by the speaker will be such that he will presumably infer that if more immigrants arrive, the unemployment rate among the residents will persist—and not, say, that the immigrants themselves will not find work, or that there will be any housing crunch, or that there will be a drain on public services. And upon hearing of new immigrants he might be inclined to carefully look over the "Help Wanted" section of the newspaper, though not to inquire at a local real estate office. Though the fixed content thus redounds in the speaker's psychology, it is not determined by any dictionary entry for "absorb"—though it is consistent with the entry "take in or utilize" (*The Random House Dictionary of the English Language*, unabridged).

What we are imagining here is the tip of an iceberg of possibilities: with further imagination we could conjure up such possibilities indefinitely. In everyday discourse such possibilities are realized spontaneously as circumstances dictate, in unpredictable ways. Conceptual indeterminacy has to do with the ever-present potential. Here is a preliminary list of additional words for which I would take the heuristic to succeed.

basic	frame	internal	core
emerge	pure	diffuse	win
stagnate	establish	clever	involved
level	amicable	earn	struggle
connect	extend	burden	collapse
undercurrent	direct	status	transfer
beyond	blend	advance	transition
touch	flow	entrenched	safe
curtail	depend	overwhelm	prepare
danger	summit	impede	system
elevate	timeless	civilized	isolate
navigate	expand	support	society
compatible	complete	strengthen	develop
private	solid	love	direct
subordinate	adhere	develop	shift
control	resonate	boost	essence
spirit	cleanse	commit	status

(Synonyms, antonyms, and morphologically-related forms, e.g. "stabilize," are also included.) What these words have in common is at least one "abstract" dictionary meaning, as opposed to "concrete" in the sense of "dog," "chair," "black," or "kick." Not abstract in the sense of e.g. "integer": these are empirical words, applicable directly to the world. But their referents are not direct to the senses. One can see a dog, but it is only in an extended sense of "see" that one can see freedom.

It might be thought that what was imagined above for "The state cannot absorb any more immigrants" is metaphor. But as noted, "take in or utilize" is a standard entry for "absorb," as in "The market absorbed all the automobiles we built." So any metaphor would be "dead," having entered the lexicon as a word meaning. I take this to be the disambiguation that would be presupposed in an inquiry into what a speaker means by "The state cannot absorb any more immigrants." Similarly for many of these words: an "abstract" meaning is provided by a once-metaphorical meaning now lexicalized ("solid argument," "emotional collapse," "cleansing thoughts").

But "live" metaphor is of a piece with the relevant phenomena. Consider "The new financial report is a knife," by which a speaker might mean that the report has very bad news. This is a genuine metaphorical usage. But just as in Al's non-metaphorical usage, the content fixed by the speaker is reflected in his inferences and behavior, in easy-to-imagine ways. And as before the content appears to be just one among unlimited possibilities, such as

The report gets right to the point.
The report is going to get us all fired.
The report will be used to separate marketing from sales.

A consequence of viewing metaphor as conceptual indeterminacy is that not only are "abstract" terms within my area of concern, but so are terms for "concrete" objects and events: while the literal usages of "dog," "chair," "kick," etc. are limited, their metaphorical usages are robust. This makes the phenomena of concern yet more pervasive.

Conceptual indeterminacy in the current sense, involving the above cluster of related issues, has not to my knowledge been systematically studied in philosophy or linguistics.[7] Yet the issues seem to be important. To begin with, they pertain to what Donald Davidson calls "a primary task of the philosophy of language," namely the elucidation of a certain tension in the description of language use. "To emphasize the role of intention is to acknowledge the power of innovation and creativity in the use of language; seeing [the history of the uses to which the language has been put] as dominant is to think of language as hedged by—even defined by—rules, conventions, usage" (1991, 1). I've acknowledged both perspectives in my characterization of speaker's meaning (without assuming a speaker's meaning to be any kind of intention): creative multiplicity on the one hand, constraints on the other.

But while Davidson's dichotomy is well-known, I propose to show that analysis of conceptual indeterminacy displays it in a new light. The reason is simply that not much attention has been paid specifically to abstract words (though quite a bit has been paid to metaphor). Linguistic usage and competence require distinctive analysis for these words, I think, because it is especially hard to say what is expressed by speakers and what if anything speakers share; whereas for words like "chair," "tiger" or "black," there are objective referents and shared beliefs with which to start. I take it to be precisely because of these difficulties that careful accounts of lexical competence sometimes explicitly limit their area of concern to "concrete" words.[8] So I take the need for a distinct (and largely non-competing) account to be clear, even if one disagrees with my own.

My goal in this book is to better illuminate conceptual indeterminacy. I will proceed by further analyzing each of the four main issues introduced above (more or less in order). In so doing I will offer answers to a host of questions raised by the analysis so far. What is the essence of "speaker's meaning" in the broad sense which includes disambiguation, implicature, etc.? How does it differ from other notions of speaker's meaning which have been advanced? What is the nature of speaker's meaning in the "fixing" sense? What underlies the distinction between what is said and what is believed? How can the disquotational principle be repaired? How does conceptual indeterminacy differ from other varieties of "non-specificity" such as ambiguity and ellipsis? What is the nature of constraints on speaker's meanings in the "fixing" sense? How if at all do they exist at the lexical level? How do speakers operate under them? Which constraints are relevant to competence, and are there others? How does metaphor fall under the rubric of conceptual indeterminacy? How does it resemble literal usage of abstract terms, and how does it differ?

Here is a prospectus. In the next chapter I will analyze the notion of speaker's meaning as we find it in everyday discourse. I will argue that a speaker's meaning is inherently fitted to dialectic, inasmuch as it answers a question: in particular, a question expressed by "What-do-you-mean?" (WDYM). My claim is not that a question must always be explicitly asked, but rather that whenever we specify a speaker's meaning it is to address at least tacit puzzlement, which may be represented as a question. I will present an analysis of WDYM-questions, from which an analysis of speaker's meaning falls out as an account of question answers. At issue will be the broad concept of speaker's meaning: questions may arise in response not only to conceptual indeterminacy but also to numerous other types of puzzlement. The various puzzlement types are characterized by various values of question parameters. But the question structure is held in common. I will compare the overarching concept with Grice's concept of speaker's meaning, which I will argue is distinct in virtue of its metalinguistic status. Gricean speaker's meaning is not however the same thing as Gricean implicature, which is not metalinguistic. I will accordingly propose a subsumption of implicature as a constrained answer to a distinctive WDYM-question (with a focus on relevance implicatures).

In chapter three, I will elaborate the question-answer apparatus in connection with conceptual indeterminacy. We've seen that the "fixing" sort of speaker's meaning relates to the speaker's inferences and behavior, and that therefore the content of the speaker's meaning is reflected in what is believed. In contrast, the meaning of the sentence is reflected in what is said. For proper perspective I will begin by analyzing two types of puzzlement in which the speaker's meaning has to do with what is said. Thus I will analyze disambiguation and the resolution of ellipsis in terms of WDYM-questions. Using the example of mentalistic terms, I will then analyze the kind of speaker's meaning relevant when conceptual indeterminacy motivates the question as a certain kind of reason. I term this a "conceptual reason." I will suggest reformulations of the disquotational principle, so as to take the possible presence of a conceptual reason into account. The reformulations will make out a conceptual reason as a reason, not for a belief, but for believing that a sentence is true. The presence of such a reason implies that, consistently with the speaker's sincerity, what is said is not the same as what is believed. I will address the apparent consequence that we often don't "mean what we say," and then revisit the distinctions with ambiguity and ellipsis.

Chapter four is devoted to the issue of competence. I will begin by extending Burge's view that many concepts involve a commitment to capture sample referents. I will suggest that linguistic competence in such cases has to do with knowing constraints on perceived essential properties that can be projected from samples. I argue that such "projection constraints" are what account for the common competence of speakers whose stocks of sample referents diverge. I further argue that they are operative across not only speakers' idiolects but also across a given speaker's occasions of usage, where a "usage" has to do with projecting from samples that are peculiar to the context. Accordingly I will spell out how projection constraints bear on conceptual reasons, though will also note that another constraint is needed. The chapter concludes with a discussion of psychological indeterminacy, in the sense of multiple actual meanings of a speaker, not just possible ones.

In chapter five I take up metaphor. I will first defend the common view that the content of a metaphorical usage is that of a speaker's meaning, substituting my own notion of speaker's meaning. I will then extend the account in terms of conceptual reasons and the disquotational principles proposed in Chapter 3, contrasting it with the view that metaphorical usage is a kind of speech act. I will show that the account makes it unnecessary to appeal to the problematic notion of similarity (with one significant caveat). I will then analyze the demarcation of a speaker's meaning as metaphorical. I will portray the constraints on a metaphorical speaker's meaning in terms of projection constraints, and an additional constraint having to do with norms of reasoning. Finally, I will defend the implication of my account that there is a sense in which what a metaphorically-minded speaker means must be expressible literally.

Before proceeding, it's worth repeating that I propose to analyze conceptual indeterminacy in part by analyzing phenomena distinct from it, within the general framework of WDYM-questions and answers. This is necessary for two reasons. First, if I were to simply introduce the framework and then apply it in detail only to conceptual indeterminacy, my solution could justifiably be considered *ad hoc*. The framework needs to be independently motivated, which means demonstrating in some detail how other phenomena studied in pragmatics can be analyzed as well. Second, part of the task of characterizing conceptual indeterminacy (or anything else) is to contrast it with apparently similar phenomena. So, specifically, part of the analysis of conceptual indeterminacy as a WDYM-question type is the contrast with analyses of other phenomena as different types. I hope the reader will be persuaded that these other analyses are not only necessary for my purposes but also potentially useful in their own right.

These goals do, however, pose a certain difficulty of presentation: for anyone reading the book straight from beginning to end, the main thread of the analysis might get lost. What I suggest is a two-stage reading process. For the main thread one can read Chapter 2, sections 1, 2, and 3; Chapter 3, sections 1, 3, 4, and 5; Chapter 4, sections 1 through 4; and Chapter 5, sections 1, 2, 4, and 5. All other sections can be skimmed or skipped until a later time.

CHAPTER 2

THE CONCEPT OF
SPEAKER'S MEANING

In philosophical studies of meaning, use is sometimes made of the notion of speaker's meaning. Though a speaker does not of course mean something the way a sentence means something, nonetheless the notion has been considered crucial to the analysis of sentence meaning. This stems from the work of H. P. Grice, who initiated a program in which meaning is analyzed in terms of speaker's meaning, in turn analyzed in terms of communicative intentions (Grice 1957). But Grice's influence extends beyond the efforts of "Griceans." For example, in his reconstruction of Wittgenstein's view of meaning Saul Kripke argues that attributions such as "Jones means plus by 'plus'" are not descriptive of genuine facts (Kripke 1984). What is common to the Gricean conception here is the status of speaker's meaning as *metalinguistic*. For example, "Jones means plus by 'plus'" is not uninformative even though we and Jones are all presumably speakers of English, because "by 'plus'" attributes to Jones an uninterpreted string. That the language to which the string belongs coincides with the understood metalanguage is incidental; but for the convenience of addressing an English speaking audience, Kripke could just as well have used "Kasparov means plus by 'plyuf'" or "The natives mean plus by 'rrng'," since from a metalinguistic stance the attributed utterance is just a string of noises or marks. To be centrally relevant in a theory of meaning, the concept of speaker's meaning *must* be metalinguistic. If the meaning of "plus" were presupposed simply in its attribution, adverting to speaker's meaning in the theory would be question-begging. Meaning (i.e. of sentences or words, as henceforth) is the object of study, not a given.

Whatever the value of the metalinguistic notion, it is not the one we use in ordinary discourse. The everyday notion of speaker's meaning is *intralinguistic*. It is a notion employed among peers as they try to understand each other from within a shared language. Typically we have already endowed the speaker's words with an assumed meaning when we are specifying what a speaker means. So a locution like "Jones means plus by 'plus'" would not normally be informative, since it does not surpass what we would already have gathered from the attribution to Jones of "plus." More typical is something like "By 'plus' Jones means adding after taxes," e.g. in reference to Jones's saying "You'll be making eighty thousand plus extras." Here Jones is presupposed to be using "plus" with its usual meaning. The speaker's meaning report addresses a cognitive shortcoming which could arise in the context despite the shared knowledge of meaning. In fact it could not arise without this background, because if you don't know what "plus" means to begin with, you're not going to wonder about the tax distinction. Such shortcomings are commonplace, and it is for these that speaker's meaning is specified in everyday discourse. When we are trying to understand the speaker we use all relevant knowledge at our disposal, with semantic knowledge assumed as part and parcel of ground zero.

It appears to me that the everyday notion of speaker's meaning has not been systematically analyzed by philosophers. This seems odd, given how pervasive it is in our linguistic lives. And it surely must be considered a fundamental notion of pragmatics, i.e. the study of the relation between language and its users. So for example Bach characterizes pragmatics as the study of speaker's meaning and speech acts, though "speaker's meaning" for him is the broadly Gricean concept having to do with communicative intention (1987, 4, referring to Bach and Harnish 1979). I hope to show that substituting the everyday notion yields a different and potentially useful picture of large areas of pragmatics (not directly including speech acts, for reasons to be discussed), and thus that careful attention to the notion is worth the trouble. But it should not be expected to contribute centrally to a reductionist theory of meaning as the strict Gricean notion does. By its nature it cannot, just as metalinguistic speaker's meaning cannot contribute intralinguistic explanations of the phenomena I propose to treat. My enterprise and Grice's are not competitive but complementary, a matter to which I will return at length.

I am going to approach speaker's meaning by studying a certain class of questions, those which begin "What do (does) you (he, she, I) mean" (henceforth, WDYM-questions). They arise in any number of contexts, such as the following.

> Example 1. Al and Bo are rehearsing a scene that they've rehearsed many times before; after a certain line of Bo's, Al is supposed to say: "Children are all alike." This time Bo gives his line but Al says: "Kids are all the same." Bo stops acting and demands: "What do you mean, 'Kids are all the same'?"
>
> Example 2. In the course of a conversation with Bo, Al utters gibberish. Seeing that Al has remained serious and intent, Bo asks: "What do you mean, 'Bleegh blugh'?"
>
> Example 3. Al says something that seems irrelevant to Bo. Bo, assuming that Al has not changed the subject, asks: "What do you mean?"
>
> Example 4. Al, a student of Bo's, has consistently attempted to manipulate Bo into improving his grade, extending deadlines for him, and so forth. On this occasion he walks into Bo's office and announces that he's been feeling depressed. Bo reacts with annoyance: "What do you mean?"
>
> Example 5. Al says that it's going to rain. Bo, who has heard the forecasts for snow and thinks that Al has too, says: "What do you mean, it's going to rain?"
>
> Example 6. In response to a question about John's age, Al says: "He's old." Bo, an insurance agent needing exact information for a file, says: "What do you mean, 'old'?"
>
> Example 7. Al says that John is clever. Knowing that John is clever in some ways but foolish in others, Bo presses for a precise sense: "What do you mean, 'clever'?"

As these examples illustrate, WDYM-questions can express different sorts of puzzlement that arise in everyday discourse. It will become clear that if we let the everyday be our guide, preconceived notions fall to the wayside: I have in mind not only the idea that speaker's meaning locutions report word or sentence meaning, but also that speaker's meaning must have to do with communicative intention. (In any case, I would ask the reader to hold any preconceptions in at least temporary abeyance as the analysis proceeds.) My goal, however, will not be to catalog the diversity of everyday usage. What I want to do instead is develop a way of bringing order to the diversity, by identifying the essential nature of WDYM-questions. I want to articulate a common underlying structure, which hopefully will enable not just cataloguing of cases but their understanding. (It is because of this common structure that the title of this chapter refers to "the" concept of speaker's meaning.) In this manner I will be aiming, here and in subsequent chapters, for a broad analysis of speaker's meaning covering a range of phenomena.

I will proceed as follows. First, I will review Bas van Fraassen's work on why-questions. Then I will relate van Fraassen's analysis to WDYM-questions in two stages, first considering the examples and then offering a systemic overview. I will then discuss answers to WDYM-questions, and will characterize a speaker's meaning as such an answer. In the final sections, I will contrast this notion of speaker's meaning with the Gricean notion, and apply it to Gricean implicature.

1. Van Fraassen on Why-Questions

Van Fraassen (1980) develops his analysis of why-questions as a theory of explanation, his rationale being that an explanation is an answer to a why-question. Like other questions, a why-question can be regarded as an abstract entity expressed by an interrogative form. It is distinguishable by the nature of the entity, consisting of parameters which constitute the question expressed in a given context. There are three such parameters.

First there is the topic, that which needs explanation. For example, the topic of the question expressed by "Why is this conductor warped?" is the proposition that a certain conductor is warped.

Second, there is the "contrast-class." Consider "Why did Adam eat the apple?" This can be construed in various ways:

(1) Why was it Adam who ate the apple?
(2) Why was it the apple that Adam ate?
(3) Why did Adam *eat* the apple?

These are distinguishable by their contrasts. Thus, (1) asks why it was Adam, rather than somebody else, who ate the apple. (2) might ask why Adam ate the apple rather than some other fruit in the garden. (3) might ask why Adam ate the apple rather than toss it to Eve.[1]

The third parameter is the "relevance relation":

the respect-in-which a reason is requested, which determines what shall count as a possible explanatory factor, the relation of explanatory relevance. In the [conductor] example, the request might be for events 'leading up to' the warping. That allows as relevant an account of human error, of switches being closed or moisture condensing on those switches...On the other hand, the events leading up to the warping might be well known, in which case the request is likely to be for the standing conditions that made it possible for those events to lead to this warping: the presence of a magnetic field of a certain strength, say. Finally, it might already be known, or considered immaterial exactly how the warping is produced, and the question (possibly based on a misunderstanding) may be about exactly what function this warping fulfills in the operation of the power station (142).

The relevance relation partly captures the interest-relativity of causation. Van Fraassen quotes N. R. Hanson:

There are as many causes of x as there are explanations of x. Consider how the cause of death might have been set out by a physician as a "multiple hemorrhage," by the barrister as "negligence on the part of the driver," by a carriage builder as "a defect in the brakeblock construction," by a civic planner as "the presence of tall shrubbery at that turning" (125).

He remarks: "In other words, the salient feature picked out as 'the cause' in that complex process, is salient to a given person because of his orientation, his interests, and various other peculiarities in the way he approaches or comes to know the problem—contextual factors" (125).

So a why-question can be regarded as a three-tuple $<P,X,R>$, with P the topic, X the contrast-class, and R the relevance relation. A "direct" answer to a why-question has the form:

P in contrast to (the members of) X because A,

where "because" signifies that A bears R to $<P,X>$.[2] For example,

suppose you ask why I got up at seven o-clock this morning, and I say "because I was woken up by the clatter the milkman made." In that case I have interpreted your question as asking for a sort of reason that at least includes events-leading-up-to my getting out of bed, and my word

"because" indicates that the milkman's clatter was that sort of reason...Contrast this with the case in which I construe your request as being
specifically for a motive. In that case I would have answered "No reason,
really. I could easily have stayed in bed, for I don't particularly want to do
anything today. But the milkman's clatter had woken me up, and I just got
up from force of habit I suppose." In this case, I do not say "because" for
the milkman's clatter does not belong to the relevant range of events, as
I understand your question (143-144).

A direct answer is defined as follows:

> *B* is a direct answer to question $Q = <P,X,R>$ just when there is some
> proposition *A* such that *A* bears *R* to $<P,X>$ and *B* is the proposition
> which is true just when (*P*; and the members of *X* are false; and *A*) is
> true.

A presupposition of a why-question is a proposition entailed by every
direct answer (140). So we have as presuppositions:

P1: *P* is true,
P2: the members of *X* are false, and
P3: at least one of the propositions that bear *R* to $<P,X>$ is true.

These are true if and only if there is some true direct answer. A non-direct
answer that denies a presupposition is a "corrective" answer.

2. WDYM-Questions

2.1. *Examples*

I now want to show how van Fraassen's analysis can be applied to the
WDYM-questions in our examples.

In example 1, Bo is interested in an explanation of why Al uttered a
certain sentence. In particular he wants Al's motive, or reason for doing
this. Also, he wants to know why Al uttered this sentence as opposed to the
one in the script, which Bo had expected. We can sum up by saying that
Bo's question is

Q1: <Al says "Kids are all the same," Al says "Children are all alike," p-reason>,

where this identifies the topic, contrast, and relevance relation, respectively, of Bo's question. By "p-reason," I mean practical reason, or reason for doing something, as opposed to reason for believing something.

In example 2, Bo is interested in knowing why Al uttered a certain string, and again wants a practical reason. But one of a particular sort. For even though Al has uttered gibberish, from Al's seriousness Bo infers that Al intended to communicate something by it, and he wants to know what this something is. We can put this by saying that Bo is interested in a "communicative" p-reason, i.e. something fitting the schema:

Al said "Bleegh blugh" in order to communicate that _____ .

In addition, he is interested in knowing why Al has uttered gibberish as opposed to something intelligible, i.e. the conversational norm—and not, say, as opposed to getting up to leave, or saying "Bleck blugh." Bo's question can thus be rendered as:

Q2: <Al says "Bleegh blugh," Al says something intelligible, communicative p-reason>.

Note that a different question is possible here as well. Bo might be requesting a p-reason, without presupposing that Al was trying to communicate something. For example, Bo might want to know if Al wanted to confuse him. In that case the relevance relation would be just as in the previous example.

In example 3, Bo is interested in why Al said something. Suppose the conversation is:

Bo: Smith doesn't seem to have a girlfriend these days.
Al: He wants to be a lawyer.
Bo: What do you mean, "He wants to be a lawyer"?

Here Bo wants to know, not merely why Al uttered the sentence "He wants to be a lawyer," but why Al said that Smith wants to be a lawyer. For Bo is puzzled at Al's apparent irrelevance, and this irrelevance is dependent on the meaning of Al's sentence. In contrast, Bo's puzzlement in the previous two examples is not so dependent: in example 1, the play-acting context makes the utterance of one sentence rather than a synonymous sentence puzzling, while in example 2 the uttered string has no meaning. But as in the latter example, the relevance relation is a communicative p-reason. Bo wishes to know what Al meant to communicate by saying that Smith wants to be a lawyer, hoping to thereby extract something relevant from Al's remark. For example, Al may have wanted to communicate that Smith has been too busy with his legal studies to date women. If we again take the contrast to represent the unmet expectation of a communicative norm, we have:

> Q3: <Al says that Smith wants to be a lawyer, Al says something of immediate relevance, communicative p-reason>.

Contrast this with conversational implicature, e.g. the example of Grice's from which the current one is adapted:

Bo: Smith doesn't seem to have a girlfriend these days.
Al: He's been paying a lot of visits to New York lately.

Here Bo can presumably grasp the implicature that Smith may have a girlfriend in New York, triggered by the apparent irrelevance of what Al says and assumed maxims enjoining cooperation and relevance. I regard such implicatures and others as subsumable under the framework of WDYM-questions: an implicature is an answer to a WDYM-question which a listener tacitly poses and spontaneously answers. This dovetails with van Fraassen's view that an explanation is an answer to a question, if one regards an implicature as an explanation for an apparently uncooperative utterance. The parameters of the WDYM-question are just as for example 3; the difference is in the spontaneous inferability of the answer. Note that the contrast does not represent the expectation that the maxim of relevance be observed, for Bo assumes it to be observed throughout. The unmet expectation of "immediate" relevance is rather that Al say something which is relevant as it stands, not via an inference. Though not a maxim, this is nonetheless a persistent conversational goal in that if an utterance is not immediately relevant the hearer is normally motivated to infer something which is. Thus when Bo infers that Al meant that Smith might have a girlfriend in New York, answering the tacit WDYM-question, he establishes Al's compliance with the maxim of relevance via the immediate relevance of the speaker's meaning. (For a similar account, see Dascal 1979, 156.)

The claim of subsumability is not very bold. It is not controversial that implicatures presuppose what is said, or that they involve the speaker's communicative intentions, or that they may be regarded as explanations; what I propose so far amounts to a way of organizing these observations. But important details remain to be elaborated, centrally that property of an answer which explains its spontaneous inferability. I will revisit implicature in section 5 below.

In example 4, Bo's question has the sense of "What are trying to get me to do this time?" Bo is requesting Al's motive for saying that he is depressed, assuming that this motive has something to do with getting Bo to grant some academic favor. Setting the contrast as the negation of the topic, the question may be represented

Q4: <Al says that he is feeling depressed, Al doesn't say this, (p-reason)>.

The parentheses around "p-reason" indicate that Bo is interested specifically in a p-reason of the form

Al said that he's depressed in order to get Bo to _____,

where the blank is to be filled in by some favor-granting action. Note that Bo is not requesting a communicative p-reason. Bo knows all about Al's devious ways, and thus assumes that Al's statement is not meant to communicate that he wants Bo to excuse him from the final exam, say, not even indirectly. Rather, Bo supposes that Al intended his statement to make Bo feel sorry for him, hopefully thus inclining Bo to grant a favor.

In example 5, Bo wants to know, not why Al said that it's going to rain, but why Al believes that it's going to rain; correspondingly, he wants Al's reason for his belief, i.e. an epistemic as opposed to practical reason (henceforth "e-reason"). Thus Bo might like to know that Al heard a recent weather report on the radio. Bo's surprise stems from the fact that he expected snow on the basis of evidence he thinks Al has as well, and this is captured by taking the contrast to be the proposition that Al believes it's going to snow. That is, Bo would like to know why Al thinks it's going to rain as opposed to snow.[3] Thus we have as Bo's question:

Q5: <Al believes that it's going to rain, Al believes that it's going to snow, e- reason>.

In general, the assertion of a surprising proposition can prompt a WDYM-question: "Einstein was a fool," "The U.S. won the Vietnam War," "Sylvia will not graduate." In such cases, the question requests evidence for the surprising belief. But one need not be surprised to be interested in evidence.

In example 6, Bo again wants to know the reason Al has for believing something, in particular why Al believes that John is old. Here though he wants an e-reason of a certain sort: a belief of Al's regarding John's age in years. Bo would like to know, say, that Al thinks John is old on the basis of thinking that John is fifty years old. The quotes in Bo's interrogative indicate that he is dissatisfied with the imprecision of the word "old" in particular, and this can be captured by letting the contrast be the proposition that Al believes that John is not old. Thus we have:

Q6: <Al believes that John is old, Al believes that John is not old, (e-reason)>,

where the parentheses surrounding the relevance relation indicate that Bo is interested in an e-reason of the sort described. (Later I will revise the contrast analysis.)

Example 7 is in essential respects like the scientology example considered at the outset. Bo does not wish to know the meaning of "John is clever," but rather any of such items as that John is quick-witted, that he is good at math and other technical subjects, that he is able to manipulate people, and so on. The possibilities are apparently unlimited, unlike the meanings of an ambiguous word, but are also constrained; for instance, Al may not mean that John has a big nose.

Previously I suggested only that the possible "senses" are speaker's meanings rather than meanings. I now suggest more specifically that they are e-reasons of a certain sort. That they are e-reasons at all implies a continuity with possible evidence for the proposition that John is clever: John's being quick-witted, being good at math and other technical subjects, and so on. But the sort of e-reason Bo is requesting entails that the speaker fixes the content of his belief. Consider

Al: Well, he's quick-witted. He's not too bright in other respects, but all I mean is that he's quick-witted.

Al does not indicate here that he takes John's being quick-witted as evidence for John's cleverness. Rather, for him this is apparently a necessary inference on this occasion. I will say that he has a "conceptual" e-reason. Treating the focus in Bo's interrogative as in example 6, reflecting Bo's interest in the word "clever," we have

Q7: <Al believes that John is clever, Al believes that John is not clever, conceptual e-reason>.[4]

(This analysis will be revised and elaborated in section 2.4, and in subsequent chapters.)

It might be thought that there is an alternative analysis, in which the topic is an utterance and the relevance relation a communicative p-reason. That is, perhaps Bo can be construed as requesting the sense of "clever" that Al wanted to convey by his utterance. But this might require that Bo assume Al to be irrational. In this example, there are by stipulation no contextual clues indicating what particular sense of "clever" Al has in mind, and this is a matter of common knowledge for Bo and Al. So it is also common knowledge that Al could not likely succeed in communicating any specific sense of "clever" just by saying that John is clever. If Al is rational, then, he would not have intended to do this.

The point is especially clear when the sense is complex. Imagine a philosopher beginning a lecture: "Our actions are predetermined. Let me tell you what I mean." She goes on to expound a theory of free will. This is an answer to the WDYM-question that she anticipates. But her theory is surely not what she intended to communicate by saying that our actions are predetermined; there are not even conceivable contextual clues. She knows all too well that her theory could not be conveyed this way, and in fact this is what leads her to elaborate. Since the philosopher does not intend to communicate her meaning by her utterance, the WDYM-question that she anticipates and answers does not request a communicative p-reason.

So far the argument is that a question arising in response to conceptual indeterminacy need not request a communicative p-reason. I would go further: I think it never does. Where there is potential resolution of conceptual indeterminacy, it lies in a speaker's conceptual e-reason. As we will see, this entails a certain mental state of the speaker's which constitutes the nature of his usage. It is incidental whether it's also a matter of common knowledge that the content of this state could reasonably be expected to be communicated by his utterance. So my intuition is that when this *is* a matter of common knowledge, an interest in resolution is still an interest in the content of a conceptual e-reason, not a communicative intention.

2.2. *The Topic of a WDYM-Question*

Let me now move to an overview. I will consider the topic, relevance relation, and contrasts in turn.

Topics so far have been of different sorts. These represent different stages of speech processing at which puzzlement has arisen. The rough idea is conveyed by Austin's analysis of the "locutionary" act, broken down into the "phonetic" act, "phatic" act, and "rhetic" act. These are, respectively, the act of uttering "certain noises," the act of uttering "noises of certain types, belonging to and as belonging to, a certain vocabulary, conforming to and as conforming to a certain grammar," and the act of "using those vocables with a certain more-or-less definite sense and reference" (Austin 1962, 95). I wish to say likewise that the asker of a WDYM-question has attributed to the speaker an act whose description reflects the asker's conception of the utterance as having properties characteristic of a stage of linguistic analysis.

Much of this analysis I take to derive from a grammar in the Chomskyan sense: an internalized system of rules and principles which relates sounds to meanings, constituting a user's knowledge of a language. Language users parse each other's utterances by accessing such a grammar—as well as by employing algorithms for building hypotheses, managing memory, etc.—and when successful recover an utterance's meaning as a function of its phonetic, lexical, and syntactic representations. I take parsing to be the work of a "language module" in the sense of Fodor (1983): a cognitive mechanism responsible for the fast specialized processing invoked reflexively upon speech apprehension, such that a native speaker of e.g. English cannot help but hear an utterance in English not as noise, but as structured and meaningful.

Austin's taxonomy is not however adequate for describing the possible processing stages. (He himself recognized the need for further refinement, but did not pursue it because he was interested in locutionary acts not for their own sake, but only as a foil for illocutionary acts.) First, the phatic act lumps together vocabulary and grammar, whereas a distinction should be drawn for the sake of cases where lexical but not syntactic analysis has applied (e.g. "What do you mean, 'Blue seven'?", asked of a child cryptographer). Second, Austin thought of the phonetic, phatic, and rhetic as aspects of the locutionary act, entailing ultimately successful attribution of linguistic meaning and reference. However, WDYM-questions may be asked when utterances are not interpretable in this sense. Third, a topic utterance is typically hybrid in its perceived linguistic properties, thus fitting none of Austin's categories, because it is not a sentence but a constituent thereof which is found problematic. For instance, "What do you mean, you're 'gurgly' with relief?" expresses a question arising at a stage in which interpretation has been partly but not fully achieved.

Finally, Austin's "rhetic act" encompassing meaning and reference glosses over a significant distinction. Anyone who speaks English has some sort of timeless understanding of "The bridge is out," but it takes context to construe its utterer as saying that the Key Bridge is not passable, and thus also to discern reference and truth-conditions. I wish to use "meaning" and "content," respectively, for that which is attributed in each case. This sense of "meaning" respects the notions that the grammar relates sound to meaning, and that linguistic competence, stemming from internalization of a grammar, entails knowing meanings. I will use "proposition" interchangeably with "content" for that which is determined from the meaning of an uttered sentence and the context, and which determines truth-conditions.

So the "rhetic" act crosses distinct processing stages. Note in particular that the attribution of content outstrips parsing, because it is dependent upon extralinguistic context. I will use the term "interpretation" for the attribution of meaning or some later stage (e.g. implicature, as in section 5), relying on context to make the relevant stage clear. I will use "semantic interpretation" either for the attribution of meaning, or for both meaning and content when the distinction doesn't matter.

In sum, a departure from Austin is called for. To describe the various stages at which a WDYM-question may arise, I will use ordinary locutions together with a convention on interpreting quotes. A direct discourse report in which an utterance is enclosed entirely in quotes represents a presemantic stage, where the non-semantic properties which are attributed are determined by the furthest extent to which processing *can* be taken short of semantic interpretation. So for example

Mary said "The bridge is out"

indicates processing through phonological, lexical, and syntactic stages; and

Mary said "Blue seven"

indicates only phonological and lexical. Phonological processing only is indicated by special notation; e.g.

Mary said "seez e/ neym/"

indicates an utterance resolvable as "C's a name" (programming instructor) or "Seize n' aim" (gun instructor).[5] An indirect discourse report indicates semantic interpretation, with quoted material attributed the properties as close as possible to but short of content. For instance, in

Mary said that the Key Bridge is not passable

meaning and content is attributed to "The bridge is out"; and in

Mary said that "the bridge" is not passable,

content is attributed except for "the bridge," to which meaning only is attributed. Finally, a belief report may be derived from an indirect discourse report and the assumption that the speaker is sincere and has not misspoken:

Mary believes that the Key Bridge is not passable.

Though I take my terminology here to be natural as far as it goes, it is also partly a matter of regimentation. "What is said" is a notoriously slippery notion, and can be taken for instance to include only syntactic or phonological properties, or implicature:

Okay, so Rhonda's work is not up to par. What are you saying?
I'm saying that she's fired.

This is not included in my provisional notion, since the proposition that Rhonda is fired is not the meaning or content of "Her work is not up to par." Of course, "meaning" and "content" are also slippery. Let me reiterate that my identification of meanings with assignments of an internalized grammar implies that meaning is "in the head": i.e. that it is known by competent speakers.[6]

Given this scheme, a WDYM-question can now be characterized as an expression of puzzlement arising at some stage of speech processing. The relevant stage is represented by a topic specifying direct or indirect discourse, or belief attribution.[7] Note that the stage at which puzzlement arises need not be identical to the stage to which the listener has progressed. In example 1, Bo has semantically interpreted Al's utterance, but what puzzles him is preinterpretive. In example 3, Bo has attributed to Al the belief that Smith wants to be a lawyer, but what puzzles him is Al's having said this in the course of their conversation.

A prime purpose of WDYM-questions is to request content. Sperber and Wilson (1995, 176-193) among others have proposed that determining what is said consists of disambiguation, reference assignment, and "enrichment." In all three cases, a WDYM-question might be asked upon failure. One might ask "What do you mean, he sees a 'bat'?" to resolve lexical ambiguity; "What do you mean, 'it' doesn't work?", to determine if "it" is the printer or printer cable; or "What do you mean, Susan 'will' finish the report?", wanting to know if it's meant that Susan will finish very soon. In these cases the topic is represented by an indirect discourse report, in which however there is quoted material indicating that semantic interpretation is incomplete, e.g.

Al says that "it" doesn't work.

("Enrichment" will be discussed in the next chapter.)[8]

In contrast, a WDYM-question is not a good device to address shortcomings of one's competence. In the case of word meaning, this is roughly tantamount to saying that a WDYM-question does not aptly take the place of consulting a dictionary. If one doesn't know the meaning of, say, "deliquescent," then it is more natural to ask "What does 'deliquescent' mean?" than "What do you mean by 'deliquescent'?"[9] This is not to say that a WDYM-question may not request a meaning, as in disambiguation: one might ask "What do you mean, he sees a 'bat'?", requesting a meaning of "bat." But the questioner's uncertainty does not reflect on her linguistic competence, just her inability to know which meaning pertains on this occasion. What would reflect on her competence would be not knowing the various meanings of "bat," in which case a WDYM-question would not be the best device for enlightenment.[10]

Note that in cases of uncertainty as to the proper disambiguation, it doesn't matter whether the questioner is for some reason unable to exploit contextual clues, or there are no clues; neither failing would reflect on her competence. Similarly for reference assignment. But sometimes the ability to reason properly with context does so reflect. Knowing the reference of "I" in a context does: in the case of certain indexical terms, the associated function that assigns referents given a context (the "character") corresponds to the dictionary definition, as David Kaplan (1989) has observed. Thus a WDYM-question wouldn't be an apt way to request a reference assignment to "I" (presumably by someone for whom English is a second language).[11]

In an important sense we may regard a WDYM-question as a why-question with an appropriate topic, since I am claiming that the same analysis applies to both. The question expressed by a WDYM-interrogative must be expressible also by a why-interrogative. However, there is a difference having to do with etiology: a question expressed by a WDYM-interrogative arises for someone during the process of speech perception, whereas the same question expressed by a why-interrogative need not.

To illustrate, consider example 5. The same question might have been expressed by "Why do you think it's going to rain?" But consider "I didn't say that it was going to rain" as a response to the WDYM-question. This is not a corrective answer in the sense earlier defined: it doesn't deny any presupposition of the question expressed, e.g. that Al believes that it is going to rain. Yet it still seems to be corrective in some way. It appears that Bo could not reasonably respond: "Perhaps not, but answer my question: what do you mean, it's going to rain?" That is, Bo couldn't acknowledge the answer without giving up his question. But as an answer to the why-question, it would not be corrective in any way. Bo could respond: "Perhaps not, but answer my question: why do you think it's going to rain?" (perhaps with an emphasis on "think").

I account for this difference by distinguishing between pragmatic and semantic presuppositions, following Stalnaker (1999, 47-62). Take the latter to be the presuppositions of the question expressed. The semantic presuppositions of Bo's WDYM-question are identical to those of the corresponding why-question, since the questions are the same. But whereas a semantic presupposition is a relation between propositions, a pragmatic presupposition is a propositional attitude. For a question, it is a belief without which the question doesn't arise. The utterer of a WDYM-interrogative presupposes not only what the question does, such as that the topic is true, but also beliefs formed prior to the topic during speech processing. Bo thus presupposes not only that Al believes that it's going to rain, but also that Al said "It's going to rain" and that Al said that it's going to rain. He does not presuppose the latter two when asking the correspond-ing why-question. Hence the corrective nature of "I didn't say it was going to rain" as a reply to the WDYM-question: while denying no presupposi-tion of the question, it denies a presupposition of the questioner.[12]

2.3. Relevance Relations

There are two basic types of relevance relation for WDYM-questions, p-reasons and e-reasons. The former are appropriate for questions with topics represented by direct or indirect discourse reports, the latter for questions with belief topics. Both types further subdivide; one may seek a particular sort of p-reason or e-reason, depending on one's interests in a context. A subtype can be not only contextual but idiosyncratic, as examples 4 and 6 indicate.

Whenever the relevance relation is a p-reason of some sort, the questioner assumes that the speaker had some goal which he intended his utterance to achieve. In such a case, there are thus *prima facie* grounds for saying that the request is for the intended "perlocutionary effect" of an utterance. But note that WDYM-questions cannot request the intended "illocutionary force" of an utterance, which has to do with *how* an utterance is meant, e.g. as a warning, not with what is meant (Austin 1962, 98; also 116-118 for why effects are not always perlocutionary). Perceived absence of "preparatory" or "sincerity" conditions for an illocutionary act (Searle 1969, 54-71) can however prompt a WDYM-question. For example, if you order me to shut the window, and I think you know the window is already shut, I'm likely to ask: "What do you mean, 'Shut the window'?" This is not a request for the illocutionary force, which I've already perceived, but for your intention in ordering me to do something when you know that a precondition for carrying out the order doesn't hold. Similarly, if you order me to break the window, then doubting your sincerity I might ask what you mean.

Since WDYM-questions do not request illocutionary force, they do not request the force of any speech act, direct or indirect. Suppose Al says "You could be more cooperative," indirectly requesting that Bo be more cooperative. The request is indirect because the utterance has the force of an assertion, not a request. But an explanation of the utterance in terms of the indirect force, e.g. "By saying 'You could be more cooperative' Al meant to request that Bo be more cooperative," though perfectly in order, is not an answer to a WDYM-question because what is meant—a propositional content—is not at issue.[13] Strictly speaking, how the utterance is meant is not at issue either, since it is understood as an assertion. We may however advert to how the utterance is *also* meant, or how an additional act is meant.[14] In any case, the question is not what but how.

Some indirect speech acts do involve modification of propositional content. Consider "Can you reach the salt?" as a way of requesting that the salt be (not reached but) passed. But the difference in content here is an uninteresting corollary of the difference in illocutionary force, such that one would not query after the former independently of the latter. As Searle (1979, 43-45) remarked for this sort of example, the connection between the question and the request is systematic in that the former concerns the preparatory condition of the latter; thus, querying the precondition naturally associates with making the request. Since it is a precondition of requesting that the salt be passed that the requestee be able to reach it, the "indirect content" here is not of interest independently of the indirect force. However, Lycan (1984, 170-171) has pointed out cases involving change of content with *no* change of force. "Don't let me catch you scarfing the parsnip pudding" may be used as an order to not scarf the parsnip pudding, though the apparently "direct" order is merely to not let one be caught; the difference is only in content. In such cases, it seems to me that WDYM-questions do have application. "By 'Don't let me catch you scarfing the parsnip pudding' I meant 'Don't scarf the parsnip pudding'"—in response say to the smart-aleck reply "OK, I won't let you catch me again"—is an answer to a tacit WDYM-question.[15] But in such cases, a question about the "indirect force" is not about how something is meant; arguably the term "indirect force" doesn't even apply here.

Indirect force aside, processing a speaker's utterance in general involves the attribution of both conventional meaning and force. And though neither can aptly be requested by a WDYM-question, disturbances or curiosities which arise during processing can prompt a question. For force these include apparent failure of preparatory or sincerity conditions. I have been focusing on the special case of assertions, where one such possible failure is that the speaker has evidence for what he asserts (Searle 1969, 66), as in example 5. Another is perceived lack of sincerity, as in "I wish I weren't so happy." But failure of an illocutionary precondition is not necessary for a question to arise, as examples 3, 6, and 7 illustrate. This is true also for speech acts other than assertion. Suppose Bo's father tells him to stop seeing Esther. Bo sees nothing problematic about this as an order; he is in fact seeing Esther, is able to stop seeing her, acknowledges his father's authority, supposes he is sincere, etc. But Bo's relationship with Esther has been so decorous that he cannot imagine what objection his father might have, and accordingly asks "What do you mean, 'Stop seeing Esther'?" The problem is not preparatory or sincerity conditions, but the lack of evident rationale—which, as any boot camp recruit could attest, is no part of the concept of an order.

Relative to WDYM-questions assertions are unique among speech acts in one crucial respect: namely, the sincerity condition gives rise to a possible question topic distinct from the speech act, namely a belief whose propositional content matches that of the act. Thus p-reasons can be requested for any speech act, e-reasons only for assertions.

In the case of an e-reason the near-synonymy between WDYM-questions and why-questions is especially clear. Consider this exchange from a Bill Moyers interview:

> Moyers: You said once that everyone who's concerned about the future ought to have contact with a real flesh and blood child. Why?
> Bateson: Because children are the carriers of the future. The most important thing in raising a child is not to try to put the stamp of the past on that child, but to give that child freedom to grow and explore...

Offhand it might seem that Moyers is asking Bateson why she said that everyone who's concerned about the future ought to have contact with a real flesh and blood child. If this were the case though, it would be hard to make sense of the answer, since her saying this isn't explained by children being carriers of the future. Nor could Bateson be taking Moyers to have asked for a communicative intention, because he would have to be supposing that she is irrational: that she intended to communicate that children are carriers of the future, etc., just by saying that everyone who's concerned about the future ought to have contact with a real flesh and blood child.

Bateson's answer is intelligible only as her reason for *believing* that everyone who's concerned about the future ought to have contact with a real flesh and blood child. And Moyers' question is presumably why she believes this. Thus the "Why?", as addressed to Bateson and assuming her sincerity, is "Why do you believe that everyone who's concerned about the future have contact with a child?" Moyers could have expressed the same question with "What did you mean?", where he would have presupposed that Bateson said that everyone who's concerned about the future ought to have contact with a child.

Another difference is in the possible replies: an initial "because" is permitted in the case of a why-question, as in Bateson's reply, but not in the case of a WDYM-question. A "because" can be explicit in the latter case, though in other circumstances. One is an interrogative which suggests an answer: "You mean because...?", as in "You mean because children are the hope of the future?" Another is an answer that reiterates the topic, as in:

> Moyers: You said that democratic politics is always dangerous. What do you mean?
> Bellah: Democratic politics is dangerous precisely because it leaves the decisions to the people. We have to rely on the people to have both common sense and what would have been called in the eighteenth century public virtue. And that's a big risk.

Here Moyers could have asked "Why?" and gotten the same reply; in either case, Bellah would be giving his reason for believing that democratic politics is dangerous.

"Why" is easier as a variant of "What do you mean" when an e-reason is requested than when a p-reason is requested because when "why" is juxtaposed to an uttered declarative S, the tacit default construal is "Why do you believe that S?" Since this is a default, it is not necessary to express the topic explicitly, just as with the corresponding WDYM-interrogative. But if the topic is an act, then for clarity a why-interrogative must express it explicitly. This is possible; in example 1, Bo might have asked "Why did you say 'Kids are all the same'?" But the greater effort makes this option less attractive.

Interviews such as Moyers' which are concerned with the discussion of ideas are likely settings for inquiry into e-reasons, because they have to do with beliefs and reasons for belief. Similarly for honest debate, in which the goal is to understand and discuss opposing views (as opposed to maintain a posture and make an opponent look foolish, as in political debate), or any rational discussion of opinion. WDYM-questions requesting e-reasons accompany a general presumption of rationality in such arenas, for as Bertrand Russell once remarked, rationality has to do not so much with what you believe, but how you believe it—i.e. how you get to it from your reasons.

I am claiming more generally that WDYM-questions always presume rationality: they always ask for a reason, either for a belief or for an act. This is another respect in which "Why?" is not synonymous with "What do you mean?" One can imagine contexts in which "Why do you believe that democratic politics is always dangerous?" requests not a reason but a *cause*. For instance, it might be directly answered "Because my parents drummed it into my head." Similarly, "Why did you say 'Kids are all the same'?" might in some contexts be directly answered by "Because of certain nerve impulses in my larynx." But these would not directly answer the corresponding WDYM-questions. So WDYM-questions are not synonymous with why-questions not only because of distinctive pragmatic presuppositions, but also because of a narrower range of relevance relations. It is not so much synonymy as isomorphism: that is, questions expressed by "what do you mean" and those expressed by "why" have the same *structure*. Or so I am attempting to show.

2.4. Contrasts

In general, any constituent of an uttered sentence might be found problematic by a listener. The function of a contrast often is to capture a WDYM-question's focus on a particular constituent. Thus "What do you mean, 'we' are in big trouble?" and "What do you mean, we are in 'big trouble'?" do not express identical questions. The former might be asked by someone wanting to know why the speaker thinks that they are all in trouble as opposed to just him, the latter by someone wanting to know what the big trouble is. Accordingly, what counts as a direct answer differs: for example, "If I'm found guilty, you will be considered my accomplices" answers the former but not the latter.

Sometimes a contrast corresponds to a prior expectation of the questioner. This is the case when the apprehension of the topic causes surprise, which entails the incompatibility of the topic with the expectation. Examples 1, 2, 3, and 5 are illustrative, where 2 and 3 involve the expectation of a broad communicative norm.

But contrasts do not always represent prior expectation. In examples 6 and 7 the questions are not prompted by surprise, but by a desire for greater "precision." A book I've seen has a chapter entitled "Toward a Unified Cognitive Theory of Science," in which the author has these subtitles: "Why a *theory* of science?" and "Why *cognitive* and why *unified*?" Under each he explains his usage of the three italicized words, thus answering the

three questions in turn.[16] The topic of each question is the same but the
contrasts differ, capturing the anticipated interests in different words.

Quotes in the interrogative often help us identify the contrasts, as a set
of propositions differing from the topic exactly with respect to the quoted
constituent. (I will say that the contrasts "stem from" the constituent.)
Which set? In the examples I took a simple way out, letting the contrasts
consist of a single proposition which negates the predication of the topic
proposition. But this was *ad hoc*; it suffices to note that "not" isn't always
syntactically qualified to modify a quoted expression.

We can begin a more systematic approach by considering intonational
stress. It is well-known that stress is semantically relevant, since the truth-
conditions of a sentence can vary with stress placement in an embedded
constituent. Taking an example of Rooth (1985), suppose that John
introduced Bill and Tom to Sue and did no other introductions. "John
introduced Bill to *Sue*" and "John introduced *Bill* to Sue" are both true, and
moreover have the same truth-conditions. But "John only introduced Bill
to *Sue*" is true, while "John only introduced *Bill* to Sue" is false. A
semantic theory should thus be capable of representing some component of
a constituent's meaning which is a function of stress. Then this component
would be available to an operator on the constituent, such that the semantic
effect of stress is manifest after the operation. Rooth proposes that the
stress-dependent meaning component of "John introduced Bill to *Sue*" is
the set of propositions

{John introduced Bill to y | y is an entity of the same type as Sue},

i.e. all the propositions derivable from "John introduced Bill to y" by
substituting values for y of the appropriate type (in an as-yet undefined
sense of "type"). Suppose, following Rooth further, that the meaning of
"John only introduced Bill to *Sue*" is roughly "If John has some property
of the form 'introduced Bill to y', then it is the property of introducing Bill
to Sue." For this meaning to be capable of compositional generation, the
"only" operator must have available to it the properties of the form
"introduced Bill to y," so they can be quantified over. On Rooth's proposal,
these properties are available because they are a component of the meaning
of the constituent "introduced Bill to *Sue*." Rooth calls this component the
"p-set." The possibility of a different truth value for "John only introduced
Bill to Sue" is explained by the fact that the p-set of "introduced *Bill* to

Sue" is different (in the obvious way), resulting in quantification over a different set of properties when the "only" operator is applied.[17]

Like stress, quotation serves to focus a sentence constituent. For example, in both "What do you mean, John is 'clever'?" and "John is *clever*," special attention is brought to the item "clever." This is not just an analogy: the quoted constituent in the clause following "WDYM" (what I'll call the "WDYM-clause") is pronounced with stress.[18] It is natural then to postulate a component of a WDYM-clause's meaning which is dependent on quote placement. We may hypothesize that the application of a "WDYM" operator results in the contrasts of the resulting WDYM-question being formed from the quote-dependent component. And just as the meaning of a sentence formed by an operator adjoined to a sentence constituent may differ from that of a sentence which is identical except for stress placement in the constituent, so the question expressed by an interrogative formed by "WDYM" adjoined to a clause may differ from that expressed by an interrogative which is identical except for quote placement in the clause, in virtue of different contrasts.

So far so good, but just what is the stress-dependent component of meaning? In particular, what is the required notion of "type"? It could not be a syntactic category. "Sue" is a noun phrase, but if any noun phrase could take its place—"sheet metal," "a red rocking chair," "the late morning session of intermediate calculus"—the domain of quantification for "only" and other operators would be too large. Rooth defines p-sets in terms of Montague's theory of semantic types. But the theory is based on a metaphysics which does not help. To be of the same semantic type as "Sue," an expression must refer to some element of the set of "individual entities," which includes sheet metal, the late morning session of intermediate calculus, etc.[19] Evidently, what is required is a category which entails some kind of semantic coherence. Returning to WDYM-questions, the questioner in e.g. example 7 is not asking for Al's reason for thinking that John is clever as opposed to silly, rectangular, combustible at high temperatures, etc. Intuitively, the relevant contrasts are psychological properties, related to mental acuity. They should be expressed by monolexemes like "clever," so as to rule out indefinite generation of complex properties: stupid in an ingenuous sort of way, slow to realize when a relationship is beginning to sour, etc.

It appears to me that the desired concept here is that of a "semantic field." Following the exposition of Grandy (1987, 1992), a semantic field is a set of meaningful expressions of a common syntactic category, and in virtue of their meanings both cohere to and contrast with each other. (It is because these are semantic relations that Grandy uses the term "semantic" field rather than "lexical" field.) Moreover, a semantic field constitutes a kind of linguistic knowledge: in particular, knowing the meaning of a word entails knowing the field to which it belongs. So for instance

> <day: Monday, Tuesday, Wednesday, Thursday, Friday, Saturday, Sunday>

is a semantic field, with "day" the "covering term." The field elements are coherent in that each element falls under the covering term, but are also contrasts. These relations are a matter of "common linguistic belief." For example, we would question the competence of anyone who thought that Monday was not a day, or overlapped with Tuesday, or followed Saturday. Knowing the meaning of "Monday" entails knowing the field to which it belongs, where the field is conceived of as structured by the covering term and the contrast relations (Grandy 1992, 107). Thus a semantic field has psychological reality, which Grandy argues manifests itself in a numerous ways, such as organization of memory as inferred from experimental subjects' responses to queries. When asked to name kinds of animal a subject might respond: "Lion, tiger, leopard, cheetah, panther, cougar, ocelot, lynx, ..., elephant, rhinoceros, hippopotamus ..." (where "..." indicates a pause).[20] So the existence and identity of semantic fields is an empirical matter.[21]

There are puzzling aspects of semantic field theory. Consider a field proposed by Kittay (1987, 245):

> <fishing: angling, trolling, harpooning, fishing with a net>.

I think I know what "harpooning" means, notwithstanding my ignorance of "trolling," which makes me think that this is merely a kind listing with no psycholinguistic significance. Grandy is careful to say that fields are objects of linguistic belief, not necessarily knowledge:

> ...quizzed about the relations among the meanings of "swamp," "bog," "fen," and "marsh," many people believe them to be synonyms or believe that they contrast but disclaim knowledge of the nature of the contrast...In this case as in many others, speakers have beliefs about the general field

relations among the terms without having precise or accurate knowledge of the specifics of the relations (1992, 107).

But if so, what makes these field relations, since the field is supposed to represent competence? Grandy himself regards the issue of how to define competence over a heterogeneous population vis-à-vis semantic fields as "a difficult empirical question" (1992, 105). The program is nonetheless well-motivated. From my perspective what is important is not to attempt further or different articulation, but to properly relate the program to the semantics of focus. Keeping to WDYM-questions, we may hypothesize that the contrast of example 7, say, is determined by the WDYM-interrogative's stress-dependent component of meaning, which is determined by the semantic field to which "clever" belongs. That is: a certain set of propositions is determined by substitution instances of "John is P" with P an element of the semantic field to which "clever" belongs, and the contrasts are determined by this set of propositions and the topic propositional attitude. The field presumably contains monolexemes descriptive of mental acuity: "ignorant," "brilliant," "stupid," etc.

How generally can semantic fields be adverted to here? Recalling that arbitrary WDYM-clause constituents may be quoted, two dimensions of generality should be considered: syntactic category and constituent complexity. Though most research on semantic fields has focused on nouns, verbs and adjectives (e.g. kinship terms, cooking verbs, colors), no parts of speech are ruled out—though for any category the exact makeup of the field to which a given item belongs may not be obvious. Note also that a semantic field may be cross-categorial, in the sense of derivationally related to an isomorphic set of a different syntactic category (e.g. "What do you mean, he did it 'cleverly'?"). As for constituent complexity, while words as opposed to phrases have received most attention—semantic field theory being a theory of word meaning—a phrase also may have a semantic field (Barsalou 1992). How often is open to serious question: e.g. to what field might "worn rear rotor blade that Sue has in her basement" belong? But I would speculate that for complex constituents the contrasts are usually determined by the questioner's particular interest in a context. I am not appealing to fields in these cases.[22]

Let me conclude by emphasizing this point. To repeat, the contrast of a WDYM-question is in general determined by the interests of the questioner in the context, such as those formed by prior expectation. So it can be idiosyncratic, and thus not coincident with any linguistic category, semantic field or otherwise. The questioner of example 5 happens to have heard predictions for rain, determining the contrast, but "rain" and "snow" do not constitute the semantic field, which presumably also includes "sleet," "hail," etc. Nor could the field be regarded as providing a set of candidates for the contrasts, to be narrowed by contextual interests. Contrasts may incorporate elements not in a field at all. Consider "What do you mean, Bill Cosby 'was' a funny guy?", where the contrast is the proposition that Bill Cosby is a funny guy. That is, the questioner wants to know why the speaker thinks Cosby is no longer funny. So far as I am aware, no one has proposed that a verb's semantic field consists of its various tensed forms.

Moreover, contrasts may not stem from the quoted constituent at all. In the 1984 debate of vice-presidential candidates, Geraldine Ferraro responded to a condescending remark of George Bush by saying that she was "almost" offended. One newspaper columnist opined that the modifier was peculiar, a sentiment she might have expressed by "What did Ferraro mean, 'almost' offended?" Here the contrast is not determined by any subset of items with an affinity to "almost." The columnist's concern was why Ferraro said that she was almost offended rather than, simply, offended.

Thus the semantic field does not in general determine the contrasts, either wholly or partly. What I am proposing is that it determines the contrasts only in some contexts.[23] It's not that the contrasts do not represent any questioner interests in these contexts. But the represented interests are non-specific, entailing no belief or expectation of any particular contrast. While the semantic field is then not psychologically real in the sense of relating to a contextual attitude of the questioner, it is still psychologically real in a broader sense, not peculiar to the context, if indeed semantic fields represent an aspect of linguistic competence.[24]

2.5. *WDYM-Interrogatives*

I conclude my account of WDYM-questions with a look at the interrogatives which express them.

The following is a list of the various forms that a WDYM-interrogative might take:

1. What do you mean?
2. What do you mean by that?

3. What do you mean, S?
   (e. g. What do you mean, he wants to be a lawyer?)
4. What do you mean, "S"?
5. "S" ? What do you mean?
6. What do you mean by "S"?
7. "S" ? What do you mean by that?
8. What do you mean, ... "W" ...?
   (e. g. What do you mean, John is "old"?)
9. ... "W" ...? What do you mean?
10. ... "W" ...? What do you mean by that?
11. What do you mean, "W"?
12. What do you mean by "W"?
13. "W" ? What do you mean?
14. "W" ? What do you mean by that?

It simplifies matters to take (3), (4), and (8) as primitive forms, (1) and (2) as a variant for any of these, (5), (6), and (7) as variants for (4), and (9) through (14) as variants for (8). Thus, I take a basic form of a WDYM-interrogative to consist of "what do you mean" followed by a clause, which may be unquoted, quoted, or partially quoted. This is what I'm calling the "WDYM-clause."

My tentative conclusions on the topics expressible by the three primitive forms are these: form (3) expresses a question with a believing-that topic, form (4) can express a question with either a direct or indirect discourse topic, and form (6) can express a question with either an indirect discourse or belief topic. Thus the WDYM-interrogative serves as a partial indicator of the stage of speech perception at which the question arises.

An apparent difficulty arises. Forms (4) and (6) contain quotation marks; yet I say that they may express questions with topics in which no quotation marks appear (saying-that or believing-that). How can it be that the WDYM-clause is quoted or partially quoted when the question expressed arises after semantic interpretation?

This would be a genuine difficulty if quotation marks always functioned to merely mention an expression, i.e. always merely transformed an expression into a name of the expression. But they don't always function this way. Consider:

According to *Z Magazine*, Clinton "will make no difference."

Here the quoted expression is mentioned, since the intent is to attribute the expression to *Z Magazine*. But it is also being used; otherwise the sentence would not be grammatical and would not make sense, as intuitively it does.[25] The quotes in a WDYM-interrogative are sometimes like this, as in examples 6 and 7. Sometimes the quoted expression is partly mentioned, attributed to the utterer because it is found problematic in some way, and partly used with a certain interpretation. Hence from the fact that quotes appear in a WDYM-interrogative it doesn't follow that the question expressed arises for the questioner at a presemantic stage, i.e. that the topic of the question is given by a direct discourse report, in which the quotes are mention-quotes. The converse, however, is true: for a presemantic topic, quotes must appear in the interrogative. In that case the quotes are mention-quotes.[26]

3. Answers to WDYM-Questions

I turn now to examining the variety of locutions which express answers to WDYM-questions, beginning with the examples.

Example 1:
(By saying "Females are very similar") Al meant to irritate Bo. (Parentheses indicate optionality.)
Example 2:
(By saying "Bleegh blugh") Al meant to convey that what Bo said was nonsense.
(By "Bleegh blugh") Al meant that what Bo said was nonsense.
Example 3:
(By "He wants to be a lawyer") Al meant that Smith is too busy with his legal studies to date women.
(By saying "He wants to be a lawyer") (By saying that Smith wants to be a lawyer) Al meant to communicate that Smith is too busy with his legal studies to date women.
Example 4:
(By saying "I'm depressed") (By saying that he was depressed) Al meant to get Bo to excuse him from the final exam.
Example 5:
Al heard on the radio that it was going to rain.
Example 6:
(By "old") Al meant more than sixty.

(By "John is old") Al meant that John is more than sixty.
Example 7:
(By "clever") Al meant quick-witted.
(By "John is clever") Al meant that John is quick-witted.

I would venture the following generalizations. First, a "by" adjunct is optional whenever it is possible at all. Any quotes found therein should be interpreted, i.e. as mention-quotes or hybrids, in the same way as corresponding quotes in the WDYM-interrogative. (Note also that the indexical "that" is always available to stand in for quoted material in the adjunct.) Second, "meant to," with optional "by saying" prefix, is appropriate just when it expresses a p-reason, i.e. when its content clause expresses the content of a goal in saying something. Third, "meant that" is appropriate to express a communicative p-reason or specific sort of e-reason. For reasons I don't understand, a generic e-reason can't be so expressed, as in example 5. Note that communicative p-reasons may thus be expressed by either "meant to" or "meant that," with corresponding optional adjuncts.

Essential to the thesis that a speaker's meaning is an answer to a WDYM-question is an account of the various constraints or metrics on answers which explain various intuitive properties of speaker's meanings. To begin with: whereas I intend for the thesis to pertain to *attributions* of speaker's meaning, "the" speaker's meaning in the sense of what the speaker in fact means is a *true* answer to a WDYM-question.

There are a number of other metrics that will be of concern. In the examples so far the answers are all direct, providing exactly the information requested. Hence they are all elliptical for

P in contrast to (the members of) X because A,

where the WDYM-question $<P,X,R>$ has arisen in the context, and where "because" signifies that A bears R to $<P,X>$, with P a direct or indirect discourse act or a belief, R a p-reason or e-reason, and A giving the content of a p-reason or e-reason. For example, "By 'John is clever' Al meant that John is quick-witted" is elliptical for

Al believes that John is clever, as opposed to believing that John is stupid, believing that John is ignorant, etc. because Al believes that John is quick-witted, where "because" indicates that Al's believing that John is quick-witted is his conceptual e-reason for believing that John is clever (see note 2). Since the answer can be abbreviated "Because A," A can be called the "core" of the answer (following van Fraassen); I will sometimes simply refer to it as the answer.

An answer may be corrective in either a semantic or pragmatic sense. In the semantic sense, an answer is corrective just when it denies a presupposition of the question. But as we've seen, an answer denying a presupposition of the questioner only is also corrective in an important sense. For instance, "What did Rizzutto mean, Clemens can't pitch?" might be answered "Rizzutto never said Clemens can't pitch." On one likely construal, the questioner asks for reasons Rizzutto believes that Clemens can't pitch. The respondent denies the questioner's presupposition that Rizzutto has said that Clemens can't pitch. The question therefore cannot arise, just as would be the case if a presupposition of the question were denied.

Recall that the question presuppositions are entailed by every direct answer:

P1: the topic is true,
P2: the members of the contrast class are false, and
P3: at least one proposition that bears the relevance relation to the topic is true.

But this will not do as a definition of a questioner's presupposition, denial of which is compatible with a direct answer. A questioner's presuppositions are beliefs without which the question doesn't arise: this includes not only the question presuppositions but also beliefs formed prior to the topic during speech processing.

A corrective answer may be expressed when one has misspoken. Consider

Al: The stock market sure has been bullish lately, eh?
Bo: What do you mean, "bullish"? They're selling off like crazy.
Al: Er, I mean bearish.

Here the answer to the WDYM-question denies P1, the presupposition that Al believes that the market has been bullish. Without denying that he said the market has been bullish, Al indicates that he did not express a belief.

Note that because his answer is corrective, Al cannot say "By 'bullish' I mean bearish." The "by" option entails directness.

As one might guess from the form of a direct answer, there are metrics on an answer that take the contrasts into account. Any number are possible. The simplest proposed by van Fraassen is whether the answer entails the topic and the negation of the contrasts. The metrics with which I will be concerned are most naturally introduced in the context of phenomena which the metrics explain, and are hereby deferred.

As van Fraassen stresses, a request for explanation can be rejected; so with WDYM-questions. For example, to the question of example 7 Al might respond (with annoyance) "I mean that he's clever," because he is using "clever" with no particular sense in mind. In this case rejection comes of denying question presupposition P3—here, that the speaker has a conceptual e-reason for the belief that John is clever. Note that rejection is a pragmatic notion, since the answer itself entails no such denial. Van Fraassen cites examples in the history of science where a why-question is rejected because an explanation to some phenomenon is considered outside the bounds of currently-accepted theory.[27] Rejection of a WDYM-question likewise does not entail that the rejector is unreasonable. He may be, though. For instance, a speaker might deny a request for a conceptual e-reason not because he doesn't think there is one, but because he doesn't want to undertake the effort to articulate it. This is one interpretation of the scientologist introduced at the outset.

Rejection need not be denial of a presupposition. Another possible basis for rejection is thinking that the questioner already knows the answer, as in:

Al: That cop is pretty reckless.
Bo: What do you mean, "reckless"?
Al: What do you mean, what do I mean? You saw how he sped through the light.

Al does not deny that he has a reason for the belief that the cop is reckless, nor does he deny any other presupposition; still he rejects the question. Any rejection might be expressed by "What do you mean, what do I mean?" (with greater stress on the first "mean" than the second). A full analysis of WDYM-questions prompted by questions is outside my current scope; but clearly, the question goes beyond the rejection to a request for the reason the original WDYM-question was asked.

Appreciation of rejections helps to contrast everyday speaker's meaning with notions of speaker's meaning prevalent in philosophy. Searle for instance has remarked:

> The simplest cases of meaning are those in which the speaker utters a sentence and means exactly and literally what he says...But notoriously, not all cases of meaning are this simple: in hints, insinuations, irony and metaphor—to mention a few examples—the speaker's utterance meaning and the sentence meaning come apart in various ways. One important class of such cases is that in which the speaker utters a sentence, means what he says, but also means something more. For example, a speaker may utter the sentence "I want you to do it" by way of requesting the hearer to do something. The utterance is incidentally meant as a statement, but it is also meant primarily as a request, a request made by way of making a statement (1979, 30).

But expressing the coincidence of speaker's meaning with what the words mean, as in "So-and so meant (just) what he said," is a rejection of a WDYM-question. It does not inform or explain relative to the interests represented by the question.[28] These interests do not include the meanings of words. If the question's topic is at a semantic interpretation stage or later, the meanings are presupposed; in any case they are part of the assumed background, and one cannot aptly request them with a WDYM-question (though as we've seen, in disambiguation one among multiple possible meanings may be requested). Regardless of how "simple" the case, the speaker's meaning is explanatory only when it "comes apart" from the conventional meaning.

Meanwhile indirect speech acts are not aptly described as "the speaker utters a sentence, means what he says, but also means something more." As we've seen, illocutionary force whether direct or indirect has to do with how something is meant, not with what is meant. Without being explicit, Searle indicates the distinction himself with his phrases "means *what* he says" and "meant *as* a statement" (emphasis added). But Searle's description makes no reference to "how."[29]

My criticism of Searle may seem unfair; for perhaps his notion of speaker's meaning is metalinguistic. "By 'John is clever' he meant that John is clever" would be informative if the attributed sentence "John is clever" is considered as an uninterpreted string; then the speaker's meaning would be explanatory even though it coincides with the meaning. But then I think he is mistaken on another score: the notion is not what is required for his purposes. Take the interpretation of metaphor. This is an intralinguistic task, one which does not arise for a hearer without presupposing the meaning (i.e. "literal" meaning) of the uttered sentence. For someone to wonder what a speaker means by "Juliet is the sun," he must apprehend "Juliet is the sun" as semantically interpreted; otherwise he would no more think of metaphor than he would for "Bleegh blugh." I take it that the notion of speaker's meaning actually used by interpreters of metaphor is the one that theorists of metaphor should concern themselves with. Moreover it is only in terms of the intralinguistic notion that one can express an important continuity between metaphor and "literal" discourse: namely, the potential of using words in novel senses (wherein the speaker's meaning and the meaning "come apart"). These issues will be revisited below in the discussion of the specifically Gricean metalinguistic perspective, and in subsequent chapters.

Returning to the answer forms, I discern four categories, as follows.

1. (By S) (By "S") x meant that p, where S is a sentence and p a propositional content
2. (By doing such-and-such) x meant to...
3. (By "W") x meant "E," where "W" and "E" are subsentential expressions
4. p

The latter expresses generic content not in the scope of a "meant," illustrated by example 5. Different locutions are appropriate for different sorts of answers—the "sorts" being the directness or non-directness of the answer, the sort of relevance relation expressed if direct, and the sort of non-directness if non-direct, e.g. corrective or a rejection. For convenience I henceforth will sometimes use "reply" for an answer locution, i.e. that which expresses an answer.

Type (3) is what Grice called "applied timeless meaning" (1989, 89). As Davis (1992b) discusses, its main distinguishing feature is that it entails no belief on the part of the speaker.[30] "By 'grass' he meant 'lawn-material'" implies no belief about lawn-material, only a thought about it. While it can thus express answers which resolve ambiguity, it can't express answers which resolve conceptual indeterminacy, at the level of what is believed—more on which in the next chapter.

This typology poses a certain dilemma since my subject of concern is speaker's meaning in the sense of *what* a speaker means. But it is not obvious that type (2) locutions can express what a speaker means, and type (4) locutions seem to not have the right form. On the other hand, since the locutions can all express a direct answer to a question which requests what a speaker means, there is a *prima facie* reason for thinking that all can express what a speaker means. So we have a choice. We can hold that all the locutions express what a speaker means, and explain why some of them nonetheless do not look to be capable of this, or we can hold that only locutions of type (l) express what a speaker means, and explain why nonetheless the other locutions can directly answer a question requesting what the speaker means. In the absence of further relevant intuitions, it seems that both alternatives are viable; both partly conflict and partly agree with ordinary usage. I will not choose between them, as it doesn't matter for type (1) which will be of prime concern henceforth.

My hypothesis is that a speaker's meaning is an answer to a WDYM-question. I take this to be now fleshed out by the account of questions and answers so far developed. Note that I am canceling the implicature of goodness or adequacy that comes with the term "answer." By this implicature a non-direct answer, say, is not an answer at all (as in "Objection, your honor: the witness is not answering the question"). But on my usage, answerhood and answer evaluation are separate issues, so that included as answers to WDYM-questions are speaker's meanings which are non-direct, or "bad" in some other way.

The hypothesis asserts a conceptual identity, which may not seem obvious fleshed out or not. Perhaps no one will dispute that an answer to a WDYM-question is a speaker's meaning. But the converse is less obvious. I claim that whenever in everyday discourse we specify the speaker's meaning, it is in a context where there is something puzzling about the speaker's utterance. This puzzlement is represented by a WDYM-question. The nature of the speaker's meaning depends on the nature of the question that it answers, which in turn depends on the questioner's interests in the context. Taking van Fraassen's view of explanation as an answer to a why-question, I can put it succinctly: a speaker's meaning is an explanation.[31] As with explanations generally, it's not essential for a question to have actually been asked; it may be only tacit. For example, one might volunteer: "What the doctor meant by 'dangerous indications' was..." The doctor's meaning is specified in order to dispel some puzzlement the listener is expected to have. It is a response to a tacit, anticipated question.

Given the account of WDYM-questions so far, this analysis of speaker's meaning is only a modest further step. Yet it may seem contentious in light of the Gricean theory of speaker's meaning. I turn to that next.

4. Gricean Speaker's Meaning

In his 1957 paper "Meaning," H. P. Grice initiated a new paradigm in the theory of meaning. Since then he and others have elaborated various theories under the paradigm, to a degree that makes it a little dangerous to speak of a Gricean viewpoint independently of particular theorists. But I take it that two features are essential. First, the meaning of a sentence in a language (one kind of "non-natural" meaning) is to be analyzed in terms of speakers of the language meaning something by uttering the sentence. Second, a speaker's meaning something by uttering a sentence is to be analyzed in terms of the speaker's communicative intention in uttering it. Planks A and B, as I will respectively call them, are all I need to distinguish Grice's notion from the notion of speaker's meaning I have analyzed. I emphasize "distinguish": my aim is not to refute or devalue, but to demonstrate compatibility.

The Gricean notion is

(G) By uttering x U meant that p,

with x a sentence—of English, let's say—U a speaker, and p a propositional content. The locution is to appear in the analysis of what it is for x to mean that p, and x is an uninterpreted string of noises or marks. Thus Gricean speaker's meaning is a metalinguistic notion. Instantiations of locution G are sentences of a metalanguage, in which the theory of meaning is expressed: when we specify that by uttering a sentence someone means something in the Gricean sense, the sentence is of an object language for which a meaning theory is being specified. This entails that attribution of the speaker's meaning cannot without vicious circularity presuppose the uttered sentence's meaning.[32]

In contrast, a WDYM-question represents the puzzlement felt by a listener in a speech context. It is motivated by the aims and problems of everyday discourse, and occurs as part of an interaction with a speaker whose language the listener shares. So the listener typically endows the sentence with its meaning in the language, and presupposes this meaning in asking the question. A WDYM-question is thus intralinguistic, as is an answer.

The point is not that metalinguistic notions aren't used in everyday discourse. If an uttered sentence contains a word one doesn't know or is in a language one doesn't know, then she might ask of the speaker: "What does such-and-such mean?" But this is not a WDYM-question, and an answer would not express the speaker's meaning. A WDYM-questioner can have a metalinguistic stance, in cases I will shortly discuss. But not typically, and in any case the interaction can be intralinguistic, whereas Gricean speaker's meaning is strictly metalinguistic. Note in this regard that it is typical and unproblematic for p to homophonically translate x in locution G, indicating the coincidence of metalanguage and object language. But as an answer to a WDYM-question this expresses not a direct answer but a rejection, as earlier remarked.

A manifestation of the distinction is the difference in the respective locutions. Locution G does not match any of the WDYM-answer locution types. In G, the act-expressing prefix "by uttering x" is followed by "meant that." As Bennett (1976, 15) has remarked, this is a mismatch which does not normally occur. Normally "by uttering x" (or "by saying x") is followed by "meant to" (my type 2), and normally if a "by" adjunct appears at all with "meant that," it is "by x" (type 1). The mismatch is resolved once the "meant that" in G is analyzed in terms of communicative intentions. But the very fact of the mismatch suggests that the notion being analyzed is not an everyday one, and indeed it is not.[33]

Consider also the difference in explananda. A Gricean theorist seeks to explain "the obvious fact that certain noises and marks have significance for individuals" (Avramides 1989, 7), and the related fact that individuals utter these noises and marks. Obviously a listener in a discourse context does not share this theoretical interest. Moreover, for her to have any vaguely similar explanatory stance would require that she *perceive* the utterance as mere noises. But interpretable utterances are not so perceived, and indeed from a psychological standpoint, cannot be; it is impossible for a speaker of English, for example, to hear a sentence of English the way someone who doesn't understand English does. (See Fodor 1983, 52-55; as he remarks, "We all know what Chinese and Swedish sound like—what does English sound like?") So it is only in the atypical case when the utterance is not interpretable, and moreover thought to belong to no public language, that the listener might wonder about the communicative intentions accompanying an utterance of noises (e.g. "Bleegh blugh"). An answer to the WDYM-question in such cases is akin to a Gricean speaker's meaning because there is no longer a distinction between intralinguistic and metalinguistic, there being no language. For the same reason, this sort of case is also not of central interest, from either a Gricean perspective or mine.

It may appear that I am overstepping my aim to distinguish rather than refute. I am claiming that Gricean speaker's meaning is not a notion of everyday discourse, and to be sure this is contrary to what Griceans have sometimes suggested. In his original paper Grice proposed to "elucidate the meaning of" certain speaker's meaning locutions, implying that the locutions represented antecedently given concepts. But as Yu (1979) has shown, other Griceans such as Schiffer and Bennett have vacillated on the question of whether the definition of speaker's meaning is analysis of a pre-existing notion or stipulation of a new notion. And some have clearly distinguished the Gricean notion of speaker's meaning from an everyday one.[34] Hence I am not refuting any explicit and unambiguous claim of the Gricean program. More importantly, it would not *matter* to the program even if I were. The concern is to analyze meaning in terms of speakers' communicative intentions, and relative to this concern the notion of speaker's meaning might just as well be stipulated. That is, a Gricean could regard G as just a handy abbreviation for an act accompanied by certain complex intentions, and put the main claims as follows: first, that acts of speaker's meaning in the stipulated sense occur, and second, that meaning can be analyzed in terms of such acts. Schiffer has in fact done just this (1982, 120-124).[35]

This point can be extended. By now it is a widely-held opinion that while plank B of the Gricean program has been fruitfully developed, plank A is hopeless—i.e. that there may be a true Gricean theory of communication but not of meaning (e.g. Schiffer's 1987 conversion; see also Lycan 1991). A notion of speaker's meaning based only on Plank B is still however metalinguistic. Lewis (1974a) for example, without endorsing plank A, accepts Gricean intentions as an explanation of "a sphere of human action, wherein people utter strings of vocal sounds, or inscribe strings or marks" (3). It does not matter for this more modest Gricean program any more than for the original if its notion of speaker's meaning is not an everyday one. The concern is to analyze the intentions that accompany a meaningful utterance, whether or not they are correctly termed "speaker's meaning" (a term not even used in Lewis's analysis).[36]

By "Gricean" speaker's meaning I have meant the notion that is relevant to Grice's reductionist program for meaning. It should not be supposed that this is the same notion relevant to Grice's theory of implicature, as some have[37]—i.e. that it pertains to what is meant in the sense of something calculable from what is said, on the basis of conversational maxims. Without being explicit on the matter, Grice himself indicated otherwise. In "Utterance Meaning, Sentence Meaning, and Word Meaning," he said that his reductionist program for meaning "arises out of a distinction between what the speaker has said (in a certain favored, and maybe in some degree artificial, sense of 'said') and what he has implicated (e.g. implied, indicated, suggested)...The program is directed toward an explication of the favored sense of 'say' and a clarification of its relation to the notion of conventional meaning" (1989, 118). But if Grice considered the reductionist program to relate to "conventional meaning" and what is said rather than to what is implicated, then the "mean" that Grice included in the family of verbs for which "implicate" was supposed to "do general duty" (1989, 24) presumably was not supposed to be the "mean" in locution G.[38]

But whatever Grice's attitude may have been, implicature is in fact bound up with speaker's meaning in the ordinary sense. For it is an intralinguistic phenomenon: the question is not "How are implicatures communicated by the utterance of marks or noises?", a fruitless question, but rather "How does one communicate an implicature by saying that such-and-such?" As all agree, implicatures happen in conversation between linguistic peers, and their recovery presupposes a semantic interpretation of the utterance in question. I thus propose to analyze implicatures as answers to WDYM-questions. Though this line of inquiry has not to my knowledge been pursued, it has been suggested. Concerning his example of a speaker B who responds to A's query of how C is doing in his new job with "Oh quite well I think; he likes his colleagues, and he hasn't been to prison yet," Grice (1989, 24) remarked:

> At this point, A might well inquire what B was implying, what he was suggesting, or even what he meant by saying that C had not yet been to prison. The answer might be any one of such things as that C is the sort of person likely to yield to the temptation provided by his occupation, that C's colleagues are really very unpleasant and treacherous people, and so forth. It might of course, be quite unnecessary for A to make such an inquiry of B, the answer to it being, in the context, clear in advance. It is

clear that whatever B implied, suggested, meant in this example, is distinct from what B said, which was simply that C had not been to prison yet.[39]

This is essentially how I view matters. The listener feels a certain puzzlement in the context, and this puzzlement is expressible by a WDYM-question: "What do you mean, he hasn't been to prison?" The implicature is an answer to the question. It is not essential that the question actually be asked. In fact in paradigm cases it would not be, as the implicature would be spontaneously inferred; but the implicature would still be an answer, one which happens to be "clear in advance." So we might expect to gain a helpful perspective on implicatures by exploring their status as answers and the nature of the questions to which they are answers, as I now propose to do.

5. Relevance Implicatures and Speaker's Meaning

I begin with a caveat: not all implicatures come under the rubric of WDYM-questions and answers. First of all, I am not concerned with so-called "conventional" implicatures, i.e. lexically-associated suppositions which are not part of truth-conditions. For instance, "Even Bill came" suggests that it wasn't to be expected that Bill would come; if this is false, then if Bill came "Even Bill came" is not false but deviant in some way. This "lexical presumption" is not calculated via conversational maxims, but is rather conventionally associated with "even." Similar phenomena obtain for a wide range of words.[40] This is not a matter of speaker's meaning. One could not construe "What do you mean, 'Even' Bill came?" as a request answerable by "It wasn't to be expected that Bill would come." The reason is precisely that this is a conventional supposition (arguably even a requirement for syntactic well-formedness—see Lakoff 1972). Since any competent speaker would already be aware of it, this is a natural extension of the impropriety of WDYM-questions for requesting items of competence. A WDYM-question can arise if the questioner disputes the supposition that Bill could not have been expected to come ("What do you mean, 'even' Bill?—He was looking forward to it for weeks"). But the request is for the speaker's justification for believing that even Bill came, as opposed to believing that Bill came—i.e. it is not for the supposition but its justification.[41]

Also excluded are implicatures whose content is a propositional attitude asserted or denied of the speaker. The reply "Somewhere in the south of

France" to a question where so-and-so lives has the implicature that the speaker does not know more precisely where so-and-so lives. This is not an answer to a WDYM-question. To be sure, "What do you mean, 'somewhere' in the south of France?" is imaginable on the part of one who wants a more exact location (say, on the witness stand during hostile cross-examination). This requests the speaker's reason for believing that so-and-so lives somewhere in the south of France, with analysis of the reason similar to example 6. But the implicature is not a direct answer to this question, and in fact the question's presupposition that the speaker has more precise information negates the assumption that the speaker is being cooperative—an assumption that is required to calculate the implicature.

A speaker's meaning can be an intention to communicate a propositional attitude, but the speaker must have asserted an attitude. For instance, "You say you 'believe' that help is coming; you mean that you don't know for sure?" requests verification of a kind of "clausal implicature" (Gazdar 1979): namely, the negation of a stronger attitude than what was asserted. But otherwise when there is an intention to communicate a propositional attitude or negation thereof, the attitude may be implicated but not meant.[42]

I also exclude the large and well-studied category of "generalized conversational" implicatures. These are implicatures which in contrast to others that are carried in virtue of special features of context, are instead carried unless special context intervenes (Grice 1989, 37). While these do involve speaker's meaning, I will not in this work be considering them as implicatures but rather as part of what is said, in the next chapter.

There are a number of remaining implicature types that I believe are amenable to analysis in terms of WDYM-questions. But here I will confine attention to relevance implicatures. I'll now develop the idea that these are answers to tacit WDYM-questions, beginning with the consideration of question parameters.

Grice thought implicatures to be based on what is said, which he took as "closely related" to the "conventional meaning" of the uttered words but dependent also on context. Identification of what one who utters "He is in the grip of a vice" has said requires competence in English, as well as contextual determination of a time reference, reference assignment to "he," and disambiguation of "grip" and "vice" (Grice 1989, 25). For the most part Grice's is the same as my provisional sense of "what is said" as attributed in a stage of speech processing. An important exception is Grice's requirement that saying that *p* entails meaning that *p* (1989, 87). For metaphor and other cases where it seems that what the speaker says and what he means differ, Grice is then led to posit "making as if to say" rather than saying-that (for discussion see Bach 1994, 143-144). But for me, saying that *p* does not entail meaning that *p*. We'll see that for metaphor, and conceptual indeterminacy generally, the speaker can say that *p* and not mean that *p*; we'll also see that this is not problematic.

In any case, for implicatures generated from apparent irrelevance, as in

Al: Smith doesn't seem to have a girlfriend these days.
Bo: He's been spending a lot of time in New York lately.

the question topic is a saying-that. The judgment of apparent irrelevance requires semantic interpretation and contextual resolution as reflected in the report

Bo says that Smith has been spending a lot of time in New York lately.

This is what needs to be explained.

Turning to the question contrast, consider first an example of Grice's for the maxims of "manner." An utterance of "Miss X produced a series of sounds that corresponded closely with the score of 'Home Sweet Home'" generates an implicature via its violation of the maxim "Be succinct," which refers not to what is said but to the syntactic form representing what Grice describes as "how what is said is to be said" (27). Parsing has progressed further than syntax, for consider Grice's paraphrase of the question that arises: "Why has the speaker selected that rigmarole in place of the concise and nearly synonymous 'sang'?" The judgment of near synonymy entails an assignment of meaning. But the question topic is the earlier stage at which the "rigmarole" is detectable: the speaker's saying "Miss X produced a series of sounds that corresponded closely with the score of 'Home Sweet Home'."

More to the current point, Grice's paraphrase of the WDYM-question explicitly indicates a contrast, namely the speaker's saying "Miss X sang 'Home Sweet Home'." This is not a prior expectation of the hearer's. In general, we expect not specific utterances but adherence to conversational maxims. For relevance implicatures I propose to take as the contrast the related expectation that the speaker say something which is in immediate accordance with the maxim of relevance. By "immediate" accordance, I mean the accordance of what is said as it stands, not via an implicature. In the girlfriend example Bo's utterance runs afoul of this expectation (as in example 3), since it is not about Smith's love life. This is what gives rise to the WDYM-question. Accordingly, what is desired in an answer is something which is immediately relevant. (For a similar formulation, see Dascal 1979, 156, 167, who uses the term "semantic" relevance as I use "immediate" relevance.)

I account for this desideratum in terms of the question's third parameter, the relevance relation (henceforth in this section R, to avoid confusion): a communicative p-reason, virtually as a point of definition. According to Grice, a speaker implicates that q by saying that p only if he believes that the hearer is able "to work out, or grasp intuitively" that the supposition that the speaker believes that q is required if the speaker can be assumed to be following the "Cooperative Principle" (31). The intention to communicate that q involves some expectation of how it is to be communicated: via the hearer's semantic interpretation of the speaker's utterance, apprehension of context, and assumption that the speaker is observing conversational maxims.[43]

We've seen that R can be narrowed by a contextual constraint, as in examples 4 and 6. I now suggest that for cases of apparent irrelevance, the communicative intention as a component of the WDYM-question comes with the constraint that q be immediately relevant. The questioner's interest is in an intention whose content meets this condition. Thus the naturalness of "By 'He has been spending a lot of time in New York lately' he meant that Smith may have a girlfriend in New York" is due to its expressing a communicative intention whose content is immediately relevant. In contrast, "By 'He has been spending a lot of time in New York lately' he meant that Smith likes New York" does not express a direct answer because it doesn't satisfy R.

Turning now to answers, what we need is a metric which explains the "calculability" of a relevance implicature: what would make an answer "clear in advance," as Grice put it. Some would argue that the metric doesn't exist, or at least has not yet been formulated. But I will discuss an attempt, that of Dan Sperber and Deirdre Wilson, whose "relevance theory" has spawned a large interdisciplinary research program. (Unless otherwise indicated, page references will be to Sperber and Wilson 1995.) Actually their theory purports to cover the full range of implicature and more, such as contextually-determined components of what is said. Here I will focus on the application to relevance implicatures.

I will be developing no commitment to relevance theory. My concern throughout is centrally with what it is for a speaker to mean something, which does not require a decision among competing views of how it is recovered—be it in implicature, disambiguation, metaphorical interpretation, or any other interpretive task. My interest in relevance theory stems from the chance to formulate the missing metric (which, let me admit, I haven't a clue how to formulate otherwise). But as it turns out, certain benefits to relevance theory itself accrue from its consideration in conjunction with WDYM-questions. Or so I will attempt to show, after briefly introducing the theory.

It is widely recognized that Grice did not propose a plausible psychological mechanism for implicature recovery. Nor is such a mechanism in sight. What Sperber and Wilson propose is an account not of the mechanism but of the constraints met by recovered implicatures (Wilson and Sperber 1986, 46-53). They suggest that a hearer's interpretation of an utterance complies with the assumption that the speaker has attempted to be as relevant as possible. Their "principle of relevance" (henceforth PR) is that every act of "ostensive-inferential communication," which includes verbal communication, conveys the presumption of its own "optimal relevance." This presumption is twofold. In the case of verbal communication, it is presumed that the content which the speaker intends to communicate is relevant enough to be worth the listener's while; and that the utterance is the most relevant one that the speaker could have used to communicate this content (158).

How are determinations made of "relevant enough" and "most relevant"? Sperber and Wilson propose a notion of relevance having to do with processing efficiency. Specifically, the degree of a proposition's relevance in a context is dependent on its "contextual implications" (as well as other "contextual effects" which for simplicity I will ignore) and on the processing effort required to derive these implications. Other things being equal, relevance is greater the more numerous the contextual implications; and other things being equal, relevance is greater the smaller the processing effort.

Consider first "contextual implications." The contextual implications of a proposition are those logical implications of the conjunction of the proposition and the context which are not implications of the proposition alone or the context alone. Take:

Peter: Does Susan drink whisky?
Mary: She doesn't drink alcohol.

Taking the context to consist of

Whisky is alcoholic,

a contextual implication of Mary's reply is

Susan doesn't drink whisky.

This follows from the reply together with the context, but not from either alone. Of course not all logical implications are eligible. Given any proposition P and any context C, an implication of $P\&C$ which is not an implication of either conjunct alone is $P\&C$. But this should not count toward the relevance of any proposition in any context, nor should any number of derivable implications: $(P\&C)\lor Q, C\&(\sim Q\rightarrow(\sim\sim P\&P))$, etc. To avoid trivial implications, Sperber and Wilson propose to restrict the allowable derivation rules to elimination rules such as *modus ponens*. Given a proposition and a context, it then also makes sense to speak of the number of contextual implications, these being finite if the context is finite.[44]

Turning now to processing effort as it figures in the proposed measure of relevance, note first that in Sperber and Wilson's scheme the context relative to which a proposition's contextual implications are derived is not a given, but rather constructed by the hearer. Assume there is an "initial" context consisting of immediately prior propositions in the discourse, and their contextual implications. The initial context may be insufficient for deriving contextual implications from an uttered proposition, in which case the context needs to be extended. For instance, to derive contextual implications from Mary's reply Peter must first add that whisky is alcoholic. This relates to processing effort. Following a paradigm in cognitive science, assume that information in memory is organized like an encyclopedia, indexed by concept. Assume also that information in a concept's encyclopedia entry is most easily accessed when that concept is contained in a proposition current in the discourse. Then the extensions to context which are easiest in terms of processing effort are those relying on information associated with concepts already used in the discourse. That whisky is alcoholic requires minimal effort because it relies on information associated with alcohol, a concept Mary has just used.

So the degree of relevance of an utterance is determined by a qualitative balancing act, between drawing as many contextual implications as possible and spending the least effort in the process. Sperber and Wilson argue that the PR, with the required notion of relevance so understood, explains successful communication. For the hearer, the task is to "construct possible interpretive hypothesis about [what the speaker intended to convey]" (165). The criterion for the best hypothesis is consistency with the PR, which means that the speaker could rationally expect it to be optimally relevant to the hearer. Again, this entails two things. The first is that the content that the speaker intends to communicate is relevant enough to be worth the hearer's while, where the degree of relevance is determined by how well the balancing act is done. The second is that the utterance is the most relevant one that the speaker could have used to communicate this content. That is, the processing of the utterance must compare favorably with the processing that would have been in involved in counterfactual utterances. For instance, instead of replying that Susan doesn't drink alcohol, why didn't Mary just say that she doesn't drink whisky, which would have been direct? The effort of the contextual extension "Whisky is alcoholic" would also have been saved. But there would also have been fewer implications; lacking would have been implications that are possible for the actual utterance, such as

Mary disapproves of drunkenness.

For Mary's utterance to be maximally relevant, such implications must be somehow worth it—say, if Peter is wondering whether to invite Susan to his wild party (Wilson and Sperber 1986, 58-60). So the actual balancing act must compare favorably with the counterfactual balancing act. This measure is also qualitative: a qualitative comparison of two qualitative measures.[45]

This has been a quick introduction to an extremely complex account, one which furthermore is difficult to lay out independently of much criticism on almost every score; the reader is referred to aforementioned sources for further details. What I hope to have achieved so far is at least sufficient clarity to lodge what I believe is a new criticism. I then want to answer the criticism in a way which I think is amicable to Sperber and Wilson while also forming the basis for handling certain previous criticisms.

Here is the new criticism. When Sperber and Wilson discuss how the PR explains communication, on the hearer's side they refer to a "hypothesis," or to an "interpretation" or "interpretive task" (e.g. 163-170). Note that their perspective on this is intralinguistic, as is appropriate for implicature. Thus they try to explain how Mary by uttering "Smith has been spending a lot of time in New York" communicates, not that Smith has been spending a lot of time in New York, but that Smith might have a girlfriend in New York. Sperber and Wilson in fact emphasize this, in different terms. For them, verbal communication has two aspects: "decoding" and "inference." The first is linguistic and on the hearer's side has to do with a reflexive parser that assigns meanings. But this "is not so much a part of the comprehension process as something that precedes the real work of understanding" (175-177). It's the "inference" aspect that the PR is intended to explain.[46]

At the same time, they attempt to explain *all* "ostensive-inferential communication," including verbal communication (162). Consider then a case where an utterance is immediately relevant:

Peter: Does Susan drink whisky?
Mary: No.

Applying the PR here would have Peter computing relevance measures by way of evaluating a hypothesis of what Mary intended to communicate. But this seems odd, because it seems that Peter has no need of any hypothesis. After decoding "No," there is no longer any interpretive task because the utterance is in order as it stands, at least with regard to relevance. So the PR should not even be brought to bear. One might discuss contextual implications, processing effort and what not, but not by way of explaining any interpretation. The point is that, in the relevant sense of "interpretation," *not every utterance requires interpretation.*

In Grice's framework, this could be put simply: no task of implicature recovery arises if there is no violation of any conversational maxim. But in Sperber and Wilson's, there are no maxims. They claim that the PR subsumes them: all implicatures are to be explained by the one principle, not a variety of maxims.[47] Moreover, whereas maxims are norms, the PR is "a generalization about ostensive-inferential communication. Communicators and audience need no more know the principle of relevance to communicate than they need to know the principles of genetics to reproduce. Communicators do not 'follow' the principle of relevance; and they could not violate it even if they wanted to. The principle of relevance applies without exception" (162). So it isn't just that it's unclear how

Sperber and Wilson would demarcate the area of non-application, it seems they deny there is any such area.

But I think this is a mistake. The proper response to our simple difficulty is to limit the PR's domain, which I think helps clarify Sperber and Wilson's program. I propose to formulate the limit in terms of WDYM-questions. Consider:

Peter: Does Susan drink whisky?
Mary: No.
Peter: What do you mean?

It's possible to imagine a motivation for the WDYM-question: perhaps Peter believed that Susan does drink whisky, and was asking only as a formality. But it's impossible to imagine the question expressing puzzlement about the relevance of Mary's utterance. That question doesn't arise here, even tacitly. Sperber and Wilson should be restricting their explanation of verbal communication to those instances when a WDYM-question arises in response to an unmet expectation of immediate relevance.

I can put it in a nutshell. The PR entails that a hearer evaluates a hypothesis. But a hearer forms a hypothesis in response to puzzlement, which is represented by a perhaps tacit WDYM-question. No puzzlement, no hypothesis; no hypothesis, no explanation of communication by the PR.

Following this path serves not only to identify what is outside the PR's explanatory domain, but also to shed more light on what is inside. The interpretive task is now defined by a WDYM-question, and a hypothesis is an answer to the question. Consistency with the PR is a metric on an answer. The story goes almost as before, with the question topic as the utterance whose relevance is to be optimized and the contrast as the counterfactual whose relevance must be lower than that of the topic. Consider again

Peter: Does Susan drink whisky?
Mary: She doesn't drink alcohol.

For Peter there is a tacit question,

<Mary says that Susan doesn't drink alcohol, Mary says something immediately relevant, (communicative p-reason)>

(where the parentheses indicate that the content of the communicative p-reason is required to be immediately relevant), to which we suppose he entertains the answer:

Mary intended to communicate that Susan doesn't drink whisky.

This is the best answer in virtue of its consistency with the PR, entailing that the effort Peter would spend drawing the contextual implication that Susan doesn't drink whisky, after adding to the context the premise that whisky is alcoholic, is worthwhile; and that this balance between effort and implications compares favorably with the corresponding balance for the counterfactual utterance that Susan doesn't drink whisky.

An apparent problem is that the counterfactual is not the contrast. So it seems the contrast doesn't figure in the metric—and in fact couldn't, because whereas processing efficiency is measured of an utterance, the contrast is not a specific utterance. However, the problem is only apparent. As the metric in question is applied to a WDYM-answer, it is a function of the answer: the answer as well as the question parameters figure in the metric. Thus we may take the comparison of processing efficiencies as that between the question topic and contrast, *given* the assumption of the answer under consideration. We compare how the relevance of Mary's saying that Susan doesn't drink alcohol compares with that of Mary's saying something immediately relevant, on the assumption she meant that Susan doesn't drink whisky. On that assumption, the appropriate immediately relevant counterfactual is her saying that Susan doesn't drink whisky.[48]

Another problem appears with respect to R. Up to now, I have not made explicit Sperber and Wilson's conception of what the speaker intends to communicate under the PR. The first part of the "presumption of optimal relevance" is the presumption that "the set of assumptions I that the communicator intends to make manifest to the addressee is relevant enough to make it worth the addressee's while to process the ostensive stimulus" (158). I includes among other things all implicated premises and all implicated conclusions. So in the whisky example, it includes both

Whisky is alcoholic

and

Susan doesn't drink whisky.

It is only the latter that we would regard as the speaker's meaning; note the oddness of "By 'Susan doesn't drink alcohol', Mary meant that whisky is alcoholic." On my account, it is distinguished in virtue of satisfying R: that is, the latter but not the former might be the content of a communicative p-reason required to provide immediate relevance. So it might appear that taking consistency with the PR as a metric on WDYM-answers is not after all consistent with Sperber and Wilson's framework.

Again, though, the problem is only apparent. The metric is indeed consistency with the PR. But this does not preclude other metrics. In particular, I have already tacitly assumed that the best answer is direct, which entails that R is satisfied. We can say that the best answer is both direct and consistent with the PR. The latter picks out the set I, as Sperber and Wilson would have it, the former the particular element of I which is immediately relevant.

I think that their framework benefits by making this clear. Some critics have pointed out that Sperber and Wilson's notion diverges from the ordinary notion of relevance by not relativizing to agents' interests: even granted that theirs is supposed to be a distinct, scientific notion, this aspect of the ordinary notion wants explaining. Sperber and Wilson have responded that there's no reason the PR can't be further developed to explain this.[49] But I think a better response would be to concede that some interests are not in the PR's domain.

Thus consider again the New York girlfriend example. Peter happens to have an interest in Smith's romantic life. This is what determines that the implicature that Smith may have a girlfriend in New York is immediately relevant. We explain its communication by specifying the WDYM-question and identifying the implicature as an answer which is (1) direct and (2) consistent with the PR. What Sperber and Wilson should say is that (2) constitutes the PR's contribution to the explanation of verbal communication in implicature. (1) entails satisfaction of R, which entails immediate relevance, which reflects Peter's interest in this context. The PR doesn't and isn't supposed to explain this aspect of communication. In this respect, the PR is partly concerned with the speaker's meaning, and partly not.

At this point we can let R revert to "relevance relation," recall that the "relevance" part has to do with the contextual interests of the questioner, and note that these are outside the domain of the PR. Note also that Sperber and Wilson have their own analysis of the communicative p-reason (60-64). Considered as a relevance relation in the appropriate WDYM-question, it bears the constraint of immediate relevance. But this constraint isn't and shouldn't be any part of Sperber and Wilson's analysis of communicative intention. That analysis is part of their explanation of verbal communication, which I suggest doesn't include the interest-relative part.

So my overall recommendation is this. The PR isn't supposed to explain verbal communication when no WDYM-question arises. When one does arise, in response to a failed expectation of immediate relevance, the PR explains the recovery of a set of assumptions intended to be communicated, but isn't supposed to explain what gets selected from the set.[50]

At least, this is a story for the spontaneously-inferable relevance implicatures, which are fully "calculable." But implicatures are generally thought to come in degrees of strength, which Sperber and Wilson account for in terms of the degree of what they call the "mutual manifestness" of one component of the speaker's communicative intention; on the hearer's side, there are degrees of confidence in the correctness of a hypothesis.[51] Following Grice they take metaphor, for example, to be a kind of weak implicature (231-236). They remark of "Robert is a bulldozer" that

> relevance...will be established by finding a range of contextual effects [i.e. modifications] which can be retained as weak or strong implicatures. Here there is no single strong implicature that automatically comes to mind, but rather a slightly weaker, less determinate range having to do with Robert's persistence, obstinacy, insensitivity and refusal to be deflected... In general, the wider the range of potential implicatures and the greater the hearer's responsibility for constructing them, the more poetic the effect, the more creative the metaphor (236).

But they do not explain why metaphor should be regarded as an implicature at all; they just try to characterize the kind of implicature it is, assuming that it is one.

This is a natural attitude, if metaphor is taken to be a matter of speaker's meaning, and speaker's meaning is taken to be a communicative intention. But as we've seen, the speaker's meaning may not have to do with communicative intention, or even practical reasoning at all. No oddness attaches to a speaker's meaning report even when it is quite unlikely as a hearer's hypothesis and as something the speaker might have intended to communicate, e.g. "By 'Robert is a bulldozer' she meant that Robert always has to clear off his desk completely before starting to work." Perhaps in metaphor, and conceptual indeterminacy generally, what the speaker means has to do in general not with communicative intention but reasons for belief. For instance, "By 'Robert is a bulldozer' she meant that Robert always has to clear off his desk completely before starting to work" might signify that she believes that Robert is a bulldozer, metaphorically speaking, on the basis of his desk-clearing habit. This need not also be what she intended to communicate by saying "Robert is a bulldozer." Such an intention might well be irrational since success isn't likely without special clues. The more "creative" the metaphor, in Sperber and Wilson's terms, the more irrational the putative intention would be. Then the intention might not exist, in which case we would have not a weak implicature but rather no implicature at all.[52]

I will return to metaphor at length in chapter 5. For now let's conclude with a reflection on the common assumption that communication is the basic purpose of language.[53] One might take it to support a weak implicature analysis: for even if communication with metaphor or other device is often not successful, the reasoning might go, the speaker still must have had some communicative intent. Otherwise why speak at all? But communicative intent broadly speaking is compatible with, say, a speaker not intending to communicate by uttering "Robert is a bulldozer" that Robert always has to clear off his desk before working. He may have intended to communicate some other content, based on such principles as exist for metaphorical interpretation, that he considers "close enough" for current purposes. Or he may intend to do better, by means of *further* utterances, perhaps as part of an interactive exchange marked by explicit WDYM-questions. Communication is sometimes dialectical. On the hearer's side, when no good explanation is available of a puzzling utterance he may decide not to bang his head against its confines, but to get the speaker to keep talking. It would be no embarrassment to Sperber and Wilson, or to any theory of how hearers do the best they can given the current state of a discourse, if this mode of interpretation is not also accounted for. But then better to recognize this than to artificially extend the theory.

CHAPTER 3

WHAT IS SAID VERSUS WHAT IS BELIEVED

I've proposed a framework for the analysis of speaker's meaning, construed as an answer to a WDYM-question. In this chapter I will narrow my focus to the kind of speaker's meaning which I've called a "conceptual e-reason" (henceforth, "conceptual reason").

I will begin by analyzing lexical ambiguity and ellipsis in terms of WDYM-questions. What these phenomena have in common, I will suggest, is that resolution transpires at the level of what is said. They are thus a useful contrast for conceptual indeterminacy and its resolution at the level of what is believed. In section 3, I will further motivate the notion of a conceptual reason, continuing with the example of mentalistic terms. Section 4 is the heart of the chapter. I will first show that there is a problem with the analysis so far, and that the solution requires recasting a conceptual reason as a reason for believing that a sentence is true. I will then propose a reformulation of the "disquotational principle" by which beliefs are attributed to speakers on the basis of their sincere utterances, so as to take into account a conceptual reason in the revised sense. It will turn out that the principle licenses the attribution of a belief which is not what has been said, despite the speaker's sincerity. I will address the apparent consequence that he does not "mean what he says." I will conclude, in sections 5 and 6, by revisiting ambiguity and ellipsis to further sharpen the contrasts with conceptual indeterminacy.

1. Ambiguity and Speaker's Meaning

One plank of the Gricean program for meaning is dedicated to the proposition that linguistic activity can be fruitfully explored via its conception as a species of human action. The strategy is to bring the framework of commonsense psychology to bear in the explanation of linguistic acts. The theory of speaker's meaning developed so far follows this tradition. When the topic of a WDYM-question is a speaker's saying something, the sort of explanation that an answer is supposed to provide is a reason for the speaker's act, just as a reason might explain any behavior. So far I've illustrated a number of cases, and now will extend the strategy to ambiguity.

As we've seen, Austin observed that an utterance can be described in multiple ways corresponding to different levels of linguistic analysis. Though I have not adopted quite his taxonomy, one can take the same view of the possible question topics I have posited corresponding to parsing stages up through what is said. Doing so enables a common explanatory mode, whereby an explanation of behavior is achieved by redescribing the behavior so as to make explicit a reason. For instance, an event described as the raising of an arm may be explained by redescribing it as a left turn signal. As Davidson (1968) comments,

> When we ask why someone acted as he did, we want to be provided with an interpretation. His behaviour seems strange, alien, outre, pointless, out of character, disconnected...When we learn his reason, we have an interpretation, a new description of what he did which fits it into a familiar picture. The picture certainly includes some of the agent's beliefs and attitudes; perhaps also goals, ends, principles, general character traits, virtues or vices. Beyond this, the redescription of an action afforded by a reason may place the action in a wider social, economic, linguistic, or evaluative context. To learn, through learning the reason, that the agent conceived his action as a lie, a repayment of a debt, an insult, the fulfillment of an avuncular obligation, or a knight's gambit is to grasp the point of an action in its setting of rules, practices, conventions, and expectations (85).

Its redescription as a turn signal explains an arm raising by giving the agent's goal in so doing: to perform an act which has significance in the context of driving conventions. But note a redescription may not entail a complete shift in context. Redescribing an advance of the king's pawn as an attack on the black rook places the action "in a wider evaluative context," though chess conventions inform both description and redescription. Again though, the redescription provides a reason: the king's pawn was advanced in order to trap the black rook.

Speaker's meaning reports which serve to resolve an ambiguous utterance are explanatory in this way, where the relevant "setting of rules" is the grammar. When described so as to reflect the stage of analysis at which the ambiguity arises, the utterance appears "disconnected" in that the grammar may derive it in more than one way. An explanation is provided by redescribing it so as to reflect a stage at which the ambiguity is resolved. The relevant stages depend on the kind of ambiguity. Consider lexical ambiguity, as in "By 'bank' he meant 'river bank'." The ambiguity appears at a stage describable as the speaker's saying that so-and-so's going to the "bank," where "bank" has been lexically identified but not assigned a meaning. The speaker's meaning report explains the act of saying that so-and-so's going to the "bank" by giving the speaker's reason for it: to say that so-and-so's going to the river bank. As Davidson comments, such an explanation is an answer to a question. The question's topic is the speaker's saying that so-and-so's going to the "bank," and the relevance relation is a p-reason. Not just any p-reason: "He said that Fred's going to the 'bank' in order to throw the police off the trail" would not express a direct answer. What is wanted is a p-reason in terms of what the speaker wanted to say, which implies truth-conditions and hence lexical disambiguation.

Reports pertaining to other kinds of ambiguity can be similarly construed. Consider the spoken report "By 'He's going to [hIt] you' he meant 'hitch you'" (not "hit you"), and "By 'They're visiting doctors', he meant that they're doctors who are visiting" (not that they're at the doctors' office building). The first is a redescription of the speaker's saying that he's going to "[hIt] you" as his saying that he's going to hitch someone, the second a redescription of the speaker's saying "They're visiting doctors" as his saying that they're doctors who are visiting. In resolving phonetic ambiguity and syntactic ambiguity (in addition to the lexical ambiguity of "visiting" as either verb or adjective), the reports likewise explain an act in terms of a reason. As an answer to a WDYM-question, each expresses a p-reason whose content resolves the relevant ambiguity.

Since both description and redescription rely upon grammatical analysis, an explanation of an ambiguous utterance is more analogous to the redescription of a king's pawn advance as a trapping of the black rook than to the turn signal explanation. As in the chess case, the description is as steeped in the "setting of rules" as the redescription. Phonetic ambiguity is no exception: phonetic analysis is a distinctively linguistic skill involving abstraction from numerous aspects of the raw signal (Garman 1990, 189-191). In short, a disambiguating speaker's meaning report is not like the turn signal explanation because it is intralinguistic, reflecting a shared grammar and associated parser. This is not to say that the description and redescription inherent in a speaker's meaning report precisely represent parsing stages. "He meant that they're doctors who are visiting" does not imply that he had in mind the syntactic structure of "They're doctors who are visiting," but rather a certain structure of "They're visiting doctors," i.e.

[S [NP [N they]] [VP [V are] [NP [ADJ visiting] [N doctors]]]]

(using standard abbreviations for "sentence," "noun phrase," "noun," "verb phrase," "verb," and "adjective"). But a speaker's meaning report, as ordinary language, is too crude a device to represent such information directly. "They're doctors who are visiting" serves to nudge one into grasping the correct structure (including the correct lexical analyses), via the synonymy of the adjectival and relative clause modifications; other tactics might do as well.

Of main concern henceforth will be lexical ambiguity. It does not matter whether we view this as multiple meanings of a single word, or as multiple homonymous words: one "bank" meaning "river bank" and a different one meaning "financial institution," that happens to sound the same. In the latter case, the quoted occurrence of "bank" in "By 'bank' he meant river bank" indicates a phonetic analysis only rather than a lexical item, and "river bank" indicates a lexical item. But either way, ambiguity is resolved at the level of what is said. Note again that the redescription's relation to underlying linguistic description may be indirect ("By 'bank' he meant the kind of place like down the street").

As always the speaker's meaning is propositional, as entailed by its status as a reason. "By 'bank' he meant river bank" is shorthand for an answer whose core is propositional: his wanting to say that so-and-so's going to the river bank. But the shorthand is especially natural here since it isolates, however roughly, the information from the grammar—specifically, the lexicon—that underlies the disambiguation.

2. Ellipsis and Speaker's Meaning

According to our current notion of what is said, its content is determined by assignment of meanings by the grammar, plus elements of context sufficient for determining truth-conditions. Uncontroversially, these elements of context must serve disambiguation and reference assignment. They must also serve the resolution of ellipsis, as in "Tonight" and "She won't continue." The first is elliptical because an adverb is not a sentence, the second because the verb "continue" has a "selection restriction" requiring an infinitive, which however is not present. Contextually-determined "enrichment" required for a proposition is properly regarded as what is said: that Dad will take everyone for ice cream tonight, or that Sheila won't continue to study at the university.

More controversial is the view taken by a number of researchers that enrichment beyond what is necessary for a proposition should also be taken as part of what is said.[1] This view's point of departure is Grice's category of "generalized conversational" implicature, which in contrast to other implicatures that are "carried by saying that *p* on a particular occasion in virtue of special features of the context" (1989, 37), are instead carried by saying that *p* absent special context. Consider "Sheila looked at the bill and fainted." On Grice's analysis, the content of what is said includes the logical conjunction reading of "and," while the implicature includes the reading "and as a result." In this way the various "meanings" of "and" stemming from its various temporal, causal, explanatory and other readings can be accounted for without positing lexical ambiguity. Note that the logical conjunction reading is sufficient for there to be a proposition.

But a number of arguments have been lodged against this analysis. Consider "If the old king died of a heart attack and a republic was declared Sam will be happy, but if a republic was declared and the old king died of a heart attack Sam will be unhappy." On the Gricean treatment the two antecedents would have the same truth-conditions, with the different temporal sequences residing only at the level of implicature. But this would makes the sentence entail a contradiction if an antecedent is true, which intuitively it does not. Similarly "He didn't steal some money and go to the bank; he went to the bank and stole some money" would be contradictory, an incorrect result. It therefore seems that "and subsequently" must be part of what is said rather than what is implicated, despite the fact that such enrichment is not necessary for a proposition. Thus the "Scope Principle":

any content that falls within the scope of a negation, antecedent of a conditional, or other logical operator is part of what is said.[2]

Together with other arguments, this principle has led to the view that what is said might include a great many types of enrichment beyond what is required for a proposition. Consider:

> At the edge of the cliff, John jumped.
> I've had breakfast.
> The park is some distance from the house.

Given disambiguation and reference assignment, a "minimal" proposition is expressed in each case. Since "jump" has no selection restriction for a prepositional phrase, the proposition does not imply that John jumped over the cliff; in the second case, there is an implicit quantifier "at some time in the past"; in the third case there is a quantifier over distances. Still, in uttering the sentence one might thereby say that so-and-so jumped over the cliff; that the speaker had breakfast today; or that the park is not within a walkable distance of the house. By the Scope Principle, these conclusions follow from the apparent fact that in each case a denial can deny the enriched proposition (e.g. "No it's not; it's right around the corner.")

The issues here are the subject of complex and ongoing debate.[3] I do not have a position in this debate, and even if I did this would not be the place to defend it. It is however pertinent to note a disadvantage of the implicature approach, Scope Principle aside: it makes the enrichment necessarily a matter of the speaker's communicative intention.

I've essentially already indicated why this is a disadvantage, at the end of the previous chapter. I argued against Sperber and Wilson's proposal to treat metaphor as a kind of weak implicature, because it would make a speaker's meaning report necessarily about the speaker's communicative intention. No oddness attaches to "By 'Robert is a bulldozer' she meant that Robert always has to clear off his desk completely before starting to work" even though the reported content is quite unlikely as a hearer's hypothesis and thus as something the speaker might have intended to communicate. This suggests that the speaker's meaning is about something else: as I will discuss in subsequent chapters, I think for conceptual indeterminacy (including metaphor) this something else is a conceptual reason. But now, note also that no oddness attaches to "By 'Tonight' Dad meant that he would take everyone for ice cream tonight" or "By 'John jumped' Sally meant that John jumped over the cliff" even in contexts where the reported content is unlikely as a hearer's hypothesis and thus also as something the speaker might have intended to communicate. Again, the speaker's meaning must be about something else: in the tacit WDYM-question to which the report expresses an answer, the relevance relation must be something other than a communicative p-reason.

Why the something else in this case is not likewise a kind of e-reason is a matter I will discuss in section 6. For now I conclude that while it is not a communicative intention, it could be another kind of intention: what the speaker intended to say. This would be consistent with the Scope Principle view.[4]

It would also make speaker's meaning reports resolving ellipsis similar to reports resolving ambiguity. Consider "Tonight," which might give rise to "What about tonight?": shorthand for a WDYM-question requesting a certain kind of p-reason for an utterance construed prior to syntactic analysis. The p-reason is such that a report expresses a redescription of the presyntactic stage in terms of what is said. Thus "By 'Tonight' Dad meant that he would take everyone for ice cream tonight" redescribes Dad's saying "Tonight" as his saying that he would take everyone for ice cream tonight. The redescription is explanatory in virtue of providing Dad's reason for saying "Tonight": to say that he would take everyone for ice cream tonight.[5]

For "By 'Sue looked at the bill and fainted' Paul meant that she looked at the bill and as a result fainted," the question topic would also be pre-interpretive, but only for lack of an optional contextual element determining an enrichment of "and." It is optional because "Sue looked at the bill and fainted" would have a syntactic structure and semantic interpretation as it stands. But a WDYM-question presupposing that there is an enrichment would not presuppose this structure, or any other, as the content of what is said. These would be inconsistent presuppositions, because if the option for enrichment is exercised the structure does not obtain.

I need a convenient cover term for the two types of case. I will use "ellipsis," with "grammatical" ellipsis meaning that enrichment is required for there to be a proposition, and "extragrammatical" ellipsis meaning that it is not. This is what I mean by "ellipsis" in the title of this section and henceforth.[6]

I would emphasize that the content of what is said is determined by the speaker, not the hearer. It is often suggested otherwise: for instance, by Carston when she remarks that this content "is a combination of linguistically encoded and contextually inferred features" (1988, 167). But suppose the hearer's inference is wrong. Is it nonetheless the inference that determines the content of what is said, rather than what the speaker in fact means?

Let's take an example of Sperber and Wilson's. Suppose that by "The child left the straw in her glass" a speaker means that the child left a cereal-stalk. And suppose the hearer hypothesizes that the child left a drinking-straw. What has the speaker said? Consider the attitudes of the principals, i.e. speaker and hearer. Following our account of disambiguation, the speaker's reason for saying that the child left the "straw" in the glass is to say that the child left the cereal-stalk in her glass. This implies that he takes himself to have said that the child left the cereal-stalk in her glass. As for the hearer, suppose she were to discover that her hypothesis is wrong. Surely she would then conclude that he said that the child left the cereal-stalk in her glass. The general attitude shows up in everyday discourse when we say "It depends on what you mean." That is: the *truth* of what you say depends on what you mean. This implies, in turn, that what you have said depends on what you mean, given the dependence of truth-conditions on content. So speaker and hearer agree: given what he meant, the speaker has said that the child left the cereal-stalk in the glass. If speakers and hearers alike consider what has been said to depend on what the speaker means, so should our theory unless there are countervailing factors; I am not aware of any. We've been considering the case where the speaker's meaning and the hypothesis thereof diverge, but the proper conclusion is that the hypothesis never determines content. Even if the hypothesis is correct, it does not determine content but simply coincides with what does.

The point isn't that the speaker's meaning entirely determines what is said, but that it is one of the contextual elements that determine what is said. Note that the speaker operates within constraints imposed by the grammar. For disambiguation the speaker may choose from among the meanings in a lexicon. For grammatical ellipsis, the constraints may leave no choice. Consider "She ate a burger and he a salad." Arguably this is derived in the grammar by a deletion operation on an underlying structure for "She ate a burger and he ate a salad" (Baker 1989, 431-432). This implies that the ellided item can only be "ate," thus that anyone uttering "She ate a burger and he a salad" has said is that she ate a burger and he ate a salad. For other grammatical as well as extragrammatical ellipsis, the constraints on speaker's meanings are looser.

I will discuss these constraints in section 6 below. For now I conclude that enrichment in the current sense resides in what is said, supporting the idea that speaker's meaning reports which address ellipsis are explanatory redescriptions at the level of what is said, just as in disambiguation.

3. Conceptual Reasons, First Considerations

We saw in the previous chapter that a speaker's meaning might be a reason for believing something. Let's now consider the particular subtype that I've termed a "conceptual reason." In this section, I will further motivate the notion; in the next section, I will revise its analysis.

I suggested in regard to example 7 that what makes conceptual reasons different from other e-reasons is that they seemingly provide necessary warrant for the belief that John is clever. I wish to say that Al fixes the content of his expressed belief, such that what he believes is that John is clever in the sense that he is quick-witted. This interest in a "sense" is often explicitly indicated in the wording of a WDYM-interrogative or reply. Consider

> Weinberg: ...These principles of symmetry have been known for a long time. They're very powerful because they dictate the form of the laws of nature. They're probably the deepest thing we know about in physics.
> Moyers: Deepest? What do you mean?
> Weinberg: In the sense that if you keep asking questions about "why," you'll wind up with the principles of symmetry...

Weinberg's "sense" is not a sense as in a possible meaning of an ambiguous sentence, nor is it what philosophers call an "intension" (Frege's "sense," as opposed to reference). I take Moyers to have already determined the intension of "deepest" when asking for the sense Weinberg has in mind.

Something like the notion of a conceptual reason was once suggested by Fodor (1975, 6-8). According to Fodor's reconstruction of Gilbert Ryle, the answer to "What makes the clown's clowning clever?" is not that the clown had such-and-such mental processes, figuring in the causation of the clown's behavior. Rather, it has to do with properties of the behavior itself: that what he does is unexpected, that the man he hit with a pie was fancily dressed, etc. But, Fodor objects, even if this sort of answer were available, it would not preclude another sort adverting to causal mental processes. The two kinds of answer, what Fodor calls the "conceptual story" and the "causal story," do not compete with each other.

The point can be put in terms of why-questions. "What makes the clown's clowning clever?" is a paraphrase of "Why is the clown's clowning clever?", one which indicates a particular contrast. "What makes..." is one of a number of devices for doing so (Ch. 2, sec. 1). Consider "Why is it the clown whose clowning is clever?", "Why is the clown's *clowning* clever?", and "Why is the clown's clowning clever as opposed to dumb?" The topic of the question is the same in each case, but the contrasts differ. "What makes the clown's clowning clever?" is synonymous with a why-question whose contrast stems from "clever." Fodor's observation can be put in terms of the relevance relation: different relevance relations are possible and equally legitimate as possible objects of interest. One such relation is the "conceptual story."

What Fodor does not emphasize is the dependence of a "conceptual story" on a conceiver. This simple fact accounts for vagaries that have been noted in the analysis of "clever" and other mentalistic predicates. Thus Ryle noted the dependence of the "dispositional analysis" of a mentalistic term—i.e. analysis in terms of behavioral dispositions—on the subject of which the term is predicated (1949, 123). For instance, "The clown is clever," "The boxer is clever," and "The chess player is clever" evidently call for different analyses: e.g. ability to amuse in certain ways, ability to feint and defend, and ability to advantageously trade pieces for position. We might say therefore that what has a dispositional analysis is not a mentalistic term, but a mentalistic term as it appears in a sentence. This takes into account the dependence of an analysis on not only the subject, but on any intrasentential influence, regardless of the term's or the influence's syntactic category (e.g. "He plays chess cleverly"). But this is not adequate. Modifying another example of Ryle's, suppose that Elizabeth is a long-time friend of Jane. Jane has learned that Elizabeth is proud in a certain complex and subtle sense. Evidently the analysis of "Elizabeth is proud" depends not just on the sentence but on Jane.

On my account, the dependencies of the analysis on the sentence and the speaker follow from construing the analysis as the content of a kind of reason for belief (though I have no commitment to Ryle's idea of dispositional analysis). It depends on the (interpreted) sentence in the way a reason depends upon the content of the belief for which it is a reason. Thus Jane's reason for believing that Elizabeth is proud is not the same as her reason for believing that her father is proud. And it depends upon Jane because her reason for believing that Elizabeth is proud may not be the same as another person's reason for believing that Elizabeth is proud.

Meanwhile the status of the reason as a kind of "analysis" is captured by taking it to be a "conceptual" reason.

One might think that the phenomena could alternatively be captured by treating a mentalistic predicate as an "attributive" adjective. This is an adjective which forms a predicate only in combination with a common noun phrase. Take "skillful." Since the respective referents of "skillful composer" and "skillful carpenter" presumably have no property of skillfulness in common, these phrases do not mean "skillful and a composer" and "skillful and a carpenter." Rather "skillful" seems to require a common noun phrase before there is any reference at all. Similarly "red" and "big" are arguably attributive, in light of "red sunset" and "red hair," and "big baby" and "big football player."[7] And similarly, it might be thought, "clever" is attributive in light of "clever clown," "clever boxer," and "clever chess player," the referents of which need not have any property of cleverness in common. This accounts for the difficulty of interpreting "clever" in isolation; with no following noun phrase, there is no predicate to interpret.

But this strategy has a number of problems. One is that it can account only awkwardly for influences on interpretation other than that of the modified common noun phrase. For the dependence of an analysis on the subject, there would have to be some underlying level of representation in which the subject is rendered as a common noun phrase. For example, "The clown is clever" is somehow rendered as "The clown is a clever clown" or "This is a clever clown." If the subject is a named individual as in "John is clever," then we would have to posit a "missing" common noun phrase, perhaps supplied by context. If the mentalistic term is not an adjective, as in "We were all impressed by the clown's cleverness," then we would have to posit some such manipulation as "We were all impressed by the clown's being a clever clown." Moreover some aspects of the dependence on a sentence can't be captured at all, awkwardly or otherwise. "Mike Tyson is a clever boxer" and "Ray Leonard is a clever boxer" call for different analyses, but the adjective-noun combination is the same in both cases. Two speakers' different analyses of "Mike Tyson is a clever boxer" is similarly unexplained. In contrast all the various sentential influences on the interpretation of an occurrence of "clever" as well as the influence of the speaker are accounted for, without awkwardness, by making out the object of interpretation to be a speaker's reason for belief.

Summing up, Fodor's point that "Why is the clown's clowning clever?" may request a "causal story" or a "conceptual story" is fine as far as it goes.[8] But a request for a "conceptual story" is elliptical for "Why do you believe that the clown's clowning is 'clever'?", because a conceptual story depends on a conceiver. In the event of an utterance the question may be expressed "What do you mean, 'The clown's clowning is "clever"?'" In either case the question's contrast stems from "clever," and the relevance relation is a conceptual reason.

I will be using mentalistic terms as a running example. They are good examples of conceptual indeterminacy because, people being complex, thoughtful application requires tailoring to the case at hand. This exemplifies a more general phenomenon for empirical abstract words, which I will discuss in the next chapter.

4. The Disquotational Principles

4.1. *A Problem*

Let's now examine the notion of a conceptual reason more closely. According to the current analysis of example 7, the question's topic is that Al believes that John is clever, and the relevance relation is a conceptual reason. Bo presupposes prior stages of speech processing, including that Al said that John is clever. Thus Bo takes what Al says and what Al believes to be the same.

To see the problem with this, consider first the "inferential role" of the belief that John is clever. Inferences such as that John is quick-witted and that John easily grasps difficult concepts in math have some degree of strength. Related to this we might expect the believer to nominate John to emcee the charity fundraiser, to ask John for help with his taxes, or to express surprise that John did not seem to grasp a plot twist in a movie. Now consider, say, the belief that John is clever in the sense of quick-witted. The inference to John's easily grasping difficult math concepts would be weaker, since wit is not particularly an indicator of mathematical acuity, and the inference to John's being quick-witted would be maximally strong.[9] And we thus would more strongly expect the believer to nominate John to emcee the charity fundraiser, but not to ask John why his phone isn't working, or to express surprise that John did not seem to grasp a plot twist in a movie. Thus the inferential role of the belief that John is clever is inconsistent with that of the belief that John is clever in the sense of quick-witted.

In posing his WDYM-question, Bo does not know the particular sense that Al has in mind. But he presupposes that Al has one or another in mind. Recall the question presuppositions

P1: the topic is true,
P2: the members of the contrast class are false, and
P3: at least one proposition that bears the relevance relation to the topic is true.

(See also Chapter 2, note 12.) For this question, P3 is the presupposition that a conceptual reason exists. Given this, he cannot be presupposing also that Al believes that John is clever. For that would be attributing to Al an inferential role which requires the *lack* of a conceptual reason. Bo does not instead an attribute a role appropriate to some particular sense of "clever," since he is not attributing any such sense to Al. Rather, he is seeking one. But this stance is incompatible with attributing to Al the belief that John is clever.

Therefore this cannot be the topic of Bo's question. The same conclusion emerges if we reflect on the status of a conceptual reason. I've suggested that this is a distinctive kind of e-reason. What makes it distinctive is that it is supposed to somehow impinge upon the content of the belief for which it is a reason. Al's having a certain conceptual reason for what he expresses with "John is clever" is supposed to account for his believing that John is clever in sense that he is quick-witted. But the latter is not constituted by some relation between the belief that John is clever and the belief that he is quick-witted. For such a relation entails that the content of the reasoned-to belief is independent of the reason: what the reason is, how good it is, or indeed whether there is any. It's in the nature of a reason that it does *not* impinge upon the content of the reasoned-to belief. If it did, how could it be a reason *for* the belief?

If this apparent incoherence in the notion of a conceptual reason has not been obvious, that is perhaps because of my characterization of it as giving rise to necessary inferences. This suggests a reason of the usual kind, but which confers upon the reasoned-to belief a maximal degree of justification: that is, not really a different kind of reason at all, only a reason with a distinctive measure of strength. But while this implicit suggestion has been heuristically useful, it must now be discarded. What I am positing is indeed a different kind of reason, one which impinges upon the content of that to which it relates. The current moral is that to be a coherent notion it cannot relate to a belief. Therefore, the topic of a WDYM-question requesting a conceptual reason cannot be a belief, since it is the topic that the relevance relation relates to.

4.2. *A Solution*

So what is it? Consider what has been termed the "disquotational principle," which in Kripke's words

> can be stated as follows, where "p" is to be replaced, inside and outside all quotation marks, by any appropriate standard English sentence: "If a normal English speaker, on reflection, sincerely assents to 'p,' then he believes that p." The sentence replacing 'p' is to lack indexical or pronominal devices or ambiguities, that would ruin the intuitive sense of the principle (e.g., if he assents to "You are wonderful," he need not believe that you—the reader—are wonderful). When we suppose that we are dealing with a normal speaker of English, we mean that he uses all words in the sentence in a standard way, combines them according to the appropriate syntax, etc.: in short, he uses the sentence to mean what a normal speaker should mean by it...The qualification "on reflection" guards against the possibility that a speaker may...assert something he does not really mean, or assent to a sentence in linguistic error. "Sincerely" is meant to exclude mendacity, acting, irony, and the like. I fear that even with all this it is possible that...a qualification [may have been] overlooked...[But] taken in its obvious intent...the principle appears to be a self-evident truth. (A similar principle holds for sincere affirmation or assertion in place of assent.) (1979, 248-249).

A version of the principle pertaining to "sincere affirmation" underlies the current analysis of the question topic. We've supposed Bo to reason that since Al is a normal speaker of English and utters "John is clever" sincerely and reflectively, he believes that John is clever. But we've just seen that if Bo is inquiring into a sense of "clever" that Al has in mind, then the attribution is incorrect. So there must indeed be some overlooked qualification.

Evidently, the attribution must be blocked if there is a speaker's meaning in the relevant sense. For Kripke, a "normal English speaker" means "what a normal speaker should mean." So this refers to speaker's meaning in a metalinguistic sense; Kripke's concern is that the speaker mean what the words mean. This condition does not then block the incorrect attribution. Consistently with the meanings of his words Al as a normal speaker might mean, in the operative intralinguistic sense, that John is quick-witted by "John is clever."

Accordingly, consider the following:

> If a normal English speaker asserts '*p*', where '*p*' is an English sentence containing no ambiguous or indexical terms, and is sincere and reflective, and by '*p*' means that *q*, then he believes that *p* in the sense that *q*.

I take it that the addition of the last condition does not make the principle any less intuitive.

A closely related principle is:

> If a normal English speaker asserts '*p*', where '*p*' is an English sentence containing no ambiguous or indexical terms, and is sincere and reflective, and there is no *q* such that by '*p*' he means that *q*, then he believes that *p*.

Something like this seems to be what is needed. If a speaker has in mind some sense of '*p*', then the last condition is not met, and the attribution of a belief that *p* is blocked.

Before further developing these principles, consider that the principle as described by Kripke can be broken into components: a subprinciple underlying an attribution of what is said and another underlying an attribution of what is believed.

> DP1': If a normal English speaker asserts '*p*', where '*p*' is an English sentence containing no ambiguous or indexical terms, then he says that *p*.
> DP2': If so-and-so says that *p* and is sincere and reflective, then he believes that *p*.

Here what we might call the "content-endowing" conditions, pertaining to disquotation per se, are applied before what we might call the "belief-endowing" conditions. This breakdown enables an intermediate attribution of what is said. But an alternative breakdown is also possible by switching the order of conditions:

DP1: If so-and-so asserts 'p', and is sincere and reflective, then he believes-true 'p'.

DP2: If a normal English speaker believes-true 'p', where 'p' is an English sentence containing no ambiguous or indexical terms, then he believes that p.

Here the intermediate attribution is an attitude toward not a proposition but a sentence, while the attribution of belief proper comes with the endowment of content.

On either breakdown, the conjunction of subprinciples entails the principle as stated by Kripke. But I take the second breakdown to carve the current problem at its joints. I propose the following variants of DP2:

DP2a: If a normal English speaker believes-true 'p', where 'p' is an English sentence containing no ambiguous or indexical terms, and believes-true 'p' on the basis of a conceptual reason that q, then he believes that p in the sense that q.

DP2b: If a normal English speaker believes-true 'p', where 'p' is an English sentence containing no ambiguous or indexical terms, and there is no q such that he believes-true 'p' on the basis of a conceptual reason that q, then he believes that p.

As required, the principles DP1 and DP2b do not permit an attribution of the belief that p if the speaker has a conceptual reason.[10]

My suggestion then is that a conceptual reason is a reason for a believed-true sentence rather than for a belief. DP2a spells out the sense in which a conceptual reason entails the speaker's fixing of content. When a conceptual reason is present, so is a belief whose content is derived from both relata in a certain way. Thus both the relational nature of a conceptual reason and the effect of the reason on content are accounted for. This resolves the paradox of accounting for both, observed in the previous section, which arises if both relata are beliefs. If what is reasoned to is not a belief but a believed-true sentence, then the content of the reason does not enter into the content of what is reasoned to. But it does enter into the content derived from the relational whole.

Falling out from all this is the topic of Bo's question: it is that Al believes-true "John is clever," attributed on the basis of DP1. This represents a kind of "way-station" for the questioner, i.e. progress toward but not yet attribution of belief. The progress consists in the satisfaction of all conditions which, if a conceptual reason were either known or known to be absent, would imply a successful attribution (DP2a, DP2b). But as it is, the questioner assumes a conceptual reason to exist without knowing what it is; so the attribution cannot proceed.

Any attributions licensed by DP1, DP2a, or DP2b are consistent with one licensed by DP1', since the various conditions are mutually compatible. Note in particular that the attribution by DP1' of what is said is unaffected by the presence or absence of a conceptual reason. Thus Bo's presupposition that Al says that John is clever is accounted for. Bo's attribution of a believed-true sentence is consistent with having semantically interpreted the sentence: the holdup in applying DP2a is not this, but the identity of the conceptual reason.

Recall the problem with analyzing the topic of Bo's question as Al's believing that John is clever: predictions of Al's inferences and behavior which are incompatible with the presupposition that Al has a conceptual reason. This problem is now solved. If the topic is Al's believing-true "John is clever" there are instead no predictions at all, because no belief is attributed. Given DP2a, the presupposition of a believed-true sentence (presupposition P1) and that a conceptual reason exists (P3) jointly imply that there is some q such that Al believes that John is clever in the sense that q. This should not be confused with the content of the belief that there is some q such that John is clever in the sense that q, i.e. the belief that John is clever in some sense, where the variable is bound within the scope of "believes." Consider the difference between the belief that John is clever in some sense and the belief that John is clever. While both are non-specific with regard to a particular sense of cleverness, there are different associated inference patterns and behavior. Whereas one who believes that John is clever might infer with a certain degree of confidence that John would be amusing as an emcee or that he has figured out how to minimize his property taxes, one who believes that John is clever in some sense would be less confident. The modifier "in a sense" makes for what we might call "promissory" content. The modified content makes inference patterns that are uniformly weaker than those of the unmodified content, but if the "promised" sense is specified then they take on firmer shape: i.e. unequal distribution of inference strengths, as earlier illustrated.

What follows from P1 and P3 is different because "believes" is within the scope of "in some sense," so the variable is free within the scope of "believes." This means that no belief content is attributed: nothing that determines truth-conditions, inferences, or behavioral ramifications, weakly or otherwise. I take this to be a correct result.

It may have occurred to the reader that the proposed principles are scarcely applicable because of the prohibition on ambiguity and indexicality. In realistic versions of the content-endowing principles, "*p*" becomes not *p* but *r*, where *r* is the result of disambiguation and other contextual resolutions. But this has no bearing on the current conclusions. Realistic principles would enable the same breakdowns, would not affect the belief-endowing principles, and could be modified so that when a conceptual reason that *q* is present the content attributed would be that of "*r* in the sense that *q*." But stating them would be more difficult and would create unnecessary distraction. For this reason I'll continue with the principles as proposed, pretending that they apply more widely than they do. Realistic principles may be mentally substituted whenever there is a suspicion of ambiguity or indexicality.

I conclude this section by addressing a possible objection. It might be thought that believing-true does have behavioral ramifications, whether or not belief content is attributed. If so, the topic of Bo's question would entail inappropriate predictions after all. Some philosophers have claimed that in general it is attitudes toward sentences rather than propositions that enter into explanations of behavior, based on consideration of indexical sentences. Perry (1979) points out that we would expect certain behavioral similarities among those disposed to say "My pants are on fire" (swear, jump up and down, etc.), even though the sentence has different truth-conditions depending on who says it (John Perry's pants are on fire, David Kaplan's pants are on fire, etc.). In such cases it would therefore seem that what explains behavior is not a believed proposition but a believed-true sentence.

Actually Perry would not put things quite this way. He calls the behavior-explaining attitude toward a sentence "acceptance," and argues that it is neither identical to nor analyzable in terms of believing-true (Perry 1980). They are not identical because the former is a three-place relation whereas the latter is a five-place relation. An agent accepts a sentence at a time. An agent believes-true a sentence at a time, but truth is itself relative to a person and time (e.g. "My meeting starts now"). Acceptance at *t* by *x* of S cannot be analyzed in terms of believing-true, for example as

At time *t*, *x* believes that S is true for person α at time τ

(where α designates x and τ designates t), because John Perry could at noon believe that "My meeting starts now" is true for John Perry at noon, but not accept at noon "My meeting starts now," and not behave in a rushed way, because he may have lost track of the time. Nor, Perry argues, can acceptance be reduced to believing-true any other way.

Let's recognize that the believing-true relation is an n-place relation involving a believer and time at which he believes, in addition to not just time and person but all the n-2 factors which determine a sentence's truth (e.g. Perry might have added place of utterance, in light of "It's raining"). These factors haven't been mentioned in the above disquotational principles because of the condition that the sentence contain no indexical terms. But following Perry I will suppose that they do not enter into the acceptance relation, and that acceptance is not reducible to believing-true.

However, the issue still arises whether my position that believing-true a conceptually indeterminate sentence does not enter into explanation of behavior is compatible with Perry's position that accepting a sentence does. In my example the sentence is both believed-true and accepted, not because there is any analytic entailment between the two but because the stipulated speech circumstance entails both. In particular, DP1 has a correlate for acceptance, to the effect that if one sincerely and reflectively asserts a sentence on an occasion then one accepts it on that occasion. My position would be peculiar were I to allow that accepting "John is clever" has behavioral ramifications, but believing-true that same sentence on the same occasion does not. At least I would owe some explanation of the discrepancy, because even though acceptance and believing-true are distinct notions they are doxastically similar stances relating to a sentence. Perry provides just such an explanation for indexical sentences: I would owe one for conceptually indeterminate sentences.

But in fact I do not acknowledge any discrepancy. I maintain rather that when a sentence is conceptually indeterminate, neither the believing-true nor the accepting has behavioral ramifications. So I dispute Perry's view. I think that acceptance explains behavior for certain indexical sentences, but not in general.

Before trying to show this, let me elaborate a bit on the view. An alternative formulation is in terms of characters (i.e. in Kaplan's sense) instead of sentences, since characters and sentences correspond.[11] The character of "My pants are on fire" is the same for all potential utterers: a function which maps the speaker in the context to the proposition that that speaker's pants are on fire. The thesis is that character, not the proposition yielded by the character given a context, is what enters into explanations of behavior. This can also accommodate natural kind terms. Recalling Putnam's thought experiment, language users on earth take "water" to refer to something that is odorless, good to drink, etc. By hypothesis the same is true of users on twin-earth. We would therefore expect certain similar behavior on the two earths, e.g. telling somebody who says she's thirsty that there's water in the refrigerator. But since "water" refers to H_2O on earth but to XYZ on twin-earth, "There is water in the refrigerator" has different truth-conditions in the two cases. Meanwhile the character of "water" is the same for us and those on twin-earth, i.e. a function which (among other things) maps earth to H_2O and twin-earth to XYZ. So again it seems to be character rather than propositional truth-conditions that enters into explanations of behavior.

There has been sophisticated debate on the adequacy of this "dual content" view of belief, with "narrow content" relevant to psychology and "wide content" to external reality.[12] But it seems to me that the basic problem with the view is very simple: it is based on too few examples. The point is not the trivial one that not all sentences have an indexical or a natural kind term, for perhaps such cases can be subsumed. Consider "eternal" sentences expressing the same proposition in every context (say, "George Gershwin was born on September 26, 1920"). If the character of a sentence yields the same proposition in every context, then it is a matter of indifference whether one appeals to the character or the propositional content when explaining behavior. So this special case does not falsify the thesis that character enters into explanation of behavior. What would falsify it would be propositional content rather than character explaining behavior when the choice is not a matter of indifference.

This can be established without even looking further than indexicals. Take the pronoun "he." We would not expect similar behavior of one disposed toward "He is about to lunge" while watching an infant, and one so disposed while confronting an intruder. It is not then the character of "He is about to lunge" that explains behavior here, since it is the same in both cases: a function mapping the first context to an infant and the second to a nearby intruder. Rather, it is the truth-conditions reflecting a particular resolution of "he" in a given context. (See Chien 1985 for a discussion of similar issues raised by the indexical "that.") Undoubtedly this relates to the earlier point that for such indexicals as "he" the character does not model linguistic competence, as it does for "pure" indexicals such as "I" or "now."[13] The bland conclusion suggested then was that perhaps a unitary account of competence is not to be had. Likewise, perhaps, for a unitary account of what explains behavior.

Returning now to our example, I would concede that if Al believes-true "John is clever," then he *might* be inclined toward the same kind of behavior he would if he believed that John is clever. This would be the case if a conceptual reason is lacking. But otherwise the behavior would be different, as already noted, and the difference follows the different belief contents expressed by the same sentence. Similarly consider two subjects each believing-true "John is clever," but one on the basis of a conceptual reason that John is quick-witted, the other on the basis of a conceptual reason that John is good at math. The different expectations of behavior (one asks John to emcee, the other for help with taxes) follow the different belief contents, whereas the sentence remains the same. Believed-true or accepted, the sentence can't explain the behavior. So I suggest that a conceptually indeterminate sentence is like a sentence with a non-pure indexical in this respect (though they differ in that resolution of the indexical is required for there to be an object of belief, whereas resolution of conceptual indeterminacy is not). Thus the attribution of Al's believing-true "John is clever" as the topic of the WDYM-question does not entail inappropriate behavioral predictions or indeed any predictions at all. For this an object of belief is required, and none is attributed: since a conceptual reason is assumed to exist but is unknown, neither DP2a nor DP2b apply.

To summarize the main points. I have proposed two modifications of the disquotational principle, one which attributes belief if a conceptual reason is present and one which attributes belief if not. The former captures the sense in which a conceptual reason implies the speaker's "fixing" of content. Both attributions are independent of the attribution of what is said. A conceptual reason is a reason for believing-true a sentence, and accordingly the topic of a WDYM-question requesting a conceptual reason is an attribution of a believed-true sentence. The questioner does not thereby attribute any belief to the speaker, so there are no behavioral ramifications.

4.3. *Saying What You Mean and Meaning What You Say*

It may seem that there is something odd about the proposed disquotational principles, simply because they imply that a sincere and reflective speaker may say one thing and believe something else. Don't good people usually say what they mean and mean what they say?

To begin with, I take the vernacular locutions "saying what you mean" and "meaning what you say" to be idioms, referring respectively to frankness and sincerity.[14] The latter does not entail the former. Consider e.g. Grice's professor, who might indeed be sincere about the job candidate's excellent penmanship, but nonetheless is not saying what he means. One might think then that "not saying what you mean" refers to the non-identity of what is said and what is implicated. Since the latter is an answer to a WDYM-question, it would so far be natural to suppose that "saying what you mean" is not idiomatic but really refers to what the speaker says and what he means. Notice, however, that if you *do* "say what you mean," there is no implicature to distinguish from what is said. If the professor said that the job candidate is no good at philosophy, the recruiter would not wonder what he meant in the implicature sense (though he may, for example, wonder what the professor meant by "no good").[15] It therefore doesn't assert the identity between what you say and what you implicate. So its negation doesn't assert the non-identity. I think "saying what you mean" simply means that you are frank, and the negation that you are not.

So on the idiomatic readings of "saying what you mean" and "meaning what you say," what is at issue is whether the general prevalence of sincerity and frankness entail that conceptual reasons are unusual. As for sincerity, a conceptual reason is not only compatible but requires it, since believing-true requires sincerity (DP1). For frankness, one would have to extend the sense of the word for it to imply the absence not only of an implicature but also of a conceptual reason. In saying that John is clever, rather than that John is quick-witted, is John not being "frank"? It seems to be the wrong word. But rather than dwelling on this, we might more profitably abandon the idiomatic readings and consider the identity of content between what is said and what is meant, taking this in context to be what is believed. Regardless of what it's called, isn't there usually such identity?

Perhaps; but if so not overwhelmingly, and not to the degree that might be thought without due consideration of conceptual reasons. Prevalence of the identity between what is said and what is believed cannot be based simply on the prevalence of sincerity. It is based upon the prevalence of sincerity, reflectiveness, and, what is less well recognized, the absence of a conceptual reason (DP1, DP1', DP2b). Whatever degree of prevalence this is, it is less than that of sincerity and reflectiveness alone. Conversely, non-identity between what is said and what is believed is more prevalent than one would think upon consideration only of misspeaking, sarcasm, joking, and other exceptions to the prevailing "convention of truthfulness" (Lewis 1974a). The possibility of a conceptual reason, which is not such an exception, must also be considered. I would suggest that it's not uncommon for there to be a conceptual reason making what is believed different from what is said.

This suggestion is not really about statistics but about the lack of mystery as to why a sincere speaker might say that p while believing that p in the sense that q. It is not that he is being obtuse, or deliberately not saying what he believes. It is simply that articulating a belief precisely can be hard. To be sure, a speaker might not be trying. He might be satisfied with only "sort" of saying what he believes, e.g. for style, brevity, or heuristic purposes. Or a speaker may not be conscious that he can do better, because he is not conscious of his belief. But even if he is trying he may easily fail, especially if his meaning has any degree of complexity. A belief is not there in our mind's eye for us to read off. Even when what one believes is not complex it can be difficult to articulate, as everyone knows. Perceptual experiences are an obvious case (Wittgenstein 1958, section 610), wherein content is arguably inexpressible in principle. But such cases aside, a belief still is often not precisely mirrored in what is seriously, reflectively, and sincerely said. The operative word is "precisely." I assume no one would deny that articulation can miss the mark. But unlike misspeaking, here the speaker gets close. This is not what linguists would call a "performance error," but rather a miss within the bounds of his competence. It is not so much an error as a vignette of the "human condition."[16]

These issues will be revisited. For now, note that the convention of truthfulness cannot be as Harman (1974, 9) paraphrases Lewis: "to try to say what is true is to say what you believe." The convention is only to *try* to say what you believe. Conforming to convention is presumably routine, not potentially a matter of difficulty or angst for those willing to conform.

5. Ambiguity Revisited

We saw earlier that the topic of a WDYM-question arising in response to lexical ambiguity is an utterance described in such a way that lexical identity but not particular meaning has been assigned. A direct answer redescribes the utterance in terms of what is said, entailing assignment of a meaning. Whereas conceptual indeterminacy is addressed at the level of what is believed, ambiguity is thus addressed at the level of what is said.

So these phenomena are compatible. Among other things this means that one cannot rule out conceptual indeterminacy by applying an ambiguity test using "reduced conjunction." For example, "Jack and Jill each went to banks, one to the river bank, another to Citibank" sounds odd except as a joke, indicating the ambiguity of "bank" as regards "river bank" and "financial institution." Similarly for "With scientology you will win your freedom much faster than the slaves did," indicating the ambiguity of "freedom" as regards spiritual and political freedom. But this outcome does not rule out conceptual indeterminacy *given* one or another of these word meanings. I've suggested that "Scientology is the road to total freedom" is conceptually indeterminate with respect to "freedom," under the "spiritual freedom" disambiguation.

An ambiguity test also could be used to establish that two "senses" are not word meanings. For example, "Scientology is the road to total freedom, be it absence of worry or removal of material wants" does not sound odd, indicating that lexical ambiguity is not the source of indeterminacy. But it doesn't follow that we have conceptual indeterminacy, for the operative foil to ambiguity covers a range of phenomena. "Sal and Robin are both neighbors, one a man the other a woman" likewise does not sound odd, indicating that "neighbor" does not have "male neighbor" and "female neighbor" as possible meanings. But what this reflects is the "non-specification" of "neighbor" with respect to gender, which does not involve an open-ended multiplicity of possibilities.

In sum, the test can establish that a word is ambiguous without ruling out conceptual indeterminacy; or that it is not ambiguous (in regard to candidate meanings) without establishing conceptual indeterminacy.[17] I emphasize the former: ambiguity and conceptual indeterminacy may be simultaneously present, with either capable of giving rise to a WDYM-question. But they are not independent, because in order for conceptual indeterminacy to be perceived ambiguity must have been resolved. One who asks a WDYM-question requesting a conceptual reason presupposes what the speaker has said and thus any required disambiguation.

My assumption that the meanings of a word are limited and pre-established is standard. But it is not universal. L. J. Cohen, for one, suggests that the semantics of natural language is "interactionist" in the sense that the meaning of a word might come not only from the lexicon but also from the sentential context. The possibilities for such meanings are sometimes open-ended, making for a kind of robust ambiguity. If Cohen were right, I would be obligated to explain why the resolution of conceptual indeterminacy doesn't transpire in such a semantics rather than in speaker's meaning. So I now want to consider his argument.

Cohen gives a number of examples. In "Most students here drop geography in their final year," "Most students here drop geography lectures in their final year," and "Most students here drop geography lectures reading assignments in their final year," "drop" means "drop studying," "drop attending," and "drop executing," respectively. The fact that "John has dropped his geography lectures and Peter has done so also" cannot be read as "dropped attending" in one case and "dropped giving" in another, except as a joke, suggests that these are multiple word meanings. It seems that many meanings of "drop" might thus be generated by the interaction of "drop" with its direct object. And "the same is true of many other verbs, like 'make', 'collect', 'establish', etc." (1986, 227-228). Cohen takes such phenomena to be incompatible with what he calls the "insulationist" view of semantics, exemplified by Tarski, Davidson, and Montague, on which "the meaning of any one word that occurs in a particular sentence is insulated against interference from the meaning of any other word in the same sentence" (223). On such a view, Cohen thinks, a great many meanings would have to be listed in the lexicon since they could not be generated in sentential context.

Cohen also has in mind attributive usages of adjectives. For example,

"good" may be said to have different, though analogous, meanings in "He has a good car" and "He has a good house," because in [the former] "good" means something like "conforms to the standards for commending cars" and in [the latter] something like "conforms to the standards for commending houses." A good guard-dog may be a bad gun-dog, and a bad philosopher may be a good driver. Nor is this use of adjectives and adverbs confined to familiar terms of evaluation or measurement, like "good" or "large." The possibility of attributive usage extends quite widely through at least the English vocabulary...A person who is called a "systematic philosopher" need not be systematic in anything but his philosophy, a "learned historian" need not be learned in anything but history, a "comfortable river cruiser" need not be comfortable on the high seas, a substance that is a "yellow stainer" need not be yellow itself, and an eighteenth century merchant who was a "triangular trader" (i.e. traded around the Britain-West Africa-West Indies triangle) was certainly never triangular himself (228-229).

In all these cases novel meanings are apparently generated when words are combined.

The apparent novel meanings are sometimes metaphorical. In one extended illustration Cohen cites a passage from Darwin:

> D. As many more individuals of each species are born than can possibly survive; and as, consequently, there is a frequently recurring struggle for existence, it follows that any being, if it vary however slightly in any manner profitable to itself, under the complex and sometimes varying conditions of life, will have a better chance of surviving, and thus be naturally selected (235).

What "naturally selected" means here, Cohen notes, is not determined by any dictionary entry for "select" in Darwin's time. Consequently it cannot be accounted for by an "insulationist" account. For "naturally selected" to mean something like "singled out by processes of nature," which, says Cohen, "is also the meaning that Darwin intended in his utterance of the sentence," it must be that the sentential context in D creates it.

I see several difficulties with Cohen's analysis. First of all, he does not demonstrate the need for a new kind of semantics. The phenomena of attributive adjectives have been well-known for a long time, in particular to Montague, Lewis and other architects of so-called "insulationist" semantic theories, who have proposed treatments. Surprisingly, Cohen does not address these. In Montague semantics, attributive adjectives are treated by associating them with a function that produces a "meaning" (an "intension" in Montague's technical sense) given the meaning of a common noun phrase. So for example "skillful" maps to a function which when given the meaning of "ballerina" produces the meaning of "skillful ballerina," but has no "meaning" itself in the sense of something implying reference. On this treatment there is no such thing as just being "skillful," and "skillful ballerina" does not mean "skillful and a ballerina." This explains the fact that a ballerina might not be skillful in anything but her ballet, without positing additional lexicon entries for "skillful." Such an account can also be applied to "good," "learned," and other adjectives considered by Cohen.[18]

As for "drop," the phenomenon can be analyzed as a kind of grammatical ellipsis. Perhaps "drop" requires in its direct object an introducing gerund, which may not appear explicitly but must appear in an underlying syntactic or semantic representation. The representation for "Most students drop geography in their final year" might be:

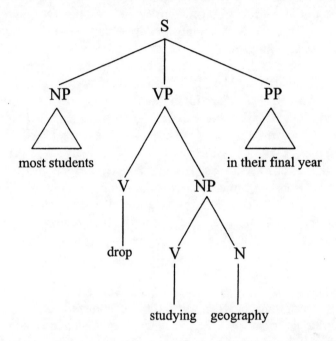

The gerund here is "studying," but any number of different gerunds might be supplied from context. This does not imply any number of different meanings for "drop." Rather, a unitary meaning can be assumed, one which is neutral as to the supplied gerund. The meaning thus implies only a placeholder in the position occupied by "studying" in the above structure. In this respect the analysis is analogous to Kratzer's (1977) analysis of modals (n. 6).

What about other verbs mentioned by Cohen such as "collect" and "establish"? Consider "Before long they established a relationship" and "The Red Sox established a lead in the pennant race." The direct object does seem to make a difference to the interpretation of "establish." Direct objects could be multiplied indefinitely, and it seems plausible that new meanings of "establish" can thereby be multiplied (Ross 1981, 103). But there is no reason why an attributive treatment for these verbs could not be appealed to instead, since a transitive verb and its direct object are siblings in syntactic structure, like an adjective and the common noun phrase it modifies (Dowty, Wall, and Peters 1981, 215-231). Thus some verbs could be analyzed as attributive in the sense of signifying a relation only in combination with its direct object. This would account for much of the phenomena, within standard compositional semantics, and without profligate lexicon meanings.

I conclude that the examples discussed by Cohen can be accommodated by existing semantic theories. I would add that it isn't clear how the phenomena would be analyzed in an "interactionist" semantics, even if there were no other option, since Cohen doesn't give details about what such a semantics would be like (as he himself recognizes). Nor has any paradigm emerged from any quarter which is comparable in scope and success to the various Tarski-based paradigms such as Montague semantics, Davidsonian semantics, situation semantics, and varieties of discourse semantics.[19] It bears repeating that "insulationist" is a misleading term for these paradigms, given the availability of attributive treatments as well as other devices for analyzing "interaction," including between non-sibling constituents (as will be discussed shortly), and between sentences in a discourse (e.g. Stalnaker 1999, 96-113).

I say that Cohen's examples "can" be accommodated by existing theories, meaning that they can capture the phenomena as he describes them. But the question arises whether they are distinct from conceptual indeterminacy; and if not, whether the treatment ought then to be within semantics rather than pragmatics, contrary to my account. From my perspective, this rather than the need for "interactionist" semantics is the main issue raised by Cohen.

The answer is mixed. I think the "drop" example does illustrate something distinct from conceptual indeterminacy, because of the privileged status of a particular construction for resolving the indeterminacy. But it is compatible with conceptual indeterminacy, which has to do with indeterminacy that remains after the gerund is supplied. Whereas the latter is part of the contextual determination of what is said, conceptual indeterminacy is resolved at the level of what is believed. Thus even supposing that one who apprehends "She dropped accepting commitments" grasps a novel meaning of "drop," one still might inquire into what the speaker means: e.g. that she no longer consciously honors commitments, that she stopped the daily efforts supporting commitment, that she now inwardly rebels against commitments that still may be imposed, etc.

With regard to "collect" and "establish," let's first review the reasons for not treating a mentalistic adjective as attributive (sec. 3). Sometimes the relevant contextual clue is the modified noun, as in "He's a clever boxer"; sometimes the subject, as in "The boxer is clever" ; sometimes the verb, as in "The way he boxes is clever." In general, it could be anywhere in the sentence ("He's got many years of experience in the boxing ring, so he's clever"). Sometimes it is not in the sentence at all, as in "He is clever." In that case, it perhaps comes from another sentence, as in "This is the first time I saw him box. He's clever." Or it may come from extralinguistic context. Even if a clue is in the sentence, it needn't determine what the speaker has in mind. Thus one speaker might have in mind one thing by "Tyson a clever boxer," another speaker another. An attributive treatment artificially singles out one sort of clue as canonical, and even in that case gives rise to further indeterminacy. Since something else is required to account for the latter in any case, why not posit only that something else and skip the artificiality?[20]

"Establish" is different in one respect: the direct object is syntactically mandatory. Whereas "John is clever" is a sentence, "They established" is not. So one can always count on the clue to be garnered from the direct object. But it still gives rise to further indeterminacy. One who apprehends "They established a relationship" still might wonder whether the speaker means that they came to trust one another, that they developed mutual expectations of fidelity, etc. For further help, clues in addition to the direct object remain possible, as in "I wouldn't worry about infidelity. They've established their relationship." So again I prefer my alternative, to posit only speaker's meaning. While the attributive treatment in this case is not syntactically artificial, it still requires a semantic departure: while formally unproblematic, it requires giving up a "default" assumption that verb meaning per se exists (implying reference), not just in combination with the meaning of a direct object. Better to do without it if something else which is required in any case can do the same job.

I'm arguing against an attributive treatment of adjectives and verbs that give rise to conceptual indeterminacy. What about other semantic treatments? For instance, some "long-distance" dependencies have been explained within Montague semantics, whereby there can be semantic influence between constituents with are not siblings in syntactic structure. Perhaps the influence of a subject on the interpretation of a mentalistic predicate, say, could likewise be explained.

To see the general idea, consider how disambiguation can apparently rely on such a dependency. Take "This unicycle has wheels" and "Unicycles have wheels." While the first is false, the second is true. This is because there are two different meanings for "wheels": one the usual meaning, the second a bound-variable reading dependent on a quantifier such as a plural noun phrase (DeMey 1981). Evidently, which meaning of "wheels" is in effect depends on the number of the subject. This creates a certain difficulty with compositionality. Consider the syntactic structure of "Unicycles have wheels":

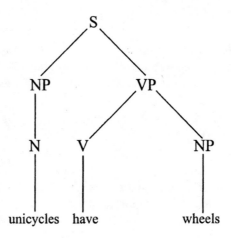

It is not obvious how the meaning of "unicycles" can influence the meaning of "wheels" if semantic derivation proceeds "bottom up," in concert with the syntactic structure (as in Montague semantics). On this assumption "wheels" is assigned a meaning which combines with the meaning of "have" at the VP node, and the composed VP meaning then combines with the meaning of "unicycles" at the top-level S node. Hence the meaning of "wheels" is determined before the meaning of "unicycles" has a chance to influence it. Chomsky (1975b) has suggested that a "top-down" version of compositionality is needed to account for such cases. Partee (1984, 287-289) on the other hand argues that a bottom-up account can posit the assignment of both the usual and the dependent meaning at the "wheels" leaf node, with both getting passed up to the S node, where the dependent meaning is selected under the influence of the meaning of "unicycles."

As it is not so clear how top-down compositionality is supposed to work as it is bottom-up, it's difficult to assess whether a top-down approach could account for the influence of "the boxer" on "clever" in "The boxer is clever." But a bottom-up approach analogous to Partee's suggestion for disambiguating "wheels" is clearly not viable. One would somehow have to represent the various senses of "clever" as the "meaning" at the "clever" leaf node, so that they get passed up to the S node where the proper sense gets selected by the meaning of "the boxer." This would also cover the case where the dependency is between siblings, as an alternative to the attributive account; the selection would just happen sooner, at the first node dominating the siblings.

But such an account would still have the problem that different speakers might mean different things by "The boxer is clever." Furthermore, extralinguistic and extrasentential influences are still left out. Furthermore, not all intrasentential influences are accounted for, e.g. "Having seen him box, I know he's clever." Here the meaning of "box" would have to likewise be passed up the tree before it could do any selection, and it is not clear how it could do the job in that case. It would have to be the meaning of "having seen him box" that selects a sense of "clever," and it isn't clear how the meaning of "box" would have to be represented and combined with other meanings so as to enable this. Finally, it is unclear how the senses of "clever" prior to selection could be modeled, particularly when the whole idea is to get the multiplicity generated by meaning composition rather than have a multiplicity of primitives.

There are perhaps other strategies for dealing with these problems, and I can't prove that none will work. But I can propose a strategy outside semantics which is intuitive and simple. If the object of interpretation is taken to be the speaker's conceptual reason, then all the facts are uniformly explained. Reviewing earlier conclusions, a reason depends on that proposition for which it is a reason. So the status of an interpretation as a kind of reason explains the all dependencies of interpretation on other propositional elements. Thus a speaker's reason for believing-true "The boxer is clever" may vary from his reason for believing-true "The composer is clever"; likewise for "He's a clever boxer," or "He's a clever composer." A reason also depends on whose reason it is, thus explaining why one speaker's reason for believing-true "Tyson is a clever boxer" might differ from another's. And there may be no overt clue to a speaker's reason at all. Thus the various possible influences on the sense of "clever" in a context can be entirely understood in terms of truisms about reasons.[21]

These points can be reinforced by considering Cohen's "naturally selected" example. It does not seem to me in this case that there is any novel word meaning. The alleged novel meaning is rather the content of the belief that Darwin expresses with sentence D (or, the last clause thereof). No doubt Cohen would agree, but add that the content originates with the interaction of "naturally selected" with the sentential context. I think instead that the content originates with Darwin. What Darwin means by "naturally selected" here is a matter of elaborate theorizing, which is only partly reflected in D. Thus, is it really so clear that the "meaning" here is "singled out by processes of nature"? With equal justice, we might say that it is "singled out by virtue of surviving the stresses of climate, competing organisms, availability of food, and other environmental factors," among many other propositions derivable from Darwin's thought. But then how can it be maintained that the *words* of D, or indeed of any other sentences containing "naturally selected," determine the "meaning"? I think that it cannot. Rather the "meaning" is determined by the speaker's reasons. It remains to explain the multiplicity of not just what a speaker might mean but of what he does mean; I will take this up in the next chapter (with metaphor deferred until chapter 5).

In the tradition of pragmatics, my analysis thus implies a certain potential for simplifying semantic theory. If the resolution of conceptual indeterminacy belongs to pragmatics, then semantic theory need not worry about the motley of resolution circumstances, but only about a general meaning operative acontextually. One benefit of the greater simplicity is less worry about how compositionality works. A source of conceptual indeterminacy can be treated under a given disambiguation as having a unitary meaning which combines with the meanings of other sentence constituents to determine the truth-conditions of the sentence, without complications pertaining to attributiveness or context-dependence (at least, not on its account). Note that a semantic theory would need such an account even if conceptual indeterminacy were within its domain, since a sentence need not contain any clue as to the relevant sense, nor need there be overt clues anywhere. That is, it would have to account for some kind of "default" interpretation: if conceptual indeterminacy is not within its domain, then this is all it has to do.[22]

With only such defaults operative in semantic interpretation, interpreting a conceptually indeterminate sentence does not thereby resolve conceptual indeterminacy. So the resulting understanding of the speaker might be found wanting. But that is how it should be. WDYM-questions in this case are triggered by the partial understanding enabled by what is compositionally derived. Building too much into the semantic account of conceptual indeterminacy would not only increase its complexity but also overlook the potentially dialectical nature of understanding. What is assigned by the semantic theory should not obviate dialectic, but enable it.

6. Ellipsis Revisited

As argued in section 2, a speaker's meaning report that addresses ellipsis is like one that addresses ambiguity in resolving puzzlement in terms of a redescription at the level of what is said. The difference lies in the level at which puzzlement arises. For grammatical ellipsis, this is a stage at which syntactic analysis is not complete, since the ellided material is required by the grammar. For extragrammatical ellipsis, the stage is likewise preinterpretive, but only for lack of an optional contextual determination—optional because the ellided material does not preclude a syntactic structure or semantic interpretation. In either case ellipsis differs from conceptual indeterminacy in that it is addressed at the level of what is said.

It follows that conceptual indeterminacy and ellipsis are compatible, since they occur at different levels: both may be present, and both may give rise to a WDYM-question. But they are not independent. Grammatical ellipsis like ambiguity must have been resolved for conceptual indeterminacy to arise. Perception of conceptual indeterminacy requires that something has been said, hence that a syntactic analysis has been completed. The same is true for extragrammatical ellipsis, except that what is required for something to be said is either that the option for resolution has been exercised or bypassed.

Whereas ambiguity involves limited possibilities stemming from the lexicon, ellipsis involves unlimited though constrained possibilities just as conceptual indeterminacy does. For grammatical ellipsis, the possibilities are grammatically based. For instance, the resolution of "She won't continue" must provide an infinitive as required by "continue." The resolution of "Tonight" must result in a sentence: "Tonight Dad will take everyone for ice cream," "Tonight there is a full moon," etc. What is missing and what counts as a resolution are specified in terms of the grammar.[23]

For extragrammatical ellipsis, the constraints are less obvious. But they do exist. Among those who take "enrichment" to be part of what is said, the consensus is that the enrichment must result in a logically stronger proposition. A speaker might mean by "Sally went to the fair" that Sally went to the fair in her imagination (one parent to another, with a wink). But it would not be a matter of what he had said: one can't say "Sally went to the fair" and thereby say that Sally went to the fair in her imagination. The problem is that Sally's going in her imagination doesn't entail that she went. Another example of what is disallowed is the "privative" adjective, whose distinguishing characteristic is that a modified construction does not entail the unmodified. Thus, "This is a fake gun" and "Morse is a former senator" do not entail "This is a gun" and "Morse is a senator." So one can't say "This is a gun" and thereby say that this is a fake gun; one can't say "Morse is a senator" and thereby say that Morse is a former senator.[24] Thus an answer to a WDYM-question arising in response to extragrammatical ellipsis is subject to a strengthening constraint.[25]

When I concluded in an earlier section that such a question requests a p-reason giving what the speaker wanted to say, rather than a communicative p-reason, I appealed to the case of metaphor where I had suggested that what is requested could be a kind of e-reason rather than a communicative p-reason. Why not likewise for extragrammatical ellipsis? Why couldn't a speaker's meaning by "John jumped" that John jumped over the cliff be analyzed in the same way as a speaker's meaning by "John is clever" that John is quick-witted?

There is a short and a long answer. The short answer is that strengthening is not a constraint on conceptual reasons. John's being clever in the sense of quick-witted entails that he is clever in some sense, but not that he is clever. Perhaps he is stupid in too many other ways for that. The long answer has to do with why strengthening isn't a constraint. A conceptual reason for believing-true "John is clever" includes a kind of conceptual "analysis": certain properties analyzing "clever," appropriate for the speaker on this occasion of trying to describe John. And this analysis bears no logical relation to such analysis as one might associate with the entry for "clever" in the lexicon. Each analysis is continuous with evidential reasoning, and subject to its vagaries. Between two of them, it would be surprising if a logical relation emerged.

The long answer obviously depends on details regarding the kind of analysis in question. I'll provide these in the next chapter.

CHAPTER 4

COMPETENCE

I have argued that speaker's meaning is a relational notion. It is not just a proposition but an answer to a question. I've portrayed the relevant sort of question as isomorphic to a why-question, analyzed as a collection of context-dependent parameters: topic, contrast, and relevance relation. So a speaker's meaning can be characterized by the parameter values of a question that it directly answers. In the case of "belief-fixing" speaker's meaning, the topic is that the speaker believes-true a sentence, and the relevance relation is a conceptual reason. This is a reason for believing-true a sentence, such that its content enters into that of the expressed belief. The homophonic rendering of the speaker's belief from his words is valid only when a conceptual reason is absent. Otherwise, there is a "gap" between what the speaker says and what he believes.

How much of a gap can there be? It could not be arbitrarily large, or there would be no distinction between speaker's meaning and stipulation. One line of attack on the notion of speaker's meaning has been to blur this distinction, implying a Humpty-Dumpty view of language whereby speakers are free to mean whatever they want.[1] But what a speaker means, in the conceptual reason sense, is bound by constraints. One cannot for example mean by "John is clever" that birds fly south in the winter. This does not imply psychological impossibility, or that a speaker might not be able to achieve some desired communicative purpose. It merely implies that fixing content in this way would violate certain constraints.[2]

Knowledge of the constraints seems to be a matter of competence. We would expect anyone who had learned the language to recognize possible speaker's meanings, and be able to think of other possibilities and rule out others. But it could be that more than competence is involved, since competent speakers have other abilities which might be reflected in our expectation. In this chapter, however, my main concern will be with such constraints as relate to lexical competence.

I will begin by reviewing work of Tyler Burge, according to which the concept associated with a word in a speaker's idiolect may involve a commitment to sample referents. I will propose an addendum in section 2, that competence entails constraints on the ways a speaker may project perceived essential properties from samples. These "projection constraints" are needed to account for what is likely shared among speakers if their stocks of samples diverge, a point I will illustrate with mentalistic concepts. In section 3, these issues will be brought to bear on speaker's meaning in two ways. I will show how the concept associated with a word in a speaker's idiolect can be the object of a WDYM-question. And I will suggest that conceptual reasons incorporate speakers' projections, based on samples peculiar to the context. Accordingly in section 4 I will spell out how projection constraints bear on conceptual reasons. I will conclude in the last section with a discussion of psychological indeterminacy, in the sense of a multiplicity of not just possible but actual speaker's meanings.

1. Burge on the Role of Examples

Tyler Burge has argued that, for many words, sample referents partly determine the individuation of their corresponding concepts (Burge 1986, 1989, 1993; henceforth references are to 1989 unless otherwise indicated). The words in question are a wide range of nouns and verbs which are non-indexical and "apply to everyday, empirically discernible objects, stuffs, properties, and events...words like 'tiger', 'water', 'mud', 'stone', 'tree', 'bread', 'knife', 'chair', 'edge', 'shadow', 'baby', 'walk', 'fight', and so on" (181). I will refer to the objects of study here as "perceptually-based" words and concepts. According to Burge, grasping such concepts is partly a matter of committing oneself to correctly describe examples. What a speaker would on reflection give as his understanding of the word—his "explication"—is consequently not all there is to the associated concept, because the enterprise of trying to get examples right is fallible.[3]

One aspect of fallibility has to do with changes in the stock of examples to which a speaker is committed. For instance, when asked to give his understanding of "chair," a speaker might mention legs and a seat. Informed of skilift chairs, he would adjust his explication accordingly.[4] Such an adjustment does not entail a change in the concept. Burge suggests that more typically one is corrected on the basis of "empirical matters about which there are cognitive rights and wrongs" (184). That an understanding of a concept might change without the concept changing has similarly long been argued by Putnam (e.g. 1988, 9-11) and Quine (e.g. 1991, 271; on whom see also Burge 1993, 312-314).

Even given a fixed stock of examples, an explication is still fallible. It is derived from examples by perceptual inference, which is fallible; perceived properties may not actually be present. And even accurate perception "need not suffice to discriminate instances of the concept from every possible look-alike" (183). For natural kind terms the nature of instances may not be perceptually accessible, in which case experts may be required for identification.[5] A further consideration which will be important in what follows is that what one projects from the examples as the essential nature is variable even if perception is accurate. Thus a speaker who has accurately apprehended certain chairs may take chairhood to be a matter of legs-and-a-seat, or just a seat. An explication is dependent not only on the examples' perceived properties but also on which of these properties are projected as essential.[6]

For all these reasons, our commitment to get examples right implies that our explications are subject to correction: "in explication one naturally alternates between thinking of examples and refining one's conceptual explication in order to accord with examples that one recognizes as legitimate" (182). While an explication sometimes legitimates an example—e.g. one determines that chairs have seats but not necessarily legs, and newly concludes that a big beanbag is also a chair—normally the interaction is in the other direction. In this sense examples "anchor" the concept, constituting the data to which a conceptual explication is accountable: "...the touchstone for evaluating attempts at conceptual explication" (182). That is, an explication is evaluated according to how well it captures examples independently recognized as falling under the concept.[7]

Following Quine and Putnam, Burge thus rejects the traditional view according to which a concept consists of necessary and sufficient conditions which determine reference and are known by competent speakers.[8] It is not just a matter of language that referents of a term have the properties specified in a competent speaker's explication of a concept. The dialectic between explication and examples is not definition-mongering but "genuine reasoning" (183), in that it results in knowledge outstripping what was known previously.

Suppose I explicate my word "chair" in such a way that requires that chairs have legs, and then come to realize that beach chairs, or deck-chairs bolted to a wall, or ski-lift chairs, are counterexamples. Or suppose I learn more about how to discriminate water from other (possible or actual) colorless, tasteless, potable liquids. Then I learn something about chairs or water that I did not know before (182).

In other words, a speaker's explication of a concept is not a "definition" but a working hypothesis about the shared nature of the example referents, in virtue of they belong to a kind. "In virtue of which" here implies "basic, 'essential', and necessarily true information" about a kind, as Burge puts it (1986, 703), though not true in virtue of meaning. "Nature" here is not meant to imply that only natural kind terms such as "water" or "tiger" are at issue, where the nature of the kind is a matter for scientific experts to discover. For other terms it might be for competent speakers to discover. Some are better at it than others: those whose grasp of the examples and whose ability to make distinctions and generalize are such that they could persuade other competent speakers (1986, 702-703).[9]

It would be a mistake to conclude from the fallibility of conceptual explication that there is nothing linguistic about an attribution of properties specified in an explication, as in "Water is drinkable," "Tigers are striped," or "Chairs have seats." A speaker's ability to make such attributions is indicative of his linguistic competence. Burge suggests that competence comes in degrees, where "minimal competence consists in conformity to the practice of others...[and] 'greatest competence' [has to do with being] persuasive to other competent speakers in the use and explication of the language." In no case is perfect knowledge required. Due to the role of examples, explications of even the most competent speakers are subject to correction.[10] Earlier, Putnam introduced a compatible notion of minimal competence in connection with natural kind terms. For purposes of communication a speaker's linguistic community requires knowledge of "stereotypical" properties, and in this sense the knowledge is linguistic. We need only bear in mind that it is not logically necessary that all, most, or even some tigers are striped, since we could be wrong about the examples (Putnam 1975, 248-251). Thus the hypothesis represented by an explication is empirical, but also has a prior plausibility deriving from the satisfaction of linguistic constraints. For community consensus creates at least some presumption of truth: "the fact is we could hardly communicate successfully if most of our stereotypes weren't pretty accurate as far as they go" (251).

So far the discussion has concerned the concept associated with a word in a speaker's idiolect. The commitment to examples entails that a speaker's explication does not exhaust the concept associated with a word even in his own idiolect. (I will henceforth sometimes use the shorthand "idiolectical concept.") Nothing so far implies that our perceptually-based concepts are shared. But they are, at least in large measure, because of

> the publicity of the examples and our shared perceptual and inferential equipment. Given that we have been exposed to substantially similar knives, chairs, water, trees, mud, walkings, and fightings, and have heard these associated with the same words, it is to be expected that we project from actual examples in similar ways. Although our kind-forming abilities may differ in some instances, it is reasonable to expect that they will typically be the same, especially with concepts that apply to entities of common perceptual experience. Normally we will be committed to the legitimacy of the same examples, and will be committed to characterizing those examples, correctly. Given that the examples are public, no one has privileged authority about their characteristics (185).

Furthermore, we frequently rely on others for access to the examples, a dependence which "grows as one's linguistic and cognitive resources widen. In some cases we depend heavily on the perceptual experiences of others (as with 'tiger', 'penguin', and 'rain', for those of us in California). In other cases we depend on theoretical background knowledge ('gene', 'cancer') or on more ordinary expertise ('arthritis', 'carburetor'). In many such cases, we intentionally take over the applications that others have made" (185).

For my purposes the remark that "it is to be expected that we project from actual examples in similar ways" deserves special attention. Why "similar" rather than "identical"? There are two reasons. First, the examples to which we are exposed are not type-identical. Second, there is leeway in what can be projected from a given stock. As noted, some speakers might project one way and others other ways, even from type-identical examples. Notice that inasmuch as projection figures in explication, the variation here is intralinguistic. An explication in Burge's sense is what a speaker would upon reflection give as his understanding of a word, to a linguistic peer; "By 'tiger' I mean tiger" wouldn't qualify.[11]

Why "similar" rather than "wildly divergent"? Burge's rationale is that one speaker's examples are similar to another's. It does not follow that the projections are similar; but as an independent point it is reasonable to suppose that there are constraints on how much difference there can be. In the case of "chair," no speaker may project weighing-less-than-a-ton, or objecthood. The point would seem to bear on the question of competence (i.e. minimal competence, as henceforth), for if a speaker did so project we would infer that he had not learned the word "chair." Similarly for Putnam. A speaker who knows only that "tiger" refers to physical objects and so cannot tell tigers from snowballs has not acquired the word. Community practice requires constrained projection from stereotypical tigers, and physical-objecthood falls outside the constraints (1975, 247-248). For Putnam a constrained projection for "tiger" includes the property of being striped, and some combination of being feline, carnivorous, fierce, etc. While variation among speakers is possible among the latter properties, constraints on the variation make for a certain similarity among speakers' projection mechanisms.[12]

2. Projection Constraints

To summarize, a speaker's perceptually-based concept is determined not just by his explication of it, but also his commitment to get exemplars right. This implies that his explication is subject to correction because the stock of examples may change. Even given a fixed stock, his perception of the examples is fallible; even accurate perception may not suffice to distinguish referents from look-alikes; nor does it determine unique projections of perceived essential properties. The commitment to getting examples right also implies that perceptually-based concepts are largely shared, because our examples and perceptual and projection mechanisms are largely shared.

Note that an explication is based on what properties a speaker projects from a stock without necessarily reflecting it exactly. Since an explication is conscious, it may also reflect faulty memory, fatigue, difficulty of articulation, etc. It is a standard point that linguistic knowledge may not be reflected in a speaker's overt "performance" because of the incursion of these extraneous factors. The caveat on explications that they be what the speaker would give "upon reflection" only partly bridges the gap between performance and linguistic knowledge. Adverting to a projection, regardless of whether or how it is articulated, avoids the gap altogether. For this reason I will often refer to projections henceforth rather than explications. I will also use "understanding"—i.e. of a concept—interchangeably with "projection."

The notion of a projection function will play an important role in what follows. I take it to be required by Burge's account of perceptually-based concepts. But it also can be motivated independently as a model of a certain kind-forming ability. It is useful to contrast it with another ability which is in some sense more basic. Assume that a kind is a set of entities.[13] Then an ability to recognize the kind might be modeled by what's called the "characteristic function" of the set: a function which returns true given any member and false given any non-member. We may think of "knowing" such a function as the ability to place an entity inside or outside the kind, if the entity were considered. This is compatible with partial knowledge of kind members insofar as members need be known as such only if considered.

The ability I have in mind is different, in that with partial knowledge of members comes some idea of the nature of the kind. Thus a projection function is a function from sample entities to hypothesized properties, in virtue of which the samples are considered to belong to the kind. Whereas the characteristic function is more basic from a metaphysical standpoint, the projection function is of greater epistemological significance if Burge's account of concepts is correct. It models how a speaker's understanding of a concept varies with the samples he accepts.

Burge (1986, 703) and Putnam take competence to be a matter of projecting from stereotypical ("normal," "good") examples.[14] But reflection on projection functions reveals a problem. Suppose Fred is acquainted only with stereotypical tigers, from which he hypothesizes that tigerhood is a matter of being striped, fierce, and feline. He is then competent on the Burge-Putnam account. But suppose further that if presented with a tame tiger, he would decide instead that tigerhood is a matter of having whiskers. Then it would seem that he is not competent after all. A speaker who has acquired the word "tiger" must be able to project acceptable properties not only from stereotypical tigers, but from arbitrary sets of tiger instances.

The point isn't that Fred is minimally competent since he has acquired the stereotype, but not to a greater degree since he hasn't learned projection from stereotypes plus non-stereotypes. Rather, he is not minimally competent. Minimal competence doesn't require actual knowledge of or actual projection from non-stereotypical instances, but it does require the potential. It requires this because the constraints on projection from stereotypes are of a piece with constraints on projection from other possible cases. "From stereotypical tigers, project the properties of being striped and feline; from other cases project whatever you want" presumably has no possible cognitive realization.

This is not to deny that there is something special about a stereotype. What's special has to do with how competence can be *conveyed*. Putnam emphasizes that "there are a few facts about 'lemon' or 'tiger'...such that one can convey the use of 'lemon' or 'tiger' by simply conveying those facts. More precisely one cannot convey the approximate use unless one gets [these] facts across" (1975, 148). Similarly Burge comments that a "definition," encompassing stereotypical properties for words like "tiger," "provide a short account of the application of the concept that meets the practical interests of someone else likely to use the term" (1993, 316). If so, then stereotypes are important. But it is consistent to add that knowing these facts about stereotypical examples does not entail that one is capable of usage (even "approximate" usage). Stereotypes provide just one test of this capability.

The relevance of a projection function to competence is more obvious when there *is* no stereotype. I now want to venture beyond Burge's domain by making this point in connection with non-perceptually-based concepts.

Notice first that these concepts also seem to involve a commitment to get examples right. Take mentalistic concepts. Defining them is impossible ("intelligent" being a notorious case): any attempt is bound to be open-ended, as for example Ryle's (1949) "dispositional" analyses were. The indefiniteness can be understood as an epiphenomenon of the variety of possible projections and the variety of possible sample sets: different sample sets are possible, and for any given set different projections are possible within the constraints. Even a fixed projection from a fixed set is not a "definition" but a hypothesis, subject to change. No wonder no one can say what it is to be intelligent. Competent speakers can have different specimens in mind, different ideas of what it is that makes any given specimen intelligent, and any speaker can legitimately change her mind about what it is that makes a specimen intelligent (without changing her concept of intelligence).

All this is true of perceptually-based concepts as well, but not to the same degree. For mentalistic terms, getting examples right is more problematic. This is not because they are natural kind terms, implying an underlying nature inaccessible to ordinary speakers. They are not. While there may well be genetic factors in personality broadly speaking, there is little reason to believe that aspects of personality as categorized by our everyday terms individually correspond to distinct genetic markers (e.g. a "proud" gene), or to any underlying features for which there is a scientific theory.[15] The reason it is more problematic to get examples right is that cleverness, for instance, is not so primitive a feature of the perceptual landscape as chairs, tigers, etc. It requires more attention, judgment, and inference to detect cleverness than to detect a chair. The problem isn't just that mentalistic properties are dispositional, so that one might be apprehending a clever person when he isn't being clever. This is not the telling difference, because an easily perceptible object or property may also be dispositional. For instance, being a certain color has to do not with the way it happens to appear, but the way it would appear under normal lighting. The telling difference has to do with the indirectness of perception. While there is certainly a sense in which cleverness can be perceived, it is not the "basic" sense in which chairs or colors can be perceived.

What is this "basic" sense? A brief review of Fodor's (1983) study of mental faculties will be helpful. On Fodor's picture, cognitive "modules" compute representations from transduced stimuli. Their most important distinguishing property is "informational encapsulation," meaning that they have access to only some of the information available to the mind as a whole. In this respect they are like reflexes. If a trusted friend thrusts her finger close enough to my eye, I will blink despite my trust, a fact which can be interpreted as the encapsulation of the eyelid reflex: it is sensitive only to motions near my eye. Similarly, a module for vision responds to optical stimuli without interaction with higher cognition, so that e.g. one will be fooled by a visual illusion even with conscious knowledge that it is an illusion. For current purposes, two features of modules related to encapsulation are especially noteworthy. First, their operation on stimuli is mandatory. One cannot look at a dog and choose not to see it. Second, they are biologically "hard-wired," which entails among other things that they define a sense in which our "perceptual equipment" is shared. Hard-wired entails innate, which entails shared (52-55, 98-99).

These reflections would not be relevant to current concerns if a perceptual module computed outputs on a preconceptual level, such as Marr's "primal sketch" (1982, 52-98). But Fodor suggests that such primitive representations are intermediate to final output couched in terms of "basic categories." What makes a category "basic" is a cluster of psychological features which appear at a particular level of a category hierarchy. Consider "poodle," "dog," "mammal," "animal," "physical object." "Dog" is the most psychologically salient, in that it is used more frequently than other categories in the hierarchy; it is learned earlier; it is the most natural candidate for ostensive definition (one can teach "dog" ostensively to a child without first having taught "poodle," but not vice versa); and it yields an "information peak" in that if a subject is asked to list information that comes to mind for, say, "animal," "dog," and "poodle," one gets many more properties for "dog" than for "animal," but only a few more for "poodle" than for "dog." Given Gricean maxims, the latter feature implies that basic categories are usually the natural ones to use for describing things. Thus in most circumstances, "There's a lady walking her dog" is preferred to "There's a lady walking her animal," "There's a lady walking her poodle," or "There's a lady walking her little black poodle." (See 93-97, citing work by cognitive psychologists Brown, Rosch, and others.)

Fodor takes such facts to reflect "a deeper psychological reality":

> Basic categories are phenomenologically *given*; they provide, as it were, the natural level for describing things *to oneself*. A glance out the window thus reveals: a lady walking a *dog*, rather than a lady walking a silver-grey, miniature etc....You might predict from these intuitions that perceptual identifications which involve the application of basic categories ought to be fast as compared to applications of either more or less abstract members of their implication hierarchies...[Furthermore] basic categories are typically the most abstract members of their implication hierarchies which subtend individuals of approximately similar appearance...So, roughly, you can draw something that is just a dog, but you can't draw something that is just an animal; you can draw something that is just a chair, but you can't draw something that is just furniture (96).

Collectively these observations suggest that the vision module, restricted to fast, maximally informational inferences from visual properties only, renders its output in terms of basic categories.

It would appear that Burge's perceptually-based concepts are just basic categories in the foregoing sense; at least, there is considerable overlap. Not just by the words he uses as examples, but his emphasis on sample referents being shared in part via the perceptual similarity of referents. Thus if one considers "furniture" rather than "chair," it is not at all clear why we should expect that different speakers tend to converge on the same samples owing to similar perceptual abilities. If Fodor's suggestion is right, it seems plausible that the perceptually-based concepts we've been considering are distinguishable from other concepts in that instances are hypothesized reflexively by a vision module—i.e. that this is what "bases" them in perception.

In particular they are distinguishable from mentalistic concepts, for which projection presumably transpires not in a module but in what Fodor calls "central systems," i.e. general-purpose reasoning.[16] One consequence is that sample referents tend less to be shared among speakers. For perceptually-based concepts, examples are perceived as falling under the concept by processing that is mandatory and hard-wired, hence largely shared among speakers. There is thus a sense in which examples are, as Fodor puts it, "phenomenologically given." But for mentalistic concepts, examples noticed by one speaker would tend less to be the same as those noticed by another, as would the properties in virtue of which any example is taken to fall under the concept—because noticing is not automatic. Rather one must use reasoning, of a sort not different in kind from the reasoning that goes into making breakfast. Everyone has his own way of doing it.

As we've seen, Burge argues for largely shared examples of perceptually-based concepts partly on the basis of "shared perceptual and inferential equipment" (185). The current conclusion is that the "inferential equipment" outside the vision module will tend less toward sharing of examples than that inside. *A fortiori* for stereotypical examples. For mentalistic concepts a given speaker need not have any stereotype, and if he does it need not be the same as another speaker's. Any shared stereotype, moreover, would be an accident, lacking the significance of a stereotype for a natural kind term: something needed to "convey the approximate use," on Putnam's account. Is there a stereotype for "intelligent"? Maybe Einstein. But the properties by which Einstein was intelligent are not particularly likely to convey the approximate usage, because they are not very prevalent. Perhaps we could do better with other candidates. But which ones? And what are their relevant properties? (Also see Rey 1999, 297.)

Summing to this point: whereas mentalistic concepts are analogous to perceptually-based concepts in that they involve a commitment to get examples right, there are also disanalogies related to the fact that they are not as directly based in perception. Because there is more divergence among speakers in terms of projections and examples, getting examples right is more problematic.

While the argument has been made for mentalistic concepts, by similar rationale these conclusions also hold for the other empirical abstract words that are my subject of concern: "freedom," "love," "society," etc. They are abstract in the way mentalistic terms are, perception of instances being a matter of general reasoning rather than a cognitive module. Admittedly, using this criterion makes my demarcation subject to empirical cognitive science. But I don't have any better pretheoretical intuition of what exactly distinguishes the sort of words I'm talking about, and even if I did I would still need to be tentative and open-minded about drawing the lines. Appealing to even tentative conclusions on cognitive modules and basic categories serves to sharpen such intuitions as I have.

I am not characterizing the words of concern simply as those which do not express basic categories. For one thing, I am not talking about abstract concepts which are not perceptual at all, like the concept of a square root. For another, a category may qualify as non-basic not only by being too abstract, but by being not abstract enough (e.g. "little black poodle"). And for another, I am not talking about the kind of abstractness that accrues to say "animal" or "furniture" in virtue of dominating other categories which are basic; there is no basic category under "clever," for example. I'm aware that more needs to be said, with lots of case-by-case discussion of examples. But I leave this for future work, while continuing to use what seem to me clear examples.

Returning to the question of competence, I've criticized the Burge-Putnam account for emphasizing capability with regard to a stereotype to the exclusion of more general capability. The criticism is now stronger, in that for abstract concepts there is not even a stereotype on which one may be tempted to focus an account. Further, the importance of the general capability comes more plainly into view. Whereas for perceptually-based concepts, shared perceptions and sample referents are two of the factors which contribute to the communal tendency of the concept, for more abstract concepts these factors are attenuated. But there remains another: similar projection functions. This is the general capability which I propose accounts for competence with respect to words across the range of Burge's concern and mine.

What is it, though, for projection functions to be "similar"? To be identical, two functions must have the same output for any given input. This is too strong: competent speakers may disagree on their projections from any given set of samples. I have in mind similarity in the sense of common constraints. Thus even if speakers disagree on their projections from given clever instances, they can agree that each other's projections are "okay," and that no one may project forgetfulness or rectangularity.

But what are shared constraints? Let's go back to the definition of a function, which includes a "domain," from which inputs are drawn, and a "range," from which outputs are drawn. Specifying a range imposes constraints on outputs in a straightforward sense: the outputs must come from the range. As a range is a set, there is nothing problematic about sameness of constraints in this sense; it is just set equality. So my suggestion is that we can think of projection functions as commonly constrained in virtue of having the same range. Thus their outputs on the same input may diverge but may not venture outside the range.[17]

To enter into an account of competence, constraints so construed must be an object of speakers' knowledge. What is it to know a set? Recall our earlier discussion of knowing a set's "characteristic function." The characteristic function for the range is one which, on any given input property, returns true if it is in the range and false otherwise. Knowing such a function is a matter of being able to classify any property as belonging to the set or not, if the property were considered. This does not entail being able to rattle off all the admissible properties, since properties need not have been considered.

Let me conclude this section by emphasizing that my present concern is only with "meaning" in the sense of what a competent speaker knows. This is therefore a kind of meaning which is "in the head," but in light of the above arguments it should be distinguished from what Putnam characterizes as in the head, i.e. stereotypical properties accounting for a speaker's competence. Without disputing that what's in the head doesn't determine reference, I'm suggesting that it's something else in the head that accounts for competence—namely, the range of a projection function. So it's this which accounts for meaning in the sense of current concern. I have no substantive disagreement with other uses of "meaning" which are consistent with this.[18]

3. Idiolects, Conceptual Reasons, and "Usage"

Before relating the foregoing to a speaker's conceptual reason, we need to consider another type of speaker's meaning for purposes of comparison. Recall the earlier principle:

DP1': If a normal English speaker asserts 'p', where 'p' is an English sentence containing no ambiguous or indexical terms, then he says that p.

"Normal English speaker" implies that when interpreting the speaker's words, we should assign their meanings in English. This ignores possible differences in idiolect.[19] If we think the speaker's idiolect differs from ours, we would not proceed by disquotation but by rendering one or more of his words into our own idiolect. One might for example report an utterer of "Chairs are ugly" to have said that armchairs are ugly, taking "chair" in his idiolect to mean what "armchair" does in ours.

Though we often assume that a speaker's idiolect is the same as ours, it's not obvious how often we're right. But the analysis of concepts we've been considering entails that we are right more often than might be thought. Suppose a speaker explains that on his concept of "chair," chairs have a seat, legs, and arms, whereas the hearer would not take arms to be necessary. So far this seems to be an idiolectical difference. But suppose further that the hearer is able to persuade the speaker that arms are not necessary, appealing to armless specimens in his dining room. On the current analysis, what changes for the speaker is his hypothesis about the nature of chairs, not necessarily his concept of chairs. He still might have all along shared the concept with the hearer, if they agree on the referents which must be taken into account.

In any case, we sometimes do assume a difference and want to know what it is. A WDYM-question would be an apt instrument. Note that presumed divergence of another's linguistic competence is not a reflection on one's own, so there is no exception here to our earlier observation that a WDYM-question is not an apt device for requesting information of which knowledge is a matter of competence. The topic of the relevant question might be:

So-and-so says that "chairs" are ugly.

This looks like the topic for a question arising in response to lexical ambiguity:

So-and-so says that Sally went to the "bank."

But the respective quotes signify different stages. In the latter case, the multiple listings of "bank" in one's lexicon are presupposed, and a particular one requested. In the former, the multiple listings are likewise presupposed, and a particular one partly attributed. Thus the listing for the chairman sense has been ruled out, and the listing for the furniture sense selected and attributed. But the entry for this listing, i.e. in the questioner's lexicon, is not attributed. The relevance relation is a p-reason giving what the speaker intended to say. Thus a direct answer provides an explanatory redescription at the level of what is said, just as in ambiguity, but in this case the redescription renders the problematic word into the questioner's idiolect.

While a speaker's idiolect can change, it does not do so quickly or often. Thus suppose we establish that "clever" in Al's idiolect is what we would call "inventive." Then if we hear "clever" from him again tomorrow, we will not likely wonder what he means in the idiolectical sense. If Al says "John is clever" we can take him to have said that John is inventive; if he says "The boxer is clever" or "Sally is clever," we can take him to have said that the boxer is inventive or that Sally is inventive. In this respect, idiolect is not a contextual factor, unlike the factors that determine a disambiguation. Rather it is a matter of one's lexicon, a component of an internalized grammar that a speaker carries around from occasion to occasion.[20]

I now want to apply the current analysis of concepts to a speaker's conceptual reason. It can't apply without modification because what's been analyzed is a concept that a speaker has as a matter of idiolect, for which the relevant sense of speaker's meaning has to do with what he intended to say. But as we've seen, a speaker's meaning in the sense of a conceptual reason has to do with the content of belief, distinct from what he has said. The content of this belief is sensitive to the occasion of use. Al's conceptual reason for believing that "John is clever" is true may differ from his conceptual reason for believing that "The boxer is clever" is true or his conceptual reason for believing that "Sally is clever" is true; he may have in mind John's wit, the boxer's ability to feint, and Sally's adeptness at problem-solving. Meanwhile the idiolectical concept is likely to be the same in each case, reflected in what he has said.

How then to apply the current analysis to a conceptual reason? The basic idea is simple. We've seen that the concept attached to a word in a speaker's idiolect is associated with a projection function, representing how the speaker's projection varies with the sample referents he accepts. I wish to maintain that a conceptual reason embodies the same concept, in that part of its content is determined by the same projection function, but operating on distinct samples peculiar to the context.

Take Al's meaning by "John is clever" that John is quick-witted. Quick-wittedness is what Al projects from the cleverness samples he has in mind on this occasion—say, John's performance in various conversations. The concept Al employs in his conceptual reason is the same as his idiolectical concept for "clever," but the property he projects is different because the sample referents are. This projection enters into the content of the conceptual reason, and is based on these samples *alone*, not on the ongoing stock as increased by the samples. The latter does presumably result, perhaps affecting how Al henceforth would explain his concept of cleverness. But the problem of projection in this context is: in virtue of what are *these* samples instances of cleverness?

This explains the fact that examples can be given in response to a WDYM-question requesting a conceptual reason. Thus Al might reply: "Well, like the way he had everyone in stitches at dinner the other night." This would be giving his "data," and inviting the interlocutor to do his own projection.[21] This has advantages and disadvantages. On the one hand, if an interlocutor knows the examples that the speaker is trying to get right, he might be able to do a better job at getting them right than the speaker. Thus an interlocutor might be able to persuade the speaker that the sense in which John is clever really has to do with his social skills, not just his wit. Or he may remind the speaker of other examples of John's behavior, likewise resulting in the speaker adjusting his projection. From the speaker's point of view, there is the additional advantage that giving an example is probably easier than articulating his projection. But on the other hand, an interlocutor may not project as well as the speaker. This is likely if the example is not the speaker's full stock, i.e. if the interlocutor's data is insufficient. Even if it is the full stock, it may be the speaker who can persuade the hearer of relevant properties to project.

John's behavior does double duty as the basis for projected properties figuring in the content of Al's belief that John is clever in the sense of quick-witted, and as justification for the belief. But a belief whose content has been fixed by the speaker need not be justified. Thus the samples need not be of John's behavior. Al might reply "Well, you know how Marcia was last night after dinner? That's how John can be," not actually knowing of relevant behavior by John. There would then be lesser justification, but no less an instance of a conceptual reason.

On the current analysis, the speaker is not the final authority on the content of his conceptual reason. His projection is a hypothesis about the nature of the samples he has in mind. It might be wrong; he might change his mind about it; someone else might be able to do better. This requires that I modify the earlier characterization of the inferential role reflective of belief content fixed by the speaker. I've said that one prominent feature of such a role is the existence of certain necessary inferences. If for instance a speaker means by "John is clever" that John is quick-witted, then his inference from the proposition that John is quick-witted to what he believes is maximally strong. But given that the projection of properties from examples is fallible, this is not quite right. The basis of an idiolectical concept in examples means that projected properties are not related as a matter of language to the word. Likewise neither are projected properties resident in a conceptual reason, even relative to this context.

Thus note the contrast between Al's believing that John is clever in the sense of quick-witted and Al's believing that John is quick-witted. The inferential roles are different: in the latter case, there obviously would be a necessary inference between what he believes and the proposition that John is quick-witted. If Al had sincerely said "John is quick-witted," he would not be exercising his concept of cleverness, and no hypothesis thereof would be involved.

Is there not a different concept here, clever-in-the-sense-of-quick-witted? I maintain that there is no such thing. To allow any such concept would be to allow any number, each capable of spontaneous creation distinct from the concept of cleverness, to which the relation would be unclear. Instead there is only the one concept, but applied to new sample referents from which new properties are projected. This constitutes the sense in which "clever" is being "used": application to new samples, not spawning of a new concept.

Meanwhile an old understanding of the concept, based on projection from an ongoing stock, coexists with the new. As noted the old understanding may change as a result of this usage, once John's behavior episodes are added to the stock. In any event it remains in the background, and persists beyond this context of utterance; whereas the contextual understanding is foremost in the speaker's consciousness, but ephemeral.

If it seems paradoxical that two understandings of a concept can exist simultaneously, consider an analogy. A tailor has an Armani suit design with default measurements for the shoulders, neck, etc. He can use the design as is, when he thinks a customer fits the defaults, or when he doesn't care about a good fit (presumably not getting paid in that case). Otherwise he can tailor the design to fit a customer. In this case, the design is still operative in that it provides the general proportions (making for a certain "look") and serves as starting point for the tailoring. The tailored design is not a new design, just the old one appropriately adjusted. Meanwhile the tailor has an understanding both of the design with defaults and the design as tailored; the first is persistent, though he may occasionally adjust the default measurements with his accumulated experience of customers' measurements, whereas the second goes out the door with the customer. Thus Al tailors his concept of cleverness to fit John, and more generally, one can tailor an abstract concept to fit a situation that one wishes to describe. This is what conceptual reasons are for.

Perceptually-based concepts can be tailored too. Suppose Al remarks of an avant-garde piece of furniture "That thing's a chair." It could be that Al would be applying only his idiolectical concept under the usual understanding, based on experience with many chairs. But alternatively, Al might have in this context an additional understanding based on this sample only. Al might believe that the thing is a chair in the sense that one can sit in it, without taking the capability of being sat upon to be the nature of chairs. He just thinks this capability is what makes *this* thing a chair (that being the best he can do). Because perceptually-based concepts have associated projection functions, they are also capable of usage in the current sense. But because they are perceptually-based, there is not as much flexibility for such usage. As samples are more shared among speakers and more objectively similar to one another than for abstract concepts, there is less occasion for encountering unique samples; and as projections from any given samples tend more to be shared, a new understanding is less likely to be required even upon such encounters.

In the introductory chapter I noted that, with ambiguity ruled out as a source of conceptual indeterminacy, it was yet to be determined whether the source was lexical at all. I'm now identifying a lexical source. Words are associated with concepts; understanding of a concept is modeled by a projection function. This is not to deny that apprehension of conceptual indeterminacy is sensitive to the sentence in which a word appears. The topic of the WDYM-question is a believed-true sentence, relative to which a word is deemed puzzling. Further, resolution of conceptual indeterminacy by specification of a conceptual reason is propositional, irreducibly so. Consider another example, a speaker's meaning by "The county cannot absorb any more immigrants" that any further jobs in the county taken by immigrants will come at the expense of native job-seekers. Conceptual indeterminacy stems from "absorb." Taking a referent of a relation to be a pair of entities, the sample referent that the speaker has in mind in this context is a county and a group of immigrants. What the speaker projects from this is a relation having to do with a non-zero-sum job market for county residents and immigrants. But unlike the clever example, what is projected does not correspond to any constituent in the content of the speaker's belief. An analogous point is well-known in connection with paraphrasing the meaning of a word as it occurs in a sentence. Alston (1971, 41) remarks that in "I ran him a close second," the meaning of "ran" is not captured by any word which can be substituted for "ran" without changing the meaning of the sentence; rather, a sentential paraphrase is required, as in "I placed second, close behind him." Thus while it is sometimes possible to report a speaker's meaning with a subpropositional constituent, as in "By 'clever' he means quick-witted," such reports are elliptical. The content of a conceptual reason is propositional, as required by its role in belief fixation.

4. Conceptual Reasons Constrained, Part One

We can now account for the constraints on conceptual reasons. I've concluded that competence with respect to a perceptually-based or abstract word means knowing the range common to speakers' projection functions, which are associated with speakers' idiolectical concepts. But we've just seen that an idiolectical concept can also be used in a given context in such a way that the function operates on samples peculiar to the context. It is the same concept, however, and the same function with the same range. So for the words in question, the latter represents the constraints not only among speakers, and not only for a given speaker's ongoing understanding of a concept, but also for a given speaker's context-dependent understanding.

Thus, far from there being anything odd about diverging not only from others' understanding of a concept but also from one's own ongoing understanding, such contextual usage is an exercise of one's competence. One version of the slogan "meaning is use" is that competence implies the ability to use words in this way.[22]

I take this to be partial account of competence: only for some words, and only an aspect of those words. So while I have opposed my account to that of Burge and Putnam, it is at least largely compatible with accounts that address other aspects. On the one hand, it is compatible with accounts of competence with respect to, say, non-empirical words and indexicals. On the other hand, it is largely compatible with accounts which analyze what it is to know an accepted meaning of a word or sentence, as opposed to what constrains usages including novel ones. Here I would include truth-conditional semantics and inferential role semantics (taken to imply that a word's meaning is its contribution to truth-conditions or to inferential role).

To take a more recent example, consider Marconi (1997), who identifies both "inferential" and "referential" aspects of competence. The former is the ability "to manage a network of connections among words, underlying such performances as semantic inference paraphrase, definition, retrieval of a word from its definition, finding a synonym, and so forth," while the latter is the mostly independent ability "to apply words to the real world [underlying] such performances as naming, answering questions concerning the obtaining situation, obeying orders such as 'Close the door!', following directions, etc." (59, 64). Marconi does not intend to cover all words; his paradigms are perceptually-based words such as "dog," "black," and "kick." For non-referential words, such as "unlikely," derive," or "nevertheless," he suggests that competence may consist of just the inferential aspect (64).

What about knowing the range of a projection function? It is not just inferential ability because projection is from referents in the world. Nor is it just referential ability, because it involves hypothesis formation, not for identifying referents but for inferring properties in virtue of which they are referents. Conceivably it might be made out as some sort of intertwining of the two aspects in a way friendly to Marconi (who allows that the aspects are not entirely independent). But I think it is better to see the problems here as symptomatic of a fundamental difference: whereas Marconi's concern is with established senses, my account entails being able to come up with novel senses. This explains not only why his account does not apply to abstract words, as it is not intended to, but also, in light of metaphor as we'll see, why his account is not complete for perceptually-based words.

Projection constraints might be considered normative in the sense of disallowing some usages and allowing others. But I take it as a fact, not a prescription, that one cannot mean by "John is clever" that John has a big nose (i.e. in the sense of a conceptual reason—it is irrelevant whether there is some context where somehow it could be communicated that John has a big nose). Projection constraints are posited to account for such facts, just as a constraint in syntax may be posited to account for an intuition of syntactic deviance.

Even considered as norms, projection constraints in my account make little contact with the debate over semantic norms. For example, Chomsky has denied that there is any such thing as public language in the sense of some common entity mastered by competent speakers; for him, there are just individual competences. He remarks:

> Successful communication between Peter and Mary does not entail the existence of shared meanings...in a public language...any more than physical resemblance between Peter and Mary entails the existence of a public form they share...It may be that when he listens to Mary speak, Peter proceeds by assuming that she is identical to him, modulo M, some array of modifications that he must work out. Sometimes the task is easy, sometimes hard, sometimes hopeless (1992b, 215).

But projection constraints are not posited on the basis of successful communication between speakers; they apply equally in cases where communication is quite unlikely. Nor are they posited as "meanings" in the sense of lexical meanings, entering into compositional rules. Finally, the variation that is constrained is as much in a given speaker's usages as between speakers. I do posit these constraints as shared, but I do not know of any existing account of norms or objection thereto which applies.[23]

This said, I recognize that positing projection constraints as shared rather than similar is an idealization. But it should be borne in mind that the posited constraints are quite permissive. Two speakers' usages and two usages of a given speaker can vary widely: I or you might, whenever, mean by "John is clever" that John is quick-witted, that he's good at manipulating people, that he has various propensities for seeing his way out trouble not of his own making, etc. Shared constraints entail that despite their various usages speakers can agree that this or that usage is "okay," whereas others are not. I expect that the idealization serves for all but the most delicate of facts about usage in the relevant sense.

Let me now be explicit about how projection constraints bear upon speaker's meanings. Suppose we have a WDYM-question

$$<x \text{ believes-true } S, x \text{ believes-true } S', \text{ conceptual reason}>,$$

where S and S' are sentences differing exactly with respect to a word w present in S but not S'. And suppose f is a projection function modeling the speaker's understanding of the concept associated with w in his idiolect. Then consider the direct answer

x believes-true S rather than believing-true S' because x believes that q,

where "because" signifies that x's believing that q is his conceptual reason for believing-true S (Ch. 2, sec. 3). For this answer to meet projection constraints, q must have abstractable content which is in the range of f.

My discussion will cover six points.

Point 1: "Abstractable" content means derivable from q by means of an abstraction operator, which forms a term expressing a property or relation by variable binding (for discussion, see Heim and Kratzer 1998, 4-9). It is available but unnecessary when the relevant content is a constituent of p, as in

$\lambda x[x$ is quick-witted$]$.

This is the set of all things such that "is quick-witted" is true of them (an "extensional" version of the property of quick-wittedness). But sometimes the mechanism is indispensable; thus

$\lambda x \lambda y[$Any further jobs in x taken by y will not come at the expense of job-seekers native to $x]$

signifies the relation which gets associated with "absorb" when a speaker means by "The county cannot absorb any more immigrants" that any further jobs in the county taken by immigrants will come at the expense of native job-seekers. So it is not required that the content subject to constraints be a constituent of q.

Point 2: I've suggested that the contrast of a WDYM-question arising in response to conceptual indeterminacy serves to capture the interest in a particular word of the uttered sentence. This suggestion bore an implicit promissory note, that an answer satisfy some constraint dependent on the contrast. The proposed constraint is so dependent in a simple way, in that the divergence of the contrast from the topic serves to determine the projection function that applies. This is of particular significance if more than one word is a source of conceptual indeterminacy, a case I will discuss presently; but even if there is only one such word, it is the contrast which serves to identify it. Note that any substitution for "clever" in the contrast would do for this purpose. My analysis of the contrast in terms of a semantic field is based as well on intuitive psychological reality (Ch. 2, sec.

2.4). For simplicity I am assuming a single contrast, but multiple contrasts corresponding to the members of a field—where each differs from S exactly with respect to w—are easily accommodated.[24]

Point 3: It is not required that abstractable content actually be projected by the speaker from any given samples, i.e. that the content be the output of the function for any samples; it need only be in the range (n. 17). So the answer

> x believes-true "John is clever" rather than believing-true "John is dull" because x believes that John is good at problem solving

would meet the constraints even if the speaker has not projected goodness at problem solving. The answer would thus not provide the speaker's conceptual reason. But the constraints are independent of this. Thus some speaker could project it, from some samples, whether or not the speaker does from any. I think this captures the intuitive sense in which the speaker's meaning here is within bounds.

Not only might an answer meet projection constraints without being a conceptual reason, it could be a conceptual reason without meeting projection constraints. Take

> x believes-true "John is clever" rather than believing-true "John is dull" because x believes that John is big-nosed.

Alternatively one might build the constraints into a conceptual reason and say that this is not a conceptual reason, but as a matter of regimentation I prefer not to do this.[25]

Point 4: An uttered sentence might have more than one source of conceptual indeterminacy. In this case more than one question might arise, e.g.

> Q1: <x believes-true "John is clever and reckless," x believes-true "John is dull and reckless," conceptual reason>

and

> Q2: <x believes-true "John is clever and reckless," x believes-true "John is clever and prudent," conceptual reason>.

The topics are the same but the contrasts differ, determining projection constraints for different words. Whether an answer is direct and meets constraints depends on which question actually arises. Both questions may arise, in which case two speaker's meaning reports are called for. Consider the report "By 'John is clever and reckless' *x* means that John is quick-witted and heedless of others' feelings." While this would satisfy each question's respective projection constraints, it would not be direct for either, providing more than what was requested. But such an answer would likely satisfy the questioner because she could infer two direct answers from it.

Point 5: Presumably a concept associated with a projection function might be expressed not by a word but by a phrase; as Fodor (1981, 261) points out, whether a concept is picked out by a word or a phrase is just a linguistic contingency. But I haven't modified the above formulation to allow for this because I'm not sure what to say about the nature of the constraints.

One question is whether and how the projection constraints for a phrase relate to the respective constraints for the constituent parts. This is not the issue of compositionality, because projection constraints are not meanings in the sense of things that enter into compositional rules. One framework which has been proposed for explaining compositionality is particularly illustrative of the distinction. The framework attempts to explain the combination of concepts as represented by structured arrangements of stereotypical properties. So the concept associated with "apple" might represented by a description with "slots" for color, shape, taste, etc. In "red apple," a complex concept is composed via the "selective modification" of the description within the color slot (Smith, Osherson, Rips, and Keane 1988). Problems arise; for one thing, a complex concept sometimes appears to have information not present in the descriptions of any constituent concepts. But note that the things combined are projections from stereotypical examples, not projection functions defined on arbitrary examples, or constraints on such functions. How or whether the projection constraints for a phrase relate to the constraints for constituents is another matter entirely.

Perhaps compositionality is nonetheless relevant. If systematic relations could be identified between the meaning of a word and associated projection constraints, and between syntactic combinations of words and manners of combination for projection constraints, then an account could perhaps "piggyback" on a theory of compositionality. Given the relations, one could compose the projection constraints of a phrase as a byproduct of composing the meaning. But this is just conjecture.[26]

Point 6: Consider

> x believes-true "John is clever" rather than believing-true "John is dull" because x believes that quick-wittedness is a virtue.

This satisfies the proposed constraints, but that quick-wittedness is a virtue does not seem to be among the speaker's meanings we want to allow. The problem revealed here is that the constrained content is required only to be present somewhere in the belief content. There is no requirement that the latter bear any particular relation to the topic, as intuitively would be implied by the status of the belief as a kind of reason.

Another constraint seems to be at work, what I will call "counterfactual inductive strength." A speaker's meaning apparently must be such that it would make for an inference of non-zero inductive strength, if it were not a conceptual reason but an ordinary e-reason. That is, the content the speaker is fixing must be drawn from the set of inferences of non-zero strength as defined by norms which are independent of his meaning. So for instance one might mean by "John is clever" that John is quick-witted, since John's being quick-witted tends to confirm that John is clever. But that quick-wittedness is a virtue does not in the least confirm that John is clever.

I would formulate the constraint in terms of a direct answer to a certain counterfactual question, whose topic and contrast are attributions of belief rather than believing-true, and which requests an e-reason rather than a conceptual reason. The answer must "favor" the topic over the contrast in a certain way. So if the question were

> <x believes that John is clever, x believes that John is dull, e-reason>,

the answer

> x believes that John is quick-witted

would favor the topic over the contrast in a sense defined by van Fraassen. If we compare the probabilities of the topic and contrast when we don't assume that x believes that John is quick-witted with these probabilities when we do so assume, we find that the probabilities shift in favor of the topic (1980, 147-148). In particular, here the probability of the topic goes up while that of the contrast goes down (though favoring might also occur if the probability of the topic goes down while that of the contrast goes down more). The same is not true of

x believes quick-wittedness is a virtue.

This captures the requisite sense of inductive strength.[27]

So are projection constraints and counterfactual inductive strength two necessary, jointly sufficient conditions? In fact counterfactual inductive strength turns out to not be necessary. Up to now I have said little about the domain of a projection function, tacitly assuming it to consist of accepted sample referents. But I think it is not just referents. If a speaker were to conclude of a stuffed animal that it is a toy tiger in virtue of being a physical object, or of a fierce person that he is metaphorically a tiger in virtue of being a physical object, then I think we would conclude not just that the speaker hasn't acquired "toy tiger" or learned to use "tiger" metaphorically, but that he has not acquired "tiger." The most natural way to account for this intuition is to suppose that a projection function can operate on non-tigers as well, hence that projection in these cases is bound by the usual constraints.

Recall my earlier suggestion that the role of projection constraints in an account of competence is more obvious for abstract words than for perceptually-based ones, because speakers tend less to share perceptions and sample referents. In light of metaphorical usage wherein these tendencies disappear, the role is equally obvious for perceptually-based words. Note in particular that perceptual modules presumably do not represent output in terms of metaphorical categories: dogs might be "phenomenologically given," but not "dogs of war." In this sense metaphor is a matter of higher cognition.

I take the idea of metaphor as subsidiary to literal usage to have been put to rest by much recent work. One aspect of its importance is confirmed if competence requires a general aptitude for projection including over metaphorical instances. But in such cases an intuitively competent usage will not give us a counterfactually strong reason. Suppose an iron is deemed "clever" in virtue of being able to shut itself off when no one is using it. This would meet projection constraints, but that an iron can shut itself off when no one is using it does not to any degree support the conclusion that it is clever.

So for now we are left with projection constraints as necessary but not sufficient, and are in need of a successor to counterfactual inductive strength as an additional necessary constraint. I will continue with this in the next chapter. Note for now that attunement to counterfactual inductive strength is a matter of not specifically linguistic but rather general reasoning ability. The same will be true of the successor. So I take projection constraints to be the constraints knowledge of which constitutes competence with regard to words giving rise to conceptual indeterminacy.

5. Psychological Indeterminacy

Conceptual indeterminacy has to do with the multiplicity of constrained speaker's meanings. The constraints do not include truth. So it is an open question whether, among the things that a speaker might mean, there can be more than one thing that he *does* mean. Let us understand by "psychological indeterminacy" the multiplicity of speaker's meanings which both meet constraints and are true. Is there such a thing?

One indication is that a speaker always can specify her meaning in various ways. Often this manifests itself in conversation: "in other words," "look at it this way," etc. But there is no more reason to suppose that relations of synonymy or paraphrase generate distinct speaker's meanings than there is to suppose that they generate distinct mental states generally. In addition to the belief that the Red Sox have been winning, I presumably do not have the distinct beliefs that the Red Sox are streaking, that the Red Sox are hot, that Boston's professional baseball team has been winning a lot of games, etc. Or if I do, this is not very interesting.

But there is a more interesting phenomenon, more clearly implying a multiplicity of mental states. The point can best be made with respect to a speaker's meaning which is complex. Take what a philosopher might mean by "Our actions are predetermined." She explains her meaning in different ways depending on the audience and circumstances. To students in a classroom, she delivers full details. To a friend not particularly inclined toward philosophy, she gives an abbreviated summary. To a colleague at a casual lunch, she gives something in between. In each case, she gives her meaning. It would seem that her meaning is not the same in every case, just expressed differently, because the differences are too dramatic. The explanations seem to reflect different "levels" not just of exposition but of her own thought. If so, then they exist independently of whether she expresses herself differently on different occasions, or at all. This would be psychological indeterminacy: multiple constrained and true answers to "What do you mean, 'Our actions are predetermined'?"

What are these "levels"? Suppose our philosopher explains to her friend that everything we do is caused. The friend turns out to be curious: "What do you mean, 'caused'?" The philosopher goes on a bit about causes; the friend prompts further; the philosopher goes on further. And so on, until the friend gets something like what the students got. What this suggests is that one speaker's meaning is "deeper" than a second if it is an answer to the last in a "chain" of potential WDYM-questions leading from the second. The questions are potential because the levels don't depend on the number of questions asked or even anticipated. The students could be getting the whole story with no question actually asked, and only one anticipated: as when the philosopher begins "Our actions are predetermined. Let me tell you what I mean." Nonetheless the meaning she expresses is deeper than what she first expresses to her friend, because of its position at the end of a potential chain.[28]

The rough notion is that questions lie in a "chain" if each takes as its topic an answer to the previous question. But there is also "branching" in that each answer can be the topic of several questions with differing contrasts. Thus in response to, say, "We are part of the universe, and the state of the universe at any time is caused by its previous state," one might inquire into "state," "caused," or "universe." An answer to a question with one contrast need be neither more nor less "deep" than an answer to another question differing only with respect to the contrast.

So the suggestion is that the true answers to a WDYM-question requesting a conceptual reason are a *structured* multiplicity. The structuring relation between propositions can be defined as follows:

> b answers a if and only if b is (the embedded content of) a direct, true and constrained answer to
> $<x$ believes-true S, x believes-true S', conceptual reason>,
> where a and b are propositions, S expresses a, and S differs from S' exactly with respect to some word or other of S.

"Some word or other" indicates variation of the contrast. Further, let A1 be the set of propositions which answer a, A2 the set of propositions which answer some proposition in A1, A3 the set of propositions which answer some proposition in A2, etc. Then the propositions "deeper" than a are those in the union of A1, A2, etc.[29]

This way of viewing matters implies that multiple actual speaker's meanings do not compete with each other, because they are responsive to different explanatory interests. By way of comparison, consider the indeterminacy of "radical interpretation." As analyzed by Quine and Davidson, the problem of radical interpretation is that of determining a theory of meaning given only a speaker's sincere utterances; "radical" means the interpreter has no advance knowledge of either the speaker's beliefs or the meanings of his utterances.[30] Such interpretation is arguably indeterminate in that multiple theories will fit the evidence equally well (Davidson 1984, 152-154). But note that these theories are competing to explain the same evidence. In what I'm calling psychological indeterminacy, the explanations are not competitors. They explain different things, and more generally satisfy different interests as represented by different WDYM-questions. So there is no reason why they might not all be true.

Note that I have somewhat expanded the notion of "explanatory interest." In the sense of the interests represented by the parameters of a fixed WDYM-question, multiple true speaker's meanings all satisfy the same interests. For instance, the true answers to "What do you mean, our actions are 'predetermined'?" all satisfy the interest in a conceptual reason for the speaker's believing-true "Our actions are predetermined," relative to a contrast stemming from "predetermined." But some also satisfy additional interests, as represented by further questions. When I refer to the different interests served by different answers, I mean these additional interests (again, not necessarily realized).[31]

Whatever psychological indeterminacy there may be in what a speaker means, whether he is able to articulate something that he means is another issue. A conceptual reason is a belief and a reason, and one need not be able to articulate any belief or reason. As Harman remarks,

> The reasons for which people believe things are rarely conscious. People often believe things for good reasons, which give them knowledge, without being able to say what those reasons are...The same point follows from the fact that in most cases we cannot say in any detail why we believe as we do. At best we can give a vague indication of reasons we find convincing. It is only in rare cases that we can tell a person's detailed reasons from what he can say about them. Indeed it is doubtful that we can ever fully specify our reasons (1973, 28-29).

These are "inductive" reasons, but Harman's remarks apply also to conceptual reasons, in a qualified way. A speaker's conceptual reason induces a belief whose content diverges from what he has said. Our words are flexible enough to accommodate such divergence; it is in virtue of meeting constraints on the usage of his words that what the speaker says is "sort of" what he believes. Still, what he believes has not been articulated, i.e. in terms whose conceptual associations are pre-established and recognizable. This might not be considered a problem as far as communication goes. A hearer might know what the speaker means, or what was said might be good enough depending on circumstances. Or the speaker might achieve other desired goals such as brevity or stylistic effect. On the other hand he might not be satisfied, in which case he may address the gap through dialectic by which he might discover one of his meanings.

But dissatisfaction might remain. Perhaps we are never at a point where a WDYM-question couldn't possibly arise, for others or ourselves. These are matters of the human condition. Bertrand Russell once wrote in a letter to Ottoline Morrell:

> It is quite true what you say, that you have never expressed yourself—but who has, that has anything to express? The things one says are all unsuccessful attempts to say something else—something that perhaps by its very nature cannot be said. I know that I have struggled all my life to say something that I never shall learn how to say. And it is the same with you. It is so with all who spend their lives in the quest of something elusive, and yet omnipresent, and at once subtle and infinite. One seeks it in music, and the sea, and sunsets; at times I have seemed very near it in crowds when I have been feeling strongly what they were feeling; one seeks it in love above all. But if one lets oneself imagine one has found it, some cruel irony is sure to come and show one that it is not really found (1991, 320).

Russell may have gotten a bit carried away in his romantic mood: it's not as esoteric as all that. Anyone could attest to the potential elusiveness of what one means, the more so the more elaborate one's ventures into the abstract.

CHAPTER 5

METAPHOR

In this chapter I will discuss some of the phenomena that go by "metaphor." Though once neglected in philosophy, the topic is vast and I will have little or nothing to say about much of it: for instance, principles of metaphorical interpretation, the role of metaphor in science, or metaphor considered independently of language. My focus will be the nature of linguistic metaphorical usage.

In particular, I aim to portray metaphor as a species of conceptual indeterminacy. I take metaphorical usage to be a matter of speaker's meaning in the sense of a conceptual reason, bound by projection constraints. There are thus essential similarities with literal usage. In itself, this is not a new idea. According to Lyons, for example,

> metaphorical creativity (in the broadest sense of "metaphorical") is part of everyone's linguistic competence. In the last resort, it is impossible to draw a sharp distinction between the spontaneous extension or transfer of meaning by individual speakers on particular occasions and their use of the pre-existing, or institutionalized, extended and transferred meanings of a lexeme that are to be found in a dictionary (1995, 59-60).

But my thesis will be a closer continuity, between "transfer of meaning by individual speakers" in metaphorical usage and such meaning in literal usage, where the latter involves creativity of an equally robust and spontaneous nature.

I will proceed as follows. First I will defend my own version of the view that the content of a metaphorical usage is that of a speaker's meaning. Next I will spell this version out more specifically in terms of conceptual reasons. In section 3, I will argue that one need not appeal to similarity relations to explain the content of a metaphor (with one important exception), and that my account should remove the temptation. In section 4, I will discuss the boundary between literal and metaphorical usage. In section 5, I will portray the constraints on a conceptual reason as projection constraints, together with an extralinguistic constraint. I will argue that the constraints constitute necessary and jointly sufficient conditions on conceptual reasons, across both literal and metaphorical varieties of "spontaneous extension." In the final section, I will examine my account's implication that metaphor gives rise to a demand for explanation, as represented by a WDYM-question. This commits me to a distant version of the discredited view that metaphor is reducible to literal paraphrase, a version that I will defend against likely objections.

1. Metaphor and Speaker's Meaning

The content of a metaphor does not come from the lexicon. Metaphor is a matter of novel usage, involving creativity as much as competence. Thus possibilities are open-ended: for "Robert is a bulldozer," they include that Robert is headstrong, that Robert likes to clear off his desk completely before working, that Robert is heedless of others' feelings, etc. It is not a matter of "bulldozer" being ambiguous, in the sense of multiple meanings listed in the lexicon.[1] While context may select a meaning of an ambiguous word (Grice's "applied timeless meaning"), the meanings are associated with the word independently of context ("timeless meaning"—Grice 1989, 89).

These matters are worth emphasizing because I think they clarify some of the debate that has followed Davidson's (1981) denial of metaphorical meanings. Davidson wrote:

> It is no help in explaining how words work in metaphor to posit metaphorical or figurative meanings, or special kinds of poetic or metaphorical truth. These ideas don't explain metaphor, metaphor explains them. Once we understand a metaphor we can call what we grasp the "metaphorical truth" and (up to a point) say what the "metaphorical meaning" is. But simply to lodge this meaning in the metaphor is like explaining why a pill puts you to sleep by saying it has a dormative power. Literal meaning and literal truth conditions can be assigned to words and sentences apart from

particular contexts of use. This is why adverting to them has genuine explanatory power (202).

Some writers have pounced on the observation about "literal meaning," pointing out the context-dependence of literal discourse. But it is a careless objection. Though Davidson does not mention Grice's distinction here, it would be reasonable to take him as claiming that literal meanings are context-independent in the "timeless" sense, which is compatible with the context-dependence of disambiguation and everything else. It is implausible to take Davidson as denying the context-dependence of disambiguation, a mere platitude: too uncharitable, or else oblivious of the relevant distinction. In any event the charitable reading stands on its own, and makes for a case against metaphorical word meanings which is not affected by the easy observation that literal discourse is broadly context-dependent.[2]

That part of the case which denies that metaphorical meanings can be lexicon entries might be taken as attacking a straw man. Black interprets Davidson this way, remarking that

> Much of [Davidson's] polemic is beside the point. I know of no theorist who claims that the words used in metaphorical remarks thereby acquire some new meaning in what Davidson calls... "the only strict sense of meaning" ...Certainly, when Wallace Stevens called a poem a pheasant he was not permanently changing the dictionary sense of "pheasant," a feat almost never accomplished by a single use of a familiar word...The question to be considered...is not the idle one of whether the words used in a metaphorical remark astonishingly acquire some permanently new sense but rather the question whether the metaphor maker is attaching an altered sense to the words he is using in context (1978, 187-188).

Two points are in order. First, there certainly are theorists who speak of words as having "metaphorical meanings." As Black would have it, this is always meant elliptically inasmuch as metaphorical meanings belong not to words but to "the metaphor maker." But many do not make this clear, and some deny it explicitly.[3] So even if Black is right that everyone excludes metaphorical meanings from the lexicon, not everyone agrees on what is the real "question to be considered." But second, and more to the current point, the thesis of Davidson's in question is just one premise of his argument. It is not just that metaphorical meanings are not word meanings, but also that if this is the case then metaphorical meanings do not have explanatory value. Surely not everyone would also grant the second premise.

I myself take the first premise to be obvious just as Black says. But I reject the second. While I agree that acontextual assignability gives meanings in the lexicon sense explanatory value, there are other avenues to explanatory value. Many implicatures are generated only in context, with the range of possibilities not fixed in advance, unlike lexicon entries. Nonetheless, adverting to implicature can have explanatory value for a contextual phenomenon, because the notion is embedded in a framework (conversational maxims, cooperative behavior, etc.) which is *motivated independently* of the appeal to implicature in this context. This subsumes Davidson's criterion: meanings in the lexicon sense have explanatory value because they too are independently motivated posits. So I take a non-semantic account of "metaphorical meaning" to be possible, i.e. an account which does not advert to lexicon meaning or anything that enters into compositionality of sentence meaning. I will not rely instead on implicature, for reasons about to be reviewed, but on (a different kind of) speaker's meaning—likewise an independently motivated notion, as I hope by now to have demonstrated.

The view that metaphorical content may be found in speaker's meaning is hardly new. According to Cooper (1986, 66), it is in fact the "standard" view. However this may be, the prevailing conception of speaker's meaning in these matters is so far as I know not just standard but universal. There are two tenets. First, speaker's meaning is what the speaker intends to communicate by his utterance. Second, the speaker's meaning normally coincides with the meaning of the uttered sentence, though sometimes speaker's meaning and meaning "come apart," as in figurative speech, irony, and indirect speech acts (Searle 1981, 249). Mine will be a non-standard version of the "standard view" because for me neither tenet holds.

Concerning the first, speaker's meaning in the everyday sense need not be the speaker's communicative intention, as we've seen. I will be arguing with respect to metaphor specifically that it has to do rather with the speaker's conceptual reason. Independently of this, it seems clear that in metaphor what the speaker means should not be analyzed as what the speaker intended to communicate by his utterance (and *a fortiori* not as an implicature). This would often require that the speaker be irrational. As all agree, the interpretation of metaphor is difficult, with such "rules" as exist hardly guaranteed to succeed.[4] Taking this to be matter of common knowledge among speakers, it follows that a speaker would often have to be irrational to expect to convey his meaning just by his utterance. If a speaker means by "Man is a wolf" that man is territorial, a hearer is not likely to guess this from the utterance absent special clues; since the speaker presumably knows this, he is not likely to have intended for the hearer to do this. The point is especially clear if the speaker's meaning is more complex.

None of this is to say that speakers are not in general concerned with communication broadly speaking. Perhaps they are. But a speaker may intend to communicate based on such capability as hearers have to interpret metaphor, satisfied that the result will be "close enough" for current purposes. Or she may intend to communicate her meaning by not just this utterance but also further utterances, perhaps as part of an interactive exchange marked by explicit WDYM-questions. Communication can be dialectical. So while what a speaker means by a metaphorical utterance might be what she intended to convey by it, this is not the general case; hence her meaning ought not to be analyzed as her communicative intention.[5]

As for the second tenet, I have argued that speaker's meaning in the everyday sense normally *does* "come apart" from the sentence meaning, and is explanatory only when this is the case. This is a reflection of its intralinguistic status (Ch. 2, sec. 3). A reply of "I meant that he's clever" to "What do you mean, John is 'clever'?" rejects the question, thus not satisfying the explanatory interests that the question represents. In those cases where a WDYM-question arises at a stage later than semantic interpretation, the questioner presupposes this interpretation in attributing what the speaker has said. So an answer does not normally give a semantic interpretation, and would not be explanatory if it did. It is only metalinguistic speaker's meaning that normally coincides with sentence meaning. But it is the intralinguistic notion that interpreters of metaphor employ in everyday discourse. For someone to wonder what a speaker means by "Juliet is the sun," he must apprehend "Juliet is the sun" not merely as a string of noises or marks but rather as semantically interpreted. Accordingly the intralinguistic notion is the more fruitful to take up in the study of metaphor, just as in implicature and other phenomena. As we'll see, one fruit will be the elucidation of certain continuities between literal and metaphorical discourse.

So from my perspective no objections that have been made to the possibility of explaining metaphorical usage in terms of speaker's meaning are strictly relevant to my enterprise, as they assume a different notion of speaker's meaning. To be sure, certain objections are still relevant in spirit. But I think that they are misguided.

I will elaborate in connection with Cooper's objections (1986, 66-89). He argues that the "standard view" makes metaphor "perverse" because it entails that in metaphor speakers violate a "transparency" convention in discourse, that a speaker should mean by his words just what his words mean. But taken as a convention on intralinguistic speaker's meaning, this amounts to an injunction that speaker's meaning should never be explanatory. (As Cooper recognizes, it is a separate issue whether there are conventions that the speaker "say what he means" and "mean what he says.")

On Cooper's view, speaker's meaning is not even relevant to interpretation. We may know what the speaker means without knowing the interpretation because

> ...a metaphor, once announced, belongs like a published poem or an exhibited painting to the world. The speaker, poet, or painter does not have exclusive rights to interpretation—and even if he did his interpretation would not have to mimic his intention at the time of composition. Suppose it turned out, on the evidence of his diary, that all Hofmannstahl intended in calling us dovecots is that we, like they, are affected by the weather. This would influence our judgment of his powers of expression, but it would not determine interpretation. People will still be entitled to offer their construals and to discuss how illuminating or otherwise the metaphor becomes on these (73).

Even if it is known that a speaker's meaning falls outside reasonable constraints, "it is [not] pointless to try and interpret the metaphors, nor [is it the case that] any old interpretation will do...[an interpreter has] some idea of what would count as reasonable or silly interpretation of [such a speaker's] metaphors" (72).

To an extent I can accommodate Cooper's concern. I can grant that there is a mode of interpretation where one aims only to satisfy oneself. Presumably this is not a matter that one can be right or wrong about, unlike interpretation of the speaker. Just as there is no "correct" reaction to a painting, in this mode there is no correct interpretation of the metaphor. I disagree only if Cooper means that this is the only mode of interpretation. I take it as obvious that an interpreter's aim is sometimes successful communication. This does not entail that the speaker has "exclusive rights," or that the hearer is not "entitled" to his own interpretation (pending further clarification of what these things mean), or that the speaker may not mean something different at another time. It simply entails that the hearer is concerned to understand the speaker.[6] Note also that it doesn't count against interpretation in this sense that it is "not pointless" to interpret metaphors which fall outside reasonable constraints. The point of such interpretation is to get the speaker right, whether the constraints have been observed or not.

I should say here that for me the word "metaphor" is no more than a cover term for various related phenomena. I can't see how there can be substance in any claim that equates "metaphor" with some phenomenon picked out from the variety. It seems to me that any such claim amounts to a stipulation as to how "metaphor" is being used, reflecting special interest in a particular aspect. Thus for Cooper's claim that "metaphor belongs to the world." Having recognized the existence of a certain mode of interpretation, I find nothing of substance to disagree with unless other modes are denied. I myself have and will continue to speak of "metaphor" as having to do with speaker's meaning, but only for convenience. For me the "standard view" simply signals an interest in the nature of a speaker's metaphorical usage (as opposed to the nature of interpretation, in particular). The important thing will be my proposed analysis of speaker's meaning as it is involved in metaphorical usage, whether what one chooses to call "metaphor" is here or elsewhere.[7]

Cooper's thesis that metaphors "belong to the world" rests further on an endorsement of Davidson's contention that there is no such thing as metaphorical content. If so, then interpretation of metaphor couldn't aim to discover the content of a speaker's meaning. I can't accommodate this position at all; I will return to it in section 6.

2. Metaphor and Conceptual Reasons

I now want to consider how the analysis of conceptual reasons elucidates metaphorical usage. Recall that modifications to the traditional disquotational principle were motivated by the need to block homophonic attribution of a belief when a conceptual reason is present (Ch. 3, sec. 4.2). For in that event, the inferences and behavior we would expect of the speaker differ from the inferences and behavior we would expect for the homophonic attribution. Hence the subprinciples DP1, DP2a, and DP2b, licensing non-homophonic attribution if a conceptual reason is present, and homophonic attribution otherwise.

> DP1: If so-and-so asserts 'p', and is sincere and reflective, then he believes-true 'p'.
> DP2a: If a normal English speaker believes-true 'p', where 'p' is an English sentence containing no ambiguous or indexical terms, and does so on the basis of a conceptual reason that q, then he believes that p in the sense that q.
> DP2b: If a normal English speaker believes-true 'p', where 'p' is an English sentence containing no ambiguous or indexical terms, and there is no q such that he believes-true 'p' on the basis of a conceptual reason that q, then he believes that p.

In the case of metaphorical usage, the need to block homophonic attribution is especially dramatic. Of one who believes that Rob is a bulldozer in the sense that he is headstrong we would expect certain behavior and inferences; of one who believes that Rob is a bulldozer, we wouldn't know what to expect. But no new principles are required. I want to emphasize four consequences of applying the principles to metaphorical usage, after which I'll address some possible objections.

First: a conceptual reason is mandatory. DP1 and DP2b entail a homophonic attribution of belief when a conceptual reason is absent, thus that a sincere and reflective utterer of "Rob is a bulldozer" believes that Rob is a bulldozer—which is not sane. In contrast, a conceptual reason is optional in literal usage. One might use "John is clever" without having any particular sense in mind. By DP1 and DP2b, one would believe that John is clever, unproblematically. The difference has to do with the unavailability of word meanings for the attribution of metaphorical content. So whereas "creative literal usage" serves to distinguish literal usage that involves content fixing from usage that does not, "creative metaphorical usage" is redundant. Even when a homophonically attributed belief would not be absurd—e.g. meaning by "The horses have left the starting gate" that it's too late in the semester to catch up with his classmates—the content of the metaphor must come from a conceptual reason.

The requirement may seem counterintuitive. Can we not contemplate "Rob is a bulldozer," "Society is a sea," or "The morning sunlight wrestled with the horizon" as metaphors without having a particular sense in mind? I will return to this in section 6.

Second: the content of a metaphorical usage is not the content of a conceptual reason, but that of the belief attributed via DP2a. It is not, for example, that Rob is headstrong but that Rob is a bulldozer in the sense that he is headstrong. The latter is cognitively distinct owing to its source, as analyzed in the previous chapter. Following Burge, I take the concept attached to a word in a speaker's idiolect to involve both sample referents to which he is committed and properties he projects from those samples. The concept is associated with a projection function, representing how the projection varies with the samples. Part of the content of a conceptual reason is determined by the same projection function, operating on distinct samples peculiar to the context. The "sense" of the speaker's words is projected from these samples, generating a new understanding of the concept. This is the nature of linguistic "usage" relevant to a conceptual reason, taken now to include metaphorical usage. Thus the projection of properties from "metaphorical samples" is fallible, not related as a matter of language to the speaker's words, even in this context. Cognitively, the belief that Rob is a bulldozer in the sense that he is headstrong is hence not a "reduction," but a state of understanding subject to change and further thought. As compared to the belief that Rob is headstrong, it conjures up more vivid imagery and leads to further comparisons.

Third: sincerity is required in metaphorical usage, since a conceptual reason relates to a believing-true. This does not entail a homophonic attribution, though, since DP2b does not apply.

Fourth: like the attribution of what is believed-true, the attribution of what is said proceeds independently of the existence of a conceptual reason. Thus the additional subprinciple

DP1': If a normal English speaker asserts 'p', where 'p' is an English sentence containing no ambiguous or indexical terms, then he says that p.

has no qualification pertaining to a conceptual reason. So there is nothing metaphorical in what is said. One who means by "Rob is a bulldozer" that Rob is headstrong has said that Rob is a bulldozer.

It might be objected that the speaker could not be saying something which he not only does not believe, but might well believe to be false; for despite the figurative turn, in metaphor speakers could be "aiming at the truth" (Martinich 1981, 508). Indeed, "lying" might be defined as saying what one believes to be false, in which case it would seem that the present account makes metaphorical usage out to be a kind of lie. But this is not a good definition, since it does not clearly distinguish lying from, say, stage acting. ("Clearly" because an actress may happen to say something that she believes; but there is a distinction even if not.) Lying is better characterized as falsely representing oneself as sincere, where this involves an intent that the hearer take one to be sincere. Such is not the case in acting (Davidson 1981, 214).

Nor is it the case in irony, understatement, or hyperbole. In these cases not only does the speaker not intend for the hearer to take him as sincere, he invites conventional and correct inferences on the hearer's part concerning what the speaker believes: the "opposite" of what has been said, something "stronger," and something "weaker," respectively. Note that these inferences are based on convention, not a conceptual reason. If one ironically intones "Mike's a barrel of laughs," one does not believe that Mike's a barrel of laughs in the sense that he is deadly boring; the belief is rather that Mike is deadly boring. In contrast, the content of a conceptual reason is taken from a multiplicity of possibilities bound but not specified by conventional constraints. The distinctiveness of metaphor among tropes in this respect is well-known (e.g. Cohen 1981, 183).

Metaphor is distinct from lying for a different reason. It isn't that the speaker doesn't falsely represent himself as sincere: he is in fact sincere. A conceptual reason relates to a believing-true; further, this relation entails a certain belief (DP2a). In these respects, a user of metaphor does "aim at the truth."

It might be objected that metaphor shouldn't require sincerity, *pace* point 3, for isn't it possible to speak metaphorically and lie at the same time? Surely I can say "Rob is a bulldozer" while not believing that Rob is a bulldozer in the sense that he is headstrong, but intending for the hearer to infer this. Note however that the same issue arises with irony, understatement, and hyperbole. I might say "Bob's a barrel of laughs" in an ironic tone while not believing that Bob is deadly boring, but intending for the hearer to infer this. Is the current account of irony therefore incorrect? I think rather that it is correct, but that this is not irony. Rather, it is lying that exploits the conventions governing irony.

This requires a further revised notion of lying. We can take it as a special case of a more general notion, perhaps "equivocating": namely, intention that the hearer incorrectly infer that which the utterance context dictates. In literal and direct usage, this is the intention that the hearer incorrectly infer sincerity, applying DP1. There may then be the further intention that the hearer incorrectly apply DP2b, or the further intention that the hearer incorrectly apply DP2a. Thus an equivocating speaker might say "John is clever," intending either that the hearer take him to believe that John is clever, or that the hearer take him to believe that John is clever in the sense that he is quick-witted. The latter is perhaps less common, because it requires that the speaker take something in the overt context to enable the hearer to make the inference. But it's quite possible. A hustling agent might say "John is clever too" during a conversation with a club owner about good comedians, referring to his client whom he knows to be dull.

For irony, understatement, and hyperbole, an equivocator's intention is that the hearer incorrectly apply, not DP1, DP2a, or DP2b, but other conventions for attributing content. He may feign irony, intending that the hearer will infer the opposite of what he says. But it's not irony, because the speaker does not believe the opposite of what he says. And one can lie while feigning metaphorical usage. But it's not metaphor, because the speaker neither believes-true his sentence nor has a conceptual reason. The nature of the deception actually more resembles one kind of equivocation in literal discourse than it resembles equivocation in irony, because of the reliance on DP2a rather than any conventional route to content. If one says "Rob is a bulldozer," intending that the hearer falsely infer that he thinks Rob is a bulldozer in the sense that he is headstrong, then like the hustling agent one's intention is that the hearer incorrectly apply DP1 and DP2a in the attribution of belief. Alternatively, the intention may be just for the hearer to infer that there is some sense in which the speaker thinks that Rob is a bulldozer (that hopefully being sufficient for concluding that Rob is unfit for the job that the speaker wants instead).[8]

A consequence of metaphor's aforementioned distinctiveness among tropes is the lesser plausibility of positing a special kind of speech act. For many speech acts, propositional content is determined by the meaning of the uttered sentence. Inasmuch as the sort of convention involved in this determination is linguistic—the sort that changes if I switch from English to French—it is not of primary interest in speech act theory. It is integral to the analysis of ordering, for instance, that the speaker be in a position of authority over the hearer, but not that "Go away" in English means go away (Searle 1969, 39-41). But some have suggested that there are speech acts wherein propositional content is not determined by sentence meaning, and for such acts the convention that determines the propositional content is the one of interest. In putative "ironical speech acts," for instance, it determines the "opposite" of the sentence meaning.[9] Whatever the plausibility of this move, I don't think a similar one is feasible for metaphor, for lack of any determination of content which can be regarded as likewise conventional.

Not everyone agrees. Bergmann (1991) is among those who argue that there is such a thing as "metaphorical assertion," what point four above rules out. The content of such an assertion is determined by "salience," which is partly a matter of "commonplaces and stereotypes," but also may depend on context. A speaker might utter "Marie is an encyclopedia" and thereby assert that Marie knows lots of things, relying on a salient characteristic of encyclopedias, or utter "That refrigerator is my cord of wood" and assert that she has paid a lot for her refrigerator, in response to someone who has just complained about how much he paid for a cord of wood. Furthermore, "what is salient for one person may not be salient for another" (487-488).

There are conditions for the success of a metaphorical assertion. "First, the audience must recognize the author's utterance as metaphor...Second, [it] must recognize the author's utterance as an assertion. And third, the audience must properly identify the proposition the author intended to assert. The audience must identify which component expressions (if any) are to be taken literally...and must identify the *correct* salient characteristics for fixing the content of the assertion" (489, my emphasis). Thus the characteristics which enter into a metaphorical assertion must be not only salient, but also the ones which the speaker has in mind. The responsibility for this success "is the author's; he...must ensure that the audience can figure out what proposition is being asserted...in short, [he] is responsible for preventing the 'richness' of a metaphor from interfering with its efficacy in asserting a specific proposition" (489). She adds that "without knowing the context in which a metaphor occurs and who its author is, it is impossible to state conclusively what the metaphor 'means' without drawing out all it could mean...but bring in a well-defined context and a real author, and matters may change drastically" (486).

We can begin to see a problem by considering the flip side: they also well may not (or, many contexts are not "well-defined"). Even if the speaker's meaning is based on salient characteristics, competing hypotheses are generated just by combinatorics. For a mere three characteristics there are seven subsets of characteristics, so each hypothesis has one chance in seven of being right.[10] Considering also the subjectivity of salience, it is easier to be pessimistic than optimistic. On Bergmann's account, a false hypothesis means that the speaker's assertion has not been successfully performed; since interpreter's hypotheses typically are false, speakers' metaphorical usages are thus typically defective in this sense. This seems odd—that defectiveness should be typical, and that such usages are defective at all. Quick communication is all well and good, but Bergmann makes it a norm: the speaker's performance of a speech act, discharging a "responsibility" to assert a "specific proposition," depends upon it. This strikes me as wrongheaded with respect to both cognition and communication.

As to cognition, consider that salience is especially inadequate if the speaker's meaning is at all complex. If by "Society is a sea" one means that most social relations, as constructions out of personal ambitions, community pressures, and general political factors, are too intricate to understand except by looking beneath the surface of everyday interactions, it's most unlikely that an interpreter is going to get the idea from the context. To have any chance of conforming to the proposed norm, one must use metaphor to express relatively simple thoughts. Surely this shows that there is no such norm. As to communication, even if a metaphorically-inclined speaker intends to communicate what he means as well as he can, this need not be an intention to communicate it by this one utterance even in conjunction with salience. Again, communication can be dialectical. An utterance intended to initiate a dialectical exchange violates no sociolinguistic norm, even if communication ultimately fails.

I conclude that salience will not do as the determinant of a metaphorical speech act's content. It is too unreliable to do the work of the needed sociolinguistic convention, and thus would entail arbitrary divisions and incorrect normative assessments of metaphorical usages. I have no alternative to propose. On the contrary, I think that Bergmann has made as good a case as can be made. I cannot discern any better candidate than salience for what determines the content of a metaphorical assertion, given that the determinant must be a matter of common knowledge. My conclusion is that metaphorical usage is not a matter of performing a speech act at all (including an indirect speech act, as Fogelin 1988 proposes). What enters into the content of what one says or asserts is just the meanings of one's words. As a consequence of what Bergmann calls the "richness" of metaphor, metaphorical content enters not at the level of a linguistic act, but only at the level of belief.

I am not the first to argue against the notion of a metaphorical speech act. Especially influential has been Cohen (1979), who has so argued on the basis of the different behavior of metaphor and speech acts in indirect reports. Whereas "Tom said that he was sorry" implies an apology on Tom's part but not the reporter's, in "Tom said that the boy next door is a ball of fire" both Tom and the reporter must be understood metaphorically. The simplest explanation, Cohen suggests, is that metaphor is not a kind of speech act. This argument seems right to me. But the point does not raise "a very serious difficulty for anyone...who wants to construe metaphor solely in terms of speaker's meaning," as Cohen further claims (65), because on my analysis speaker's meaning is not a speech act.[11]

In this section I've spelled out four consequences of taking metaphorical usage to be a matter of a conceptual reason. And I've answered several possible objections: that my account makes metaphor a kind of lie, that one can both use metaphor and lie, and that metaphorical usage is rather a matter of making a special kind of assertion.

3. Similarity

The role of similarity in metaphor has long been discussed. Here is a classic reflection of Goodman's:

> If we are pressed to say what sort of similarity must obtain between what a predicate applies to literally and what it applies to metaphorically, we might ask in return what sort of similarity must obtain among the things a predicate applies to literally. How must past and future things be alike for a given predicate, say "green," to apply literally to them all? Having some property or other in common is not enough; they must have a *certain* property in common. But what property? Obviously the property named by the predicate in question; that is, the predicate must apply to all the things it must apply to. The question why predicates apply as they do metaphorically is much the same as the question why they apply as they do literally (1981, 129).

I take there to be two points here: that similarity is of no help accounting for metaphor, and that metaphorical and literal application are alike in this respect. This is basically my stance too (with an important caveat), but my rendition will be very different.

Notice to begin with that Goodman conflates what we might call "weak" and "strong" similarity. Weak similarity is what is expressed by an *assertion* of similarity, i.e. a simile: "A is like B," "A is similar to B," "A resembles B." Strong similarity is expressed by an unmodified copula, e.g. "A is B." (When A and B are noun phrases, call this a "nominal predication.") The similarity "among the things a predicate applies to literally" is strong similarity, expressed by e.g. "Emeralds are green." But the similarity "between what a predicate applies to literally and what it applies to metaphorically" is weak similarity. So Goodman's ruminations on "green" aren't relevant to metaphor.

Similarity both weak and strong is relative to a particular respect of similarity.[12] Strong similarity is similarity relative to the property expressed by the predicate, as Goodman observes. Weak similarity is relative to properties which need not be criterial for application of the predicate; e.g. "Sid is like a policeman" might be used to express similarity between Sid and policemen with respect to being authoritative. It's the respect of weak similarity that enters into the content of a metaphor. Thus one problem with the "hidden simile" view of metaphor is that it makes the interpretation of metaphor too easy (Davidson 1981, 209); the interpretation of "Sid is a policeman" would just be that Sid is like a policeman, i.e. in some unspecified respect. What's hard in interpretation is to specify the respect.

Strong similarity entails weak, but not the converse. It might seem that we can go further: not only does weak not entail strong, it seems to entail its negation. "Sid is like a policeman" seems to imply that while there is some similarity between Sid and policemen, he is not a policeman. However, we can analyze the implication as a "quantity implicature." For example, "Some of the guests have arrived" implicates that not all of the guests have arrived, even though "some" is compatible with "all." The implicature is generated by assuming observance of a "quantity maxim," prescribing that one should be as informative as required. Thus if a speaker believes that all the guests have arrived, he should say so; having not said so, he must believe that not all of the guests have arrived. Similarly, "Sid is like a policeman" implicates that Sid is not a policeman, even though "is like" is compatible with "is." Note that the implicature can be cancelled. Just as one could say "Some of the guests have arrived, in fact they all have," one could say "Sid is like a policeman, and in fact he is a policeman."

The current account of metaphorical content accommodates all this. Consider "Sid is a policeman in a sense." This expresses weak similarity between Sid and policemen. "Sid is a policeman in a sense" implicates that Sid is not a policeman, even though "in a sense" is compatible with "is." The implicature can be cancelled, as in "Not only is Sid a policeman in some sense, he is a policeman." In short, "in a sense" is another way to express a simile.[13] Meanwhile the respect of weak similarity required to make interpretation non-trivial is expressed by "in the sense that," which on my account forms the content of a metaphorical usage.

I've been speaking as if similarity does figure in metaphor, which so far seems natural enough. But the naturalness doesn't generalize. In nominal predications, the "focus" of the metaphor (Black 1981, 65) is a noun phrase complement. The relata of similarity then are the referents of the subject and the noun phrase. But suppose the focus is elsewhere. In "The ship ploughs the waves," "we aren't calling the ship a plough. We are intuitively perceiving the similarity in two dissimilar actions: the ship does to the waves what a plough does to the ground" (Kenner, cited by Brooke-Rose 1958, 206). There are not two independent comparisons here, the ship to the plough and the waves to the ground. Rather there is one comparison, between entities with a propositional structure. But these are not the referents of any expressions in the sentence.

Miller (1979) has provided a helpful overview. He suggests that a step in the interpretation of metaphor is "reconstruction" of a similarity relation, the nature of which depends on the focus. For what he calls "predicative metaphor" wherein the focus is an adjective complement or main verb, he proposes the schema:

M1: $G(x) \rightarrow (\exists F)(\exists y)[F(x)$ is similar to $G(y)]$.

To the left of the arrow is the predication in need of interpretation. To the right is an attribution of similarity between propositional forms, in which the quantified variables represent the "omissions" in the predication to the left of the arrow. F is the omitted predication of x, and y the omitted thing of which G is predicated. So for "Their marriage suddenly vaporized" the relation is between the marriage suddenly undergoing something and something vaporizing; for "My new toaster is clever" it is between the toaster having some attribute and somebody being clever. Miller intends M1 to apply with obvious modifications to multiple-place predicates. For "The ship ploughs the waves," the similarity is between the ship doing something to the waves, and something ploughing something else.

If there were no more to interpretation than reconstruction, then Miller would be open to the charge of making interpretation trivial. But there is another step, to make good on the "omissions" (232). Thus in M1 the goal is to determine values for F and y, and the content of the metaphor is the right side of the arrow with these values substituted (and quantifiers removed).

But there is a problem. Take "Their marriage suddenly vaporized," by which one might mean that their marriage suddenly became unworkable because of mutual resentment. Herein would be a value for *F*. But we needn't consider a value for *y*, i.e. something that vaporized. Whether we envision water in a pot, an alien zapped by a ray-gun, or nothing at all, the content of the metaphor would still be that their marriage suddenly became unworkable because of mutual resentment. Similarly, an interpretation of "My toaster is clever" requires only a property of the toaster, not a specification of some person who is clever. The second relatum in M1 does not seem to be relevant to interpretation.[14]

The explanation for the asymmetry is simple. M1 analyzes predicative metaphor. So the interpretation must "unpack" the predicate in a way that's appropriate to the subject. Unpacking the subject in a way that's appropriate to the predicate is neither here nor there, since the predicate is not what the speaker is talking about. So in M1 it is only the first relatum that needs filling out. On the continuing assumption that similarity underlies metaphorical content, the moral is that similarity is asymmetric. Tversky (1977) has made this point well-known.[15]

But the assumption itself can now be questioned. A reconstructed similarity does not suffice for interpretation, and one reconstructed relatum is not relevant to interpretation. Why bother then? Why not simply regard interpretation as the result of substituting for *F* in *F(x)*, considered apart from M1 (i.e. in what Black calls the "frame")? If we can do without the second relatum, we can do without similarity.[16]

In the case of what Miller calls "sentential metaphor," this conclusion is patent. If one means by "The horses have left the starting gate" that it's too late in the semester to catch up with one's classmates, there is no subsentential focus. Thus "the entire sentential concept...must be inferred from the text or context" (233). Miller proposes the scheme:

M2: $G(y) \rightarrow (\exists F)(\exists x)[F(x)$ is similar to $G(y)]$.

Notice that the second relatum simply reiterates what requires interpretation. So on this scheme interpretation involves first reconstructing the relation between some unspecified proposition and horses having left a starting gate, then determining the unspecified proposition. Clearly the first step is doing no work. We might say, no more helpfully but at least less awkwardly, that it involves determining what the speaker means by "The horses have left the starting gate." Occam's razor dictates the elimination of a relatum and hence of similarity.

Let's return now to nominal predication, where it seemed natural to posit similarity. Miller proposes another schema:

M3. $be(x,y) \rightarrow (\exists F)(\exists G)[F(x)$ is similar to $G(y)]$.

The open sentence on the right side of the arrow is identical to the open sentence in M1, but the quantifiers differ. Here both predicates are quantified, not just F. The idea is that similarity obtains not between the referents of the two noun phrases (x and y) but between one referent's having certain properties and the other's having certain properties (230-231). The need for this is most obvious for disparate domains, such that the properties are analogous rather than shared. Suppose one means by "Rob is a bulldozer" that Rob is headstrong. The similarity is not in virtue of a shared property between Rob and bulldozers, but between Rob's being headstrong and a bulldozer's having some unspecified property. When properties are shared rather than analogous, M3 can subsume this a special case; Miller can say that Sid's being authoritative is similar to a policeman's being authoritative, rather than that Sid is similar to a policeman with respect to being authoritative.[17]

But there's the same problem: the second relatum is not relevant to interpretation. Interpretation of "Rob is a bulldozer" does not require a property of bulldozers, only a property of Rob. So M3, like M1 and M2, seems unnecessary. Interpretation can be characterized as filling out the frame (to a first approximation at least), without adverting to the second relatum and hence to similarity at all.

I take the problem to be not with Miller, but with similarity: it does not underlie the content of a metaphor. This doesn't mean that we may not informally speak of similarity, just that this doesn't do any explanatory work—not even for the case I initially considered in connection with weak similarity, i.e. nominal predication wherein properties are shared. In this case similarity need not be analyzed in terms of reconstruction in Miller's sense; but while I can accommodate the putative similarity, doing so adds no insight and doesn't generalize. "Is like" just paraphrases "in a sense"; we can but don't have to say that what is expressed is weak similarity. And the paraphrase is only for nominal predications. For "Their marriage suddenly vaporized," paraphrase with "like" would be artificial—a manifestation of the artificiality of the reconstructed similarity in M1. In contrast "in a sense" and "in the sense that" operate across the range of forms considered by Miller, requiring no "reconstructions," because they are sentential operators.[18]

In particular, "in the sense that" is operative in the content of a metaphor regardless of where the "focus" is. I equate focus with stress in a WDYM-interrogative, as already analyzed: a manifestation in surface form of a particular explanatory interest. To say that the metaphorical focus in "Their marriage suddenly vaporized" is "vaporized" is to say that this is what might pique a hearer's interest in a metaphorical interpretation. He might pursue this interest by asking "What do you mean, their marriage suddenly 'vaporized'?", expressing a question whose contrasts stem from "vaporized." In an analysis of metaphor such an interest is automatic, but in everyday life one might already have an interpretation, or not care, or care more about something else. One might wonder "What do you mean, their marriage 'suddenly' vaporized?" (didn't it happen long before now?) or "What do you mean, their 'marriage' suddenly vaporized?" (their personal relationship, yes, but aren't they both as committed as ever to the legal arrangement, for the kids' sake?). These interests would be represented by different contrasts, and thus different questions.

I began with a passage from Nelson Goodman, whom I criticized for taking strong similarity rather than weak to pertain to metaphor. But as matters so far stand I would agree with what I take to be his two main points. First, similarity is of no help in an account of metaphor. Goodman's alternative is predication, while mine is related to a certain kind of qualified predication.[19] Second, this alternative assimilates metaphorical usage to literal. All I have said about metaphorical content is based on the same principles proposed for the content of literal usage. Thus whether or not weak similarity underlies "Sid is a policeman" on a metaphorical usage, the same answer should be given for "Sid is clever" on a creative literal usage.

It would be satisfying if matters could be left here. But another issue remains to be considered, what we might call "systematicity." Take the presidential declaration "This is a war on drugs." The metaphor suggests a range of analogies between martial activity and apparent federal efforts against illegal drugs, such as in one senator's remark that "the troops are out there...All they're waiting for is the orders, a plan of attack, and they're ready to march."

The point is not simply that a long conjunction of properties may be attributed, as a given usage of "Man is a wolf" might attribute fierceness, being territorial, given to hierarchical social organization, etc. Black refers here to a "system of commonplaces" associated with "wolf" (1981, 74). Systematicity in the current sense includes this, but is broader. In Miller's terms: not only may there be a similarity between propositional entities certain constituents of which fill out omissions in a "reconstructed" similarity, but also many similarities, between entities which need not in the same sense address omissions at all. Thus the "root" similarity invoked in the "war on drugs" image is that between some kind of effort against illicit drugs and war on something or other. But other similarities may be invoked as well: between drug enforcement officers and soldiers, between laws against drug possession and martial laws, between police raiding a public housing project and an army regiment storming an enemy encampment. These can't be regarded as providing values for variables in the root similarity.

We might put it this way: systematicity entails a relation not just between entities but between domains. The basic idea is captured by the notion of a "homomorphism," or structure-preserving mapping. Take a domain to be a set of entities together with certain properties and relations that hold among them. A homomorphism between two domains entails a correspondence between entities, properties, and relations of one domain and entities, properties, and relations of the other, such that an entity's having a certain property in one domain, or entities' standing in a certain relation of the domain, correspond to their counterparts having the counterpart property or standing in the counterpart relation in the other domain. "This is a war on drugs" determines a mapping from the domain of war to that of a government drug campaign, relating such entities as soldiers, commanders, and enemy territory and such properties and relations as soldiers storming an enemy encampment, commanders' formulating an attack plan, etc. to police officers, political leaders, and urban slums, and to policemen raiding a housing project, political leaders devising plans, etc.[20]

In one regard I must accordingly temper my qualified agreement with Goodman. Not with regard to the continuity between metaphorical and literal, since in simile systematicity may underlie literal content as well. But similarity is not so clearly dispensable, at least not for the reasons I've advanced. It is still true that adverting to the "root" similarity seems dispensable—i.e. in the "war on drugs" case, to the similarity between some kind of effort against illicit drugs and war on something or other. As before, only the first relatum needs filling out; thus the interpretive question is not "The drug effort is like war against what?" but only "What kind of effort against drugs is like a war?" But systematicity entails other similarities which do not involve variables in the root. Therefore it can't be said against these similarities that providing variable values in one relatum is irrelevant to interpretation. So I concede that similarity relations in the homomorphism sense can play a role in the explanation of metaphorical content, i.e. of a conceptual reason when it displays this distinctive sort of complexity.

4. Metaphoricity

I've argued for several continuities between metaphorical usage and literal usage: conceptual reasons, disquotational subprinciples, the role of similarity. I will also suggest a common competence based on knowledge of projection constraints. In this section, though, I will say something about the difference.

As the question of what makes a usage metaphorical relates to that of how an interpreter can tell when a usage is metaphorical, I begin by reviewing the latter problem. The identification of metaphor is standardly conceived of as an initial phase of metaphorical interpretation wherein it is ascertained that metaphor is present, though not yet what its content is. Thus for example "Rob is a bulldozer," "The chairman ploughed through the discussion," and "Juliet is the sun" are patently false on literal readings, so that alternative readings are prompted. Cases such as these, where terms from disparate domains are intrasententially juxtaposed, have often been taken as paradigmatic. But it is well-known that the literal reading need not be patently false. For example, "No man is an island," "Jesus was a carpenter," "Sid is a policeman," are patently true, true, and possibly true on literal readings, respectively (in addition to being perhaps true on metaphorical readings to the effect that no man can live happily without social contact, that Jesus fashioned new spirits from old, and that Sid is authoritative).

The point is especially clear with regard to sentential metaphors. Suppose a speaker means by "The horses have left the starting gate" that it's too late in the semester for him to catch up with his classmates. Since there is no subsentential focus, the literal reading entails no incongruity between constituents, and no patent falsity.

Let's call the view that metaphors always are patently false on a literal reading the "patent falsity thesis." A number of responses to the counterexamples have attempted to minimize departure from this thesis. I'll now consider three such responses, and argue their shortcomings.

Some have expressed satisfaction that the thesis is true in most or even the "vast majority" of cases.[21] This strikes me as facile. I am not myself convinced, first of all, that the thesis is true even for most cases. Surely no one is really trying to count; statistical assessments like "most" are merely impressions based on examples with which one happens to be comfortable. But even for the well-read, these are just tiny samples from the corpus of tokened metaphors. Since the counterexamples are easy to come by, an offhand impression that *they* form the majority would seem to have an equal degree of legitimacy. Furthermore, why should the analysis be restricted to tokened metaphors, as is required for statistical claims to make sense? I don't see the relevance of this restriction or an accompanying statistical claim even if true (by accident). The philosophical question in any event remains of how to characterize metaphorical usage, including cases which do not involve patent falsity.

A second response has been to modify the thesis to require patent truth-value, i.e. patent truth if not patent falsity. This enables a uniform account, inasmuch as patent truth on a literal reading serves just as well to signal the need for a metaphorical interpretation. But the suggestion relies all-too-obviously on special cases. Thus Davidson (1981, 213) supports it with two examples, Cohen (1981, 192) with three; neither gives an argument why we should expect the same of all the counterexamples. And in fact we should not. As we've seen, examples of contingent truth-value on the literal reading are easy to come by (see also Binkley 1981, 140).

A third conservative response has been to appeal to the wider utterance context. Thus Kittay (1987, 68-74) proposes that a metaphor whose literal reading does not generate a patent falsity nonetheless does so in a suitably constructed "discourse," in virtue of "projection rules" which establish coreference relations. Consider the following example, "in which the situational context, that both speaker and hearer know that Smith is a surgeon and not a plumber, is given expression in the discourse":

Don't let Smith perform such a delicate surgical procedure.
Smith is a plumber.
His last two patients died.

Here the "projection rules" establish that "Smith," "plumber," and "his" are coreferential, so that one can convert the last sentence to

That plumber's last two patients died.

There is now an incongruity between "plumber" construed literally and "patient" because plumbers "operate only on inanimate, non-human things" (73). So even though "Smith is a plumber" taken literally is not patently false, it entails violation of selection restrictions and thus patent falsity at the discourse level. This indicates that "plumber" is to be taken metaphorically. Kittay conjectures that "whenever we decide, on the basis of some oddity in an utterance, to give that utterance a metaphorical interpretation, if we construct or reconstruct a sufficiently rich context, we shall find that the [semantic combination] rules violated turn out to be the familiar selection restrictions" (75).

Notice first that Kittay's sense of the word "discourse" is peculiar, and needs spelling out. A discourse in the usual sense entails overt utterances, but on Kittay's usage it is in general a construction, making explicit something which is otherwise implicit. What is this something? In the "plumber" example, Kittay suggests that it is relevant shared knowledge of the speaker and hearer: "that Smith is a surgeon and not a plumber." But this needs revising. It is not necessary that the hearer share the speaker's knowledge. All that is required in order to identify the speaker's utterance as metaphorical is for the hearer to be aware that the speaker believes Smith to be a surgeon and not a plumber. We might gather then that a discourse in Kittay's sense represents certain beliefs of the speaker in the context, which in cases of successful metaphorical interpretation the hearer correctly hypothesizes.

Further charitable revision is needed. It seems clear that the truth-value of "Smith is a plumber" taken literally is not an issue for a hearer in this case, in that he can settle on a metaphorical interpretation whether or not he takes Smith to really be a plumber—as a moonlighter, say. The literal reading is ruled out because it would be irrelevant, having nothing to do with patients or surgery (Wilson and Sperber 1981, 159-164). Charitably construed, Kittay's account is a proposal for how this happens: to determine that a literal reading in context generates a violation of selection restrictions is to determine that the reading is irrelevant. It does not follow that the reading is false (patently or not). To be sure, people normally have only one profession, and if such background knowledge is supposed to be part of the "discourse"—as Kittay suggests in a footnote (73-74)—then the discourse does determine the falsity of "Smith is a plumber." But it is still not this falsity that rules out the literal reading, a point that the further elaboration of the "discourse" just obscures. Even if it were known that Smith is a plumber, overriding the background knowledge, the hearer could still rule out the literal reading as irrelevant.

But Kittay's proposal seems incorrect even when charitably construed. Consider "I'd never buy lottery tickets, but you know Paul—he dreams." Note that the literal reading does not entail that Paul is asleep (unlike "He is dreaming"), just that when he is asleep he dreams. There is no violation involving a sleeping person buying lottery tickets, or any other, on which to base the irrelevance of the literal reading.

It appears to me that not only Kittay's but all attempts to keep closely to the patent falsity thesis are misguided. The correct response to the counterexamples is to give up the thesis entirely. There is no uniform means by which metaphors are identified, not even an oblique one, only a variety of means.[22] I like Bergmann's summation:

> The speaker may explicitly indicate that he or she is using metaphor. The expression used may be either semantically or contextually anomalous if taken literally. Following Grice, we may say that in this case a conversational maxim has apparently been violated: Quality (the sentence "Men are wolves," taken literally, is false) [patent falsity], Quantity (you may say of our mutual friend who has long lived in California, "Hayward is a Californian, all right") [patent truth], Relation (you may answer my question about your new automobile's road performance and gas mileage by replying "It seems I have a mule with an insatiable appetite") [irrelevance]. In each case, the literal content of the sentence is conversationally inappropriate. Or recognition of metaphor may just involve recognition of the appropriateness of a particular reading of the expression as metaphor, rather than recognition of inappropriateness of the literal reading (1988, 489).

I would add though that metaphorical interpretation is not a matter of calculating a Gricean implicature, and that a metaphor may not be identifiable at all.

Let's now turn to the question of what makes a speaker's usage metaphorical, whether or not anyone can so identify it. It will turn out that a partial answer to this question explains the unreliability of identification.

In the previous chapter I considered the notion of "counterfactual inductive strength": that a speaker's meaning be such as to make for an inference of non-zero inductive strength, if it were not a conceptual reason but an ordinary e-reason (Ch. 4, sec. 4). I surmised that it fails for metaphor. What I now want to propose is that failure is a requirement, serving as a way to demarcate metaphorical usage. More precisely:

M. A speaker's meaning is metaphorical to a given degree only if its content supports an inverse degree of counterfactual inductive strength.

Let's consider what this entails.

Note first that M gives only a necessary condition. A speaker who means by "Rob is a bulldozer" that Rob is a prime number is not waxing metaphorical in virtue of the fact that being a prime number gives zero inductive support to being a bulldozer. Other constraints are needed, as will be discussed in the next section; I will be assuming sufficiency given that they are met.

M makes metaphor a matter of degree. If a speaker means by "Sid is a policeman" that Sid is authoritative, we might think this metaphorical since the speaker is using "policeman" to describe someone who need not be a policeman. But consider that if a speaker means by "John is clever" that John is quick-witted, he is using "clever" to describe someone who need not be clever. Just as one might be a policeman in a certain sense without being a policeman, one might be clever in a specific sense without being clever (John might be slow in most other ways). So it isn't obvious just what the distinction is. But it does seem clear that it isn't a sharp one.

Let's see how M works when the degree of metaphoricity is maximal. A speaker's meaning by "Rob is a bulldozer" that Rob is headstrong is metaphorical to a maximal degree because Rob's being headstrong lends no inductive support to Rob's being a bulldozer. Notice it makes no difference if the property in question is shared or analogous. Thus if a speaker means by "Man is a wolf" that man is territorial, his usage is likewise metaphorical to a maximal degree, since that men are territorial lends no inductive support to men being wolves—even though wolves are territorial, whereas bulldozers aren't headstrong.

The paradigm examples involving patent falsity on a literal reading are on my proposal metaphorical to a maximal degree, insofar as "patent" implies that falsity is assured independently of evidence. But as Harman among others has emphasized, a little imagination often serves to undermine what seems patent (1973, 104-107). For instance in an age of genetic engineering we ought to be careful about saying that "Rob is a gorilla" has to be false. Suppose a speaker means by "Rob is a gorilla" that Rob has a lot of body hair. If we can imagine a gorilla egg successfully fertilized by human sperm, then arguably Rob's having a lot of body hair does support his being a gorilla to some negligible but non-zero degree. If so, then the speaker's usage is not maximally metaphorical; the greater the feasibility or prevalence of such engineering, the lesser the degree. So my proposal does not render the patently false cases (taking "patently" to be something weaker than "necessarily") as maximally metaphorical on all usages. I think that is as it should be.

Patently true metaphors are also maximally metaphorical according to M, on the assumption that a reasonable model for inductive strength is what has been called "statistical relevance" (Salmon 1975). The idea is that an inference is inductively strong only to the degree that the truth of the premises is relevant to the truth of the conclusion. Thus an inference from "Fred is chaste" to "Fred won't get pregnant" has no inductive strength even though the latter is certainly true, because Fred's chastity has nothing to do with it. Similarly, a speaker's meaning by "No man is an island" that no man can live happily without social contact is maximally metaphorical, since we may conclude that no man is an island irrespective of whether no man can live happily without social contact. Note that statistical relevance serves equally well as a model for the patent falsity cases, though it has not been necessary to recognize this. An inference from Rob's being head-strong to Rob's being a bulldozer has no inductive strength because the latter is false irrespective of whether Rob is headstrong. That is, degree of relevance is zero whether a conclusion is true irrespective of the premises or false irrespective of the premises (modulo suitably imagined premises as just discussed).

Not only does M thus give us a uniform account of metaphors which are patently false on a literal reading and those which are patently true, it also explains maximal degrees of metaphor where the truth-value is not patent. For instance if a speaker means by "The horses have left the starting gate" that it's too late in the semester for him to catch up with his classmates, his usage is just as metaphorical as his meaning by "Rob is a bulldozer" that Rob is headstrong. This cannot be explained if patent truth-value is required, but it is not. What is required is a degree of inductive strength, which is again zero: that it's too late in the semester to catch up with one's classmates provides no inductive support for any horses leaving any starting gate.

Now consider a case where the degree of metaphoricity is not maximal. I've suggested that the "Sid is a policeman" case is not easy to distinguish from a novel literal usage. I think that this has to do with the fact that Sid's being authoritative confirms his being a policeman to a non-zero degree, just as John's quick-wittedness confirms John's cleverness to a non-zero degree. It would seem though that the former degree is less, as the inference to policemanhood is especially weak, and this is what accounts for the usage being more metaphorical. But that there is a degree of support at all makes it less metaphorical than the "Rob is a bulldozer" case. This captures the fact that people and policemen are not so metaphysically disparate as people and bulldozers. For while "policeman" doesn't apply to non-policemen, it at least applies to people.

Whereas it is easy to quantitatively identify the metaphorical end of the spectrum I am proposing, namely by zero inductive strength, it is impossible to likewise identify the other end. I suggest that the degree to which John's quick-wittedness confirms John's cleverness makes the usage of "John is clever" maximally literal, though this is not the maximal degree of inductive strength. I can't say what degree this is. The main point to keep in mind is the rendering of metaphoricity as a continuum, with definite cases at each end.

Some have suggested that metaphoricity comes in degrees because novelty does. So in between an indisputably fresh metaphor and an indisputably dead one, there are intermediate cases whose degree of metaphoricity has to do with how widespread they are. But this is a different continuum. M applies to the content of a speaker's meaning, where this implies that it does not derive from word meanings. So it has to do with any usage novel enough to have not made it into the lexicon, and the degree of this novelty is not what it measures.

Related to this, graded metaphoricity does not affect the requirement of a conceptual reason for metaphorical usage. In the absence of a conceptual reason, the content of the belief expressed by sincere utterance is determined in part by word meanings. I earlier observed that this might imply an absurd belief on the speaker's part. We can now see that it need not, even on a maximally metaphorical usage ("The horses have left the starting gate"). And the metaphoricity may not be maximal ("Sid is a policeman"). But metaphoricity to any degree entails the speaker's departure from the lexicon.

Let me summarize in terms of a traditional observation that metaphor entails an analogy between disparate realms, where what makes for disparity is that predicates characteristic of one domain cannot apply in the other without incongruity. In the paradigm cases, the disparity is manifest by incongruity between subject and predicate, entailing patent falsity on a literal reading. Or the incongruity may be similarly manifest but negated, entailing patent truth. But the incongruity need not be manifest intrasententially, and thus need not entail patent truth-value. On my proposal the unifying notion of disparity is captured not by any kind of truth-value but by a certain dysfunctionality of inference: zero inductive support lent by metaphorical content (determined by speaker's meaning) to literal (determined by sentence meaning). Middling degrees of support reflect lesser degrees of incongruity.

It remains to reconsider the identification of metaphor. Since counterfactual inductive strength depends on the speaker's meaning, M attributes metaphoricity not to a sentence but a usage. This explains why identification is so unreliable and requires a variety of means, for a speaker does not in general wear her meaning on her sleeve. If in some cases it seems one can judge just from the sentence, that is because there is a way of inferring what one needs to know. Thus M explains why one can infer metaphoricity in the patent truth-value cases, where whatever the speaker might mean wouldn't lend support to the utterance construed literally. But the general case is that metaphoricity depends on knowing the content of the speaker's meaning, and hence on any of a variety of contextual clues to speaker's meaning. In that case, however, there is no longer any task of identification as an intermediate interpretive step; if you know the speaker's meaning, you're done. Meanwhile patent truth-value on a literal reading just makes a WDYM-question more likely. But there is nothing special in that; whenever one is after the speaker's meaning, a question must necessarily have arisen somehow. Its having arisen does not constitute an interpretive step, but simply calls forth the task: to get the right answer, in metaphor as elsewhere.[23]

5. Conceptual Reasons Constrained, Part Two

As everyone agrees, metaphor is creative. Notwithstanding that the content of a metaphor often is drawn from "commonplaces and stereo-types," as Bergmann puts it (1991, 487), in general the speaker's imagination may range over uncharted territory. Just as obvious but less often observed is that not everything goes. One might mean by "Rob is a bulldozer" that Rob is headstrong, that he is heedless of others' feelings, etc., but not that Rob is wearing a raincoat.

In this section, I'll say something about the constraints. This is not to say that I will try to *state* them, any more than I have for literal usage. I don't know whether this can be done in any general way, though some seem to try. Lakoff has proposed an "invariance principle" constraining the mapping in a systematic metaphor, whereby the "target domain" must "preserve the cognitive topology of the source domain, in a way consistent with the inherent structure of the target domain" (1993, 215). So in the pervasive metaphor wherein categories are conceived of as containers (things can be "put in" a category, "removed" from it, etc.) "interiors will be mapped to interiors, exteriors to exteriors, and boundaries to boundaries" (212-215). I don't myself understand this principle, as it seems to presuppose the metaphor rather than explain it. But in any case, I will not attempt to formulate any principles of this nature. Rather I will portray the constraints on metaphor as projection constraints in the sense of the previous chapter.

Inasmuch as constraints are the flip side of creativity, I want to begin by putting aside a mistaken account of creativity in metaphor. The mistake had its origin in this famous passage of Black (1981):

> Often we say "X is M," evoking some imputed connexion between M and an imputed L ... in cases where, prior to the construction of the metaphor, we would have been hard put to it to find any literal resemblance between M and L. It would be more illuminating in some of these cases to say that the metaphor creates the similarity than to say that it formulates some similarity antecedently existing (72).

The last sentence proved to be controversial, owing to the seeming paradox that metaphor can create similarity. As Black later pointed out, he does not quite say here that metaphor has this power, only that "it would be more illuminating" to so regard it. Nonetheless the claim does have proponents, and needs to be addressed.

Suppose for the sake of argument that similarity relations figure in the content of a metaphor. Consider then that the temptation to attribute a power to create similarity arises only for those metaphors for which it is considered that a similarity in any case *now* exists. If it does not, the question can hardly arise whether it pre-exists or is brought into existence. But suppose one means by "July is the pinnacle of summer" that July is the month of summer when most people take vacations. Suppose also that most people vacation in August. Then one would not have latched onto any similarity relation between July and a mountain. But surely the metaphor is just as creative as meaning by "July is the pinnacle of summer" that July is the most-loved month, assuming the latter to be true. The similarity is not created: if there at all, it was there all along, even if we "would have been hard put" to find it without the metaphor. Put another way, creativity in metaphor pertains not to the objective relations that make a proposition true but rather to the relation forged on this occasion between proposition and sentence (at the level of what is believed). At least, this is so on the assumption that such objective relations exist. One might question this assumption on independent grounds, but not because of the way metaphor works.[24]

But constraints must be observed whether or not reality is. If one who means by "July is the pinnacle of summer" that reptiles lay eggs is being creative, it is not in a linguistic sense. This is just as in literal usage. Specifically, what underlies the continuity with literal usage is that the constraints on metaphor are projection constraints as discussed in the previous chapter. There we saw that the concept attached to a word in a speaker's idiolect is a matter of sample referents which he accepts, and properties he projects from those samples. The concept associates with a projection function, representing how the projection varies with the samples. I argued that part of the content of a conceptual reason is determined by the same projection function, operating on distinct samples peculiar to the context. The "sense" of the speaker's words is projected from these samples, generating not a new concept but a new understanding of an existing concept. This is the nature of linguistic "usage" relevant to a conceptual reason.

Such usage is therefore bound by projection constraints. I've suggested that competence involves knowing the range common to speakers' projection functions. Constraints in this sense are not just interspeaker constraints, but are operative also across a given speaker's progressive understandings of a concept based on a stock of sample referents accumulated over time, and across his contextual understandings. These are different applications of the speaker's idiolectical concept, but involve the same function with the same range.

As I am taking metaphorical usage to be a matter of conceptual reasons, I take all this to apply. We simply recognize that projection may be not only from referents but non-referents. As earlier remarked, if a speaker were to conclude of a fierce person that he is metaphorically a tiger in virtue of being a physical object, then I think we would conclude not just that the speaker hasn't learned to use "tiger" metaphorically, but that he has not learned "tiger." The most natural way to account for this intuition is to posit not a new concept, but new application of the old—more specifically, operation of the idiolectical concept's associated projection function on non-tigers as well as tigers. Thus there is no separate, accessory competence with respect to metaphor: projection from non-instances is bound by the same constraints as for literal usage.

The point isn't peculiar to metaphor. Remarking on the applicability of "flower" to likenesses such as plastic or painted flowers, Cohen (1971) argues that "flower" is not thereby ambiguous but may be acceptably used in such cases even though there is no flower. What I take to be the measure of competence here is that what the speaker projects is within bounds: a likeness of petals and stem with the right relative proportions, but not the whiteness of the plastic. It's not just that a speaker be able to use "flower" for a plastic flower, but that he have a reasonable idea of what *makes* it useable. As in metaphor this would be an exercise of a unitary competence with respect to "flower."

The notion of projection from non-instances is problematic, though, because a projection has been characterized as a hypothesis as to what makes given samples instances of a kind. If projection is from non-instances, obviously this characterization won't do. I will say that it is a hypothesis as to what makes the non-instances "illustrative" of a kind. Being illustrative has to do with contributing to the understanding of a concept, including the ongoing understanding based on instances. Thus a speaker might change his understanding of chairs based on consideration of skilift chairs, deciding that legs are not necessary. But note that a real skilift chair is not necessary: a picture, toy, or plastic miniature could accomplish the same end. To do so, though, the right properties must be projected; projecting curvature from the miniature will not lead one to a better hypothesis about the nature of chairs. In this respect a hypothesis of what makes non-referents "illustrative" is something that one can be right or wrong about.

Similarly in science, a metaphor or model of a phenomenon can contribute to discoveries about the phenomenon itself (Hesse 1966, 157-176). But for a billiard-ball metaphor to contribute to the understanding of gas molecules, the right properties of billiard balls must be abstracted—e.g. certain behavior upon collision, but not weight of the balls. What makes billiard balls "illustrative" of gas molecules is thus a hypothesis, in that a given abstraction may or may not lead one closer to the nature of gas molecules.

It is not just the ongoing understanding of a concept that is at issue, but a contextual understanding: what I earlier called "tailoring" a concept to instances peculiar to a context. Hypothesizing about what makes non-instances illustrative can shed new light on them, whether or not it does on the concept. Here too projections are fallible, and the speaker thus not the final authority on what she means. Suppose she means by "Society is a sea" that social institutions are vast. She hypothesizes that what makes certain phenomena illustrative of seahood is vastness. But she could change her mind. Upon further reflection she might consider that it's more a matter of vast complexity, involving myriad interactions of dependence and conflict. Or it might be someone else who persuades her of this. So as an alternative to articulating her meaning, the speaker might give her examples, just as in literal usage. To "What do you mean, society is a 'sea'?" she might say, "Oh well, you know, like the way so many people use the courts for even the most trivial disagreements." The interlocutor would then have the opportunity not just to replicate the speaker's projection but to improve upon it.

So to claim that the content of her usage is that society is a sea in the sense that it is vast is not to "reduce" her meaning to vastness, as earlier observed. The content reflects a tentative state, marked by attempt rather than attainment. Unlike simply describing society as vast, the speaker's metaphor has her doing her best to abstract out features of society which make the concept of seahood apt—a task potentially shaped by any of the associations which come with that concept.

I now turn to the business of constraints left unfinished in the previous chapter. My concern will not be with those constraints on metaphor which have to do with aesthetics rather than competence. Suppose that by "Every mind contains an aviary that is stocked with birds of every sort" Socrates meant that thoughts leave unpleasant residues. I take it that by some lights this would be a bad metaphor. But this is no reflection on competence, as there would be if he meant that minds are dulled by too much food. In the first case the metaphor is not appealing, while in the second there is no metaphor. A metaphor must be competent before its artistry can even been considered.

As they say, there's no accounting for taste; anyway I don't propose to. But note that I am taking aesthetic value like metaphoricity to attach in the first instance to a usage rather than a sentence. I assume that some of the same lights would consider what Socrates actually meant by "Every mind contains an aviary that is stocked with birds of every sort," that items of knowledge are retrieved from memory rather than acquired, to be more appealing. What's judged is the usage. For a sentence, a judgment is thus doubly subjective: it's not only beauty but an imagined usage that's up to a beholder.

In the previous chapter we saw that counterfactual inductive strength is not a constraint on conceptual reasons because it fails for metaphorical usages (Ch. 4, sec. 4). This raises an issue because satisfaction of projection constraints, defined as a constraint on WDYM-answers, is necessary but not sufficient. For example, a speaker who means by "John is clever" that quick-wittedness is a virtue satisfies projection constraints, but intuitively is out of bounds. The problem then is to account for this and constrained metaphorical usage as well, without appealing to counterfactual inductive strength.

Let's first consider something that will do the work of counterfactual inductive strength when usage is non-metaphorical. Recall how this was rendered as a constraint on a direct answer to a counterfactual question, one whose topic and contrast are attributions of belief rather than believing true, and which requests an e-reason rather than a conceptual reason. The constraint on the answer is that it "favor" the topic over the contrast in a certain way. So if the question were

<x believes that John is clever, x believes that John is dull, e-reason>,

the answer

A1: x believes that John is quick-witted

would favor the topic over the contrast, in that if we compare the probabilities of the topic and contrast when we don't assume that x believes that John is quick-witted with these probabilities when we do so assume, the probabilities shift in favor of the topic. The same is not true of

A2: x believes quick-wittedness is a virtue.

The favoring metric thus captures the relevant sense of inductive strength.

Can we achieve the same outcome with another constraint? We can, with favoring as applied to the actual rather than a counterfactual question. Consider the actual question in this example:

<*x* believes-true "John is clever," *x* believes-true "John is dull," conceptual reason>.

If we consider this metric for A1 and A2, considered now as conceptual reasons, we find again that the first but not the second passes. Take the first case. Not assuming A1, the topic and contrast each have some probability; it doesn't matter what. If we now assume A1, what happens? Since the belief has the status of a conceptual reason, we are assuming that *x* is fixing the content of his belief using the content that John is quick-witted. This raises the probability that *x* believes-true "John is clever," i.e. that x is fixing the content for this sentence. Meanwhile it lowers the probability that *x* believes-true "John is dull." So assuming A1 does shift probabilities in favor of the topic. But assuming A2 doesn't shift the probabilities at all. (See also Chapter 4, note 27.)

In counterfactual inductive strength we had an explanation for the acceptability of one speaker's meaning and unacceptability of another in terms of how the speaker reasons. Now we instead have one in terms of how he uses language. But the explanation may not satisfy. One wants to know *why* assuming the first answer raises the probability that *x* believes-true "John is clever," and lowers the probability that *x* believes-true "John is dull." Apparently, it's because John's being quick-witted is an acceptable sense of "John is clever." But do we not want our constraint to explain this, rather than be explained by it?

Not necessarily. What we see here is that evaluating the probabilities for the favoring metric presupposes the projection constraints. But that's all right, because it's not required that favoring and projection constraints be independent. What is required is that they jointly explain the constraints on speaker's meanings. And this, I submit, is what they do. As noted previously, the problem revealed by A2 is that projection constraints as brought to bear on WDYM-answers only operate on part of the belief content. They do not require that the latter bear any particular relation to the topic, as is implied by the status of the belief as a kind of reason. Favoring does require this. Satisfaction of both projection constraints and favoring require that projected content in a conceptual reason be within bounds, and that the conceptual reason bear the appropriate relation to both topic and contrast.

This works for metaphorical usage as well. Suppose the question is

<*x* believes-true "The iron is clever," *x* believes-true "The iron is dull," conceptual reason>.

Then as the reader may verify, the answer

   x believes that the iron can turn itself off when no one is using it

favors the topic over the contrast, while

   x believes that being able to turn itself off when no one is using it is a
   standard feature of Kenmore toaster ovens

does not. Thus while both answers have projected content within bounds, only the first additionally bears the appropriate relation to topic and contrast.

Counterfactual inductive strength is more intuitive than favoring. It has also proven to be of independent interest as a way to demarcate metaphorical usage. But it has been a ladder that we can now kick away. I propose that projection constraints and favoring are necessary, jointly sufficient constraints on conceptual reasons. They answer a question posed at the outset of this book, namely what constrains the multiplicity of possible speaker's meanings for a conceptually indeterminate sentence. They also explain the multiplicity itself, as the robustness of hypothesis formation with regard to essential properties of sample referents, where the properties play a role in reasoning vis-à-vis what is (and is not) believed-true. The robustness is a reflection of the flexibility we have in tailoring our concepts to new things, and employing the results in thought.

The aspect of competence which is explained by knowledge of projection constraints has to do with lexical competence. What is explained by knowledge of projection constraints and favoring is not only extralexical but extralinguistic. The probabilities involved in the favoring metric have to do with general-purpose reasoning, as well as background world knowledge (Ch. 4, n. 27). So knowing the bounds on conceptual indeterminacy is a matter of both competence and intelligence.

6. The Demand for Explanation

In his 1955 paper "Metaphor," Max Black famously criticized the view that metaphor is reducible to literal discourse, a view he described as treating "the metaphorical expression (let us call it 'M') as a substitute for some other literal expression ('L', say) which would have expressed the same meaning, had it been used instead. On this view, the meaning of M, in its metaphorical occurrence, is just the literal meaning of L" (Black 1981, 68). While Black took this to be a common view in his time, nowadays I think one would be hard-pressed to find any advocates. In any case I am not one myself. However, a certain version of what I will call the "reducibility" thesis does fall out of my account. I'll conclude by elaborating on this and responding to possible objections.

Why do I reject the reducibility thesis as described by Black? To begin with, I don't think that it even makes sense, since I take metaphoricity to be a matter not of words alone but of usage, implying a speaker's meaning. I can recognize the metaphoricity of a sentence only in an elliptical way, as metaphoricity on all usages. Only sentences with patent truth-value qualify. As we saw in section 4, a speaker's meaning by "Rob is a bulldozer" that Rob is headstrong is maximally metaphorical in virtue of zero inductive support given by Rob's being headstrong to his being a bulldozer. Since anything that might be meant would have the same result, the sentence is metaphorical on all usages. Let's assume this notion of sentence metaphoricity, and take a "literal" sentence to be one that is not metaphorical. "The horses have left the starting gate" and "Sid is a policeman" are then literal, despite possible metaphorical usage.

The reducibility thesis now makes sense; but I am not committed to it. First of all, my account does not entail the existence of the literal expression. Recall the principle:

DP2a: If a normal English speaker believes-true 'p', where 'p' is an English sentence containing no ambiguous or indexical terms, and does so on the basis of a conceptual reason that q, then he believes that p in the sense that q.

The consequent here does not entail that there is a sentence expressive of q. It might be thought that nonetheless such a sentence, call it the "q-sentence," must exist. For now, let's assume this to be the case. Reducibility does not follow even so, for two reasons.

First, my account does not entail that the content of the metaphor is simply that q (sec. 2, point 2). The content of a speaker's metaphor is not the content of his conceptual reason but the belief content attributed by DP2a. To believe that Rob is a bulldozer in the sense that he is headstrong is not the same as believing that he is headstrong. As previously discussed, the former has to do with fallible projection while applying the concept of a bulldozer. Thus the metaphorical meaning of "Rob is a bulldozer" is not the literal meaning of "Rob is headstrong."[25]

Second, the very fact that I am rendering metaphorical content in terms of speaker's meaning is incompatible with the reducibility thesis, inasmuch as a speaker's meaning is tied to an occasion of utterance. What a speaker means by a given sentence on one occasion may differ from what he means on another. But making metaphoricity a property of the sentence runs it across contexts. Black comments that on the reducibility thesis "Richard is a lion" metaphorically means just what "Richard is brave" means (Black 1981, 69), but this can't be right if only because the literal paraphrase in another context might be "Richard is quick."

Consider then a modified version of reducibility, according to which for every metaphorical usage there is a literal sentence the content of which is embedded in the metaphorical content. My account is compatible with reducibility in this sense, what I will call "weak" reducibility. Continuing to assume that the q-sentence must exist, my account implies it because if the q-sentence were metaphorical, the speaker's belief would be patently false or patently true. What a speaker means by "Society is a sea" cannot be the literal meaning of "Society is held together by the waters of community," or he would have the belief that society is a sea in the sense that it is held together by waters of community, which is patently false (or incongruous).

My rationale is not affected by metaphoricity coming in degrees. By definition a metaphorical sentence is one whose usage must be maximally metaphorical. So it is not germane that one could mean by such-and-such that Sid is a policeman, with "Sid is a policeman" not expressing an absurd or trivial belief. A q-sentence with a possible literal usage is literal on the current definition. I think this is true to the spirit of the reducibility thesis; in any event, I am committed to weak reducibility only on this definition of terms.

Here is another way of looking at matters. The requirement of a speaker's meaning for metaphorical content implies the existence of a WDYM-question prompted by the speaker's utterance. The question represents an explanatory demand. Weak reducibility thus implies that a metaphorical usage must be explained in terms of a literal q-sentence. A metaphorical q-sentence won't meet the demand because, barring speaker dysfunctionality, the answer to the question would be neither true nor direct since q would not be the content of his conceptual reason.

I can imagine two objections: that the *q*-sentence need not be literal, and that there need not be any *q*-sentence at all. I consider these now in turn.

It does seem that a metaphor can sometimes be explained in terms of another. Consider

> Moyers: You said in a recent speech that the United States is in a real danger of becoming a lost land. In what sense?
> Puttnam: A nation is lost when the soul that it would wish to have becomes more and more removed from the manner in which it sees itself reflected on a day-to-day basis.

Puttnam's reply seems to indicate a metaphorical *q*-sentence, something like "The soul the United States wishes to have is removed from the manner in which it sees itself reflected." I grant that this is explanatory in some fashion. But the literal meaning of the putative *q*-sentence is not Puttnam's meaning, unless he believes that nations literally can have souls and look at themselves. So this is not the *q*-sentence, and the fact that it is metaphorical is beside the point. (Or, if "soul," "see," and "reflect" are taken to be dead metaphors suitable to nations, the *q*-sentence is not metaphorical in the required sense.)

How then can it have explanatory value? We've already seen one way that a reply can suggest a true and direct answer without expressing one. One can give an example, which is not supposed to express the content of a conceptual reason but from which the questioner can infer the content. Another way is by suggesting further avenues of inquiry. Moyers could ask how a nation can have a "soul," or how it can "see" itself. By such means Moyers might eventually get a true and direct answer to his original question, either via a reply of Puttnam's or an inference it enables.

Against this it might be maintained that a "secondary" metaphor need not be explained in *any* fashion. It might be held that Puttnam's reply expresses just as good an explanation as, say, the literal "More and more Americans have no concept of national purpose," in that it can be understood "as is"—i.e. without need of further explanation.

This brings us to the second objection to weak reducibility, for presumably the same could be claimed of the original metaphor. Just as a metaphorical *q*-sentence might be understood as is, so might any metaphorical sentence. A metaphorical sentence need not require any *q*-sentence at all, literal or otherwise. There need be no q-sentence because there need be no explanatory demand to meet.

This objection sounds plausible. But I think this is because of the pervasiveness of other phenomena which are easily confused with understanding a metaphor "as is." To begin with, it may be that what is grasped is the content of the sentence as modified by "in a sense"—e.g. not that the United States is becoming a lost land, but that in some sense the United States is becoming a lost land. But this could not be the content of a metaphor, because it's too easily true. Davidson similarly criticized the hidden simile view by noting that "everything is like everything, and in endless ways" (1981, 209). If this seems too strong, consider Goodman's "Anything is in some way like anything else" (1964, 440), i.e.

For all x and y, there is some way in which x is like y.

I take this to be synonymous with

For all x and y, there is some sense in which x is like y.

Following previous discussion (n. 13), I don't think this is distinct from

For all x and y, there is some sense in which x is y.

So the point needn't be made in terms of similarity: the reason we can be confident with the quantifiers is the multiplicity of senses. For the same reason, we can be confident in the truth of the more general "In a sense p."

Not only is there still a demand for explanation, such content amounts to a kind of weak response to it. As previously discussed, when a WDYM-question requests a conceptual reason, its presuppositions together with DP2a entail that there is some q such that the speaker believes that p in the sense that q. From this it follows that the speaker believes that in some sense p; but this is not a direct answer, just a kind of promissory note for one (Ch. 3, sec. 4.2.) Grasping such content is too trivial to count as understanding a metaphor, "as is" or otherwise. But inferring it is so easy as to be beneath notice, which I think explains how it can be confused with irreducible metaphorical content.[26]

Another phenomenon easily confused with understanding a metaphor "as is" is the difficulty of articulation, just as in literal usage. From this difficulty it of course doesn't follow that a q-sentence doesn't exist. But there may be a difficulty in principle, as arguably when content is based on sense perception. In metaphor there is another possible source. It has been observed that one purpose of metaphor is to address gaps in the lexicon, i.e. to express thoughts which are not expressible with existing lexical resources. In that case a speaker's loss for words will reflect no shortcoming of his own, but the non-existence of the words. Note that the point is about the speaker's language: whether or not there is a q-sentence in the metalanguage in which the content of his belief is attributed (DP2a), there may not be one in the language of his utterance.

Here then is where I abandon my provisional assumption that the q-sentence must exist. Acknowledging the possibility of inexpressibility in principle, I cannot hold to weak reducibility as so far defended, which assumes that a q-sentence exists and claims that it must be literal. What I do still hold is that the q-sentence must be literal if it exists, on the unchanged rationale that if it were metaphorical, the attributed belief would be absurd or trivial. I also maintain that this inexpressibility is not understanding "as is." A statement that a wine is "unassuming" causes one to puzzle over what the speaker means whether or not there are words to express it. Any grasped content doesn't obviate explanation, but rather constitutes it—though being inexpressible, a hearer might come by it only by guessing.

It might be thought that metaphor is still being undervalued. Black claimed that "we can comment upon the metaphor, but the metaphor itself neither needs nor invites explanation and paraphrase" (1962, 237), suggesting that he would not accept weak reducibility any more than reducibility as he formulates it. But the distinction is important. I can readily agree with Black that

> a memorable metaphor has the power to bring two separate domains into cognitive and emotional relation by using language directly appropriate to the one as a lens for seeing the other; the implications, suggestions, and supporting values entwined with the literal use of the metaphorical expression enable us to see a new subject matter in a new way. The extended meanings that result, the relations between initially disparate realms created, can neither be antecedently predicted nor subsequently paraphrased in prose...Metaphorical thought is a distinctive mode of achieving insight, not to be construed as an ornamental substitute for plain thought (237).

The insight enabled by a metaphor might be just as Black describes, but it comes from having an explanation. A "memorable metaphor" is not distinguishable from the sense we make of it, by way of a process that begins with puzzlement. And to say that the explanation, when not ineffable, must be expressible by a literal sentence is just to say that the "implications, suggestions, and supporting values" do not ensue from absurd or trivial belief.[27]

I have been supposing that there is such a thing as metaphorical content. But this has been denied, most prominently by Davidson (1981). On his view, the significance of metaphor lies not in the existence of any special kind of content—of words, speakers, interpreters, or otherwise—but in what it "calls to attention." This cannot be captured by a propositional content because "there is no limit to what a metaphor calls to our attention, and much of what we are caused to notice is not propositional in character" (218). Thus Davidson denies the paraphrasability of metaphor for a distinctive reason: there is no content for a paraphrase to capture. If so, this would also count against my account of metaphorical usage as the content of a conceptual reason.

But I do not accept the argument. I would generalize Bergmann's reply that an unlimited number of possible interpretations may be greatly reduced by context (1989, 486). The point isn't just about interpretation: unlimited possibilities as to what the speaker might mean do not entail unlimited things that a speaker does mean. It is independently clear that what a metaphor calls to attention should not be equated with the limitless possibilities. As previously observed, elsewhere in his paper Davidson argues that if a metaphor were a hidden simile it would be trivial because "everything is like everything, and in endless ways" (209). The moral, one would think, is that what makes metaphor non-trivial is that certain of the possibilities are picked out. But it turns out that Davidson thinks metaphors evoke not just some but endless similarities. Why, then, isn't metaphor just as uninteresting as a simile after all?

Turning to the non-propositional character of what we "notice," it is noteworthy that Davidson appeals to perception, observing that words are the "wrong currency to exchange for a picture" (218). But this is hardly unique to metaphor. It's one reason why a speaker might indicate her meaning with an example ("Here's what I mean by the 'essence' of a sunset," showing a photo). We do not conclude that there is no such thing as content in literal usage.[28] The theory of content is difficult, but it has not been shown that there is nothing to theorize about.

I have not tried to provide such a theory, but to analyze the content of a metaphorical usage as the content of a speaker's meaning—with all that this entails given the analysis of WDYM-questions, and of conceptual reasons and their constraints. My hope is that this has resulted in a better understanding of metaphor, and its place within the realm of linguistic usage.

Notes to Chapter 1

1. When I speak of "derivation from syntactic rules" I do not mean rules in any normative sense, but principles of an internalized grammar in the modern linguistic sense.
2. Higginbotham (1986, 46), citing an example he attributes to Donald Davidson.
3. Note though that if one were to inquire what the speaker means out of a desire for a particular sentence meaning on an occasion, then just as in Bo's case the inquiry would be informed by the possible meanings, known in virtue of competence. The disambiguating kind of speaker's meaning thus also contrasts with the "deliquesces" example, where one has not acquired a word. That one does not request an item of linguistic competence when inquiring into the speaker's meaning will be a recurring theme.
4. Peirce had his reasons for speaking here of implications rather than inferences generally; for a discussion, see Aune (1972). The mundane notion that propositional content is reflected in inferences, or an "inferential role," should be distinguished from the controversial view that content just *is* inferential role. Peirce's remark suggests a version of this view, which has been expounded more recently by a number of theorists (e.g. Field 1978, Block 1986, and Harman 1987); on Peirce's version, there is no content for a speaker to fix over and above the implications fixed.
5. I mean "inductive" strength, the degree to which the truth of premises compels the truth of a conclusion. The sense of this notion has long been challenged (e.g. Harman 1986, 4-6), but it simplifies my project. I believe that preferred notions (for Harman, a "change in view" which obeys various principles) could be substituted throughout without affecting the points I wish to make.
6. In *A History of Western Philosophy*, Russell defines it as "the method of seeking knowledge by question and answer" (1945, 92). For some comments on dialectic in understanding language, see Mates (1964, 73).
7. It might be suspected that this is a vacuous conclusion, since I have described the phenomena in a such a way as to already suggest my approach, to which there must be alternatives. That is, it might be suspected that the same raw

phenomena have been studied, but accounted for differently. The closest candidate I'm aware of is the analysis of an apparent multiplicity of systematically related meanings that can be generated when a word is combined with others. Consider for example the meanings of "drop" in "drop a stitch," "drop a friend," and "drop a hint," which are distinct yet related in some systematic fashion, such that one could apparently generate new meanings just by varying the sentential context. This topic was discussed by Aristotle, and in recent years by James Ross and L. J. Cohen. My concern is largely orthogonal, however. Conceptual indeterminacy arises once the meanings of words are determined, however they might be determined, and whatever relation there might be to meanings that would arise in other sentential contexts. Conceptual indeterminacy in the case of "drop," if there is such, would have to do with an unlimited number of senses in which one can drop a friend, say. But my concern is not entirely orthogonal: Ross and Cohen discuss a wide range of cases, and some of them I take to involve a multiplicity of possible speaker's meanings rather than word meanings.

I will return to this in Chapter 3, section 5. As will also be discussed there, conceptual indeterminacy only partly coincides with the phenomena that linguists have identified as a foil to ambiguity, via "ambiguity tests" (explained and defended by e.g. Atlas 1989, 73-77)—a foil designated by a variety of terms including "sense-generality," "vagueness," and "non-specificity." For example, "neighbor" is non-specific as to gender, but this is not conceptual indeterminacy in my sense: we wouldn't refer to a "neighbor in the sense of female neighbor."

8.   See e.g. Putnam (1975), Burge (1989), and Marconi (1997).

Notes to Chapter 2

1.   Van Fraassen includes the topic in the contrast-class, but for my purposes it is more convenient to exclude it. It will also often be convenient to suppress reference to a class, especially when there is only one contrast, so I will henceforth often refer to just the "contrast" or "contrasts."
2.   It may seem odd to speak of R holding between A and $<P,X>$ rather than simply between A and P. The oddness is resolved by distinguishing between R holding *qua* relation *simpliciter* and *qua* relevance relation. It is only in the latter sense that R holds between A and $<P, X>$, for relevance is relative to a question with P and X as constituents (142).
3.   Justification for a belief is surprisingly sensitive to the choice of contrast. See Dretske (1972, 429-430), and Lipton (1991), who uses the term "foil."
4.   There is an alternative stipulation of example 6 on which it too involves a conceptual e-reason. If the questioner were interested in a range of ages, such as would be provided by "I mean that he's over sixty," then he might be

requesting a sense of "old." This can't be said of an exact age, on the principle that for any sense of "old," if one person counts as old in that sense then an older person must also count as old in that sense; see Kamp (1975).

5. The phonetic representation here may not correspond to any representation in the grammar. I assume that the grammar assigns distinct sound patterns to "an aim" and "a name" (e.g. more elongated pronunciation of "a" in the latter); but my concern is with parsing, in which a listener's phonetic representation of an utterance may not match well with any assigned pattern, or may match in varying degrees with more than one.

6. For a complete statement of the methodological assumptions I adopt here, specifically regarding the grammar, parsing, assignment of meanings by the grammar, and knowability of meaning, see Larson and Segal (1995, 9-22). Knowability should not be taken to beg any questions, e.g. about natural kind terms. Though Putnam concluded his famous "twin-earth" thought experiment with "Meaning ain't in the head," the actual conclusion (as he indicated elsewhere) was that meaning ain't in the head *if* meaning is supposed to determine reference—i.e. that what is in the head does not also determine reference (Putnam 1988, 19-26). Were this not so his argument would have been weaker, since it just would have pitted some intuitive usages of "meaning," those linking meaning to reference, against others, those linking meaning to competence. But construing "meaning" as what's in the head, in accordance with the latter intuitions, is consistent with Putnam's argument, especially given the formula that meaning plus context determines content (which determines truth-conditions). So meaning alone does not determine content: if we suppose that context includes a possible world, then we can account for "water" referring to H_2O on earth but to superficially identical XYZ on twin-earth.

7. I'm assuming an intuitive ordering among parsing stages: phonological, lexical, syntactic, then semantic. But this is only for convenience of reference. Whether the actual processing is serial or parallel is a topic in empirical psycholinguistics. Even if it is basically serial, there evidently are also feedback loops whereby for instance semantic knowledge may help determine a syntactic analysis for a not-quite well-formed string, or lexical context may restore a distorted or absent phoneme. (Fodor 1983, 74-82, argues for a constraint on such loops: within the language "module," they are not informed by higher cognition, but only "dumb" processes that enable speed. On this proposal, real-world knowledge could not inform lexical analysis within the module.)

8. Arguably Donnellan's distinction between the "attributive" and "referential" uses of definite descriptions also is captured at the level of what is said. "Smith's murderer is insane" might be construed as true if there is a unique individual who murdered Smith and he is insane (attributive reading), or

alternatively as true if some particular individual is insane, where the individual is "picked out" by "Smith's murderer" even if the description isn't accurate (referential reading): in the former case but not the latter, being the murderer of Smith enters into truth-conditions. As Recanati (1989, 300) points out, accommodating the distinction in what is said does not entail that context is irrelevant to the distinction, since what is said depends in part on context. He argues that such an accommodation is superior to a standard alternative account according to which the referential reading is contextual in the sense of Gricean implicature. I do not however propose to pursue the issue. In this book I will be avoiding the issue of "speaker's reference" entirely, aside from this note. (For extensive treatments, see Bach 1987 and Recanati 1993.)

9.   WDYM-questions may in fact be asked as a way to avoid admitting that one is ignorant of a word. "What does 'prophylactic' mean?" is more embarrassing than "What do you mean by 'prophylactic'?", which might request whether the word is being taken to necessarily entail birth control or just disease prevention, a nicety ignorance of which would not reflect on one's worldliness. Since one might get an idea of the meaning from a speaker's meaning, the tactic is useful.

10.   This is Grice's (1989, 89) distinction between "timeless meaning" and "applied timeless meaning." Though he contrasted both with "utterer's occasion meaning," I am maintaining that "applied timeless meaning" is a kind of speaker's meaning, a position based on the naturalness of such locutions as "By 'grass' I meant 'marijuana,' not 'lawn material.'" Note also my assumption here that competence is shared between speaker and hearer, which is an idealization. A WDYM-question could be used to request the meaning of a word in the speaker's idiolect, as I will discuss in chapter 4.

11.   Those indexicals whose character plausibly model what is known to competent speakers appear to be limited to the "pure" indexicals "I," "now," and "here." These are terms which never behave as variables in the usual sense, because they cannot be bound (Partee 1984, 299-301). For example, "here" has no bound-variable readings, even when it means "the place where I am." Thus in "In every city I am in, I try to interview someone who has lived here all his life," "here" cannot range over the cities which the speaker is in; rather, it must refer to some fixed particular place. Other indexicals do have bound-variable readings, e.g. "Every man wishes he were rich." It is probably not an accident that in these cases, character does not seem to model competence. To establish the contextual reference of "he," it is not sufficient to have acquired "he": as is well-known, commonsense and arbitrary knowledge about the world may be required. For instance, in "Stan beat Pete up pretty bad, but he's doing okay in the hospital now," we would presumably take "he" to refer to Pete. But concluding that the victim and not the

perpetrator of a beating would probably be the one to end up in a hospital is a matter of general reasoning and knowledge. It would seem that a unitary model of semantic competence is not to be had even within the category of indexicals. The bound-variable distinction also correlates with a difference between indexicals with regard to their role in explaining behavior. Perry (1979) proposes that indexical sentences, not the propositions they express, are what enter in explanations of behavior; but his examples are based only on the pure indexicals. These issues will be revisited in the next chapter.

12.   Given the context-dependence of a WDYM-question, the distinction might alternatively be put in terms of two kinds of pragmatic presupposition: Stalnaker's, and presupposition of a sentence in context. Hardly anyone nowadays defends a purely semantic notion (Beaver 2001, 43-52). But for me "semantic" is a more convenient term (though more often I'll refer to the presuppositions of the question). It might appear that my use of Stalnaker's notion is not in keeping with his intent, in that he proposed to replace the semantic notion whereas I'm keeping it around. But for me it will often be necessary to refer to the question presuppositions P1, P2, and P3 defined at the end of section 1, and I need an easy way to refer to them. I leave open the question of whether they should be construed as propositional attitudes. Also, whereas Stalnaker characterizes a pragmatic presupposition as something an utterer takes for granted when making an utterance (48), I've modified this in application to questions: beliefs without which the question doesn't arise, as noted. I refer to them as beliefs of the speaker; Stalnaker's conception is of beliefs shared by speaker and hearer. I don't share this conception because I want to leave it open that a hearer (giving a corrective answer) might reject a presupposition of the questioner.

13.   We'll see in section 3 that an explanation of this form can however be an answer to a WDYM-question, in cases not involving illocutionary force.

14.   I assume here that so-called "indirect force" really is indirect, i.e. that it is somehow inferred from the utterance interpreted with a different "direct" force. This is what Lycan (1984, 158) calls the "conservative approach." The challenge in maintaining this view is to explain how utterances like "You could be more quiet" are *normally* used with their indirect force, a fact which makes it plausible to suppose that "You could be more quiet" idiomatically expresses an imperative, and that this is directly grasped rather than inferred (158-186).

15.   I would suggest that the topic of the question is Al's ordering Bo to not let Al catch him scarfing the parsnip pudding, and that the relevance relation is a p-reason. I construe "By 'Don't let me catch you scarfing the parsnip pudding' Al meant 'Don't scarf the parsnip pudding'" as giving Al's purpose in ordering Bo to not let Al catch him scarfing the parsnip pudding: to order Bo to not scarf the parsnip pudding. Assuming indirect force is involved here,

this is consistent with the "conservative approach" according to which Al has in fact issued the order for Bo to not let Al catch him scarfing the pudding.

16. The book is Ronald Giere's *Explaining Science*.
17. I omit here an account of just how meaning composition given the p-set takes place; for details, see Rooth's chapters 2 and 3. Different accounts are required for different operators; Rooth is primarily concerned with "only" and "even." He does not for instance propose an account for the following example of Dretske (1972). Suppose that Clyde would get an inheritance on the condition that he is married, and chooses to marry old friend Bertha. Then "The reason Clyde *married* Bertha was to qualify for the inheritance" is true, since merely remaining friends with Bertha would not be sufficient; whereas "The reason Clyde married *Bertha* was to qualify for the inheritance" is false, since Clyde could have married anyone to qualify for the inheritance, but chose Bertha because she is unintrusive, say. A treatment of what the operator "The reason __ is to __" does with an input p-set would involve an account of epistemic justification relative to alternative states of affairs—a difficult matter.
18. The focus may also be indicated by eliding the rest of the clause, e.g. "What do you mean, 'clever'?" See section 2.5.
19. I don't mean to imply that semantic types and syntactic categories mirror each other in Montague's system. For instance, adjectives, verb phrases, and noun phrases all map to the same type; see Dowty, Wall, and Peters (1981, chapter 4). But the point remains that the types are too coarse for the semantics of stress.
20   See Grandy (1992, 263), referring to studies by H. Gleitman. Grandy also suggests that semantic fields play a role in conversational cooperation, metaphor, and questions and answers. Concerning the latter, he notes that "Is Susan's car blue?" indicates a member of a field, and requests an answer drawn from the field, e.g. "No, it's green." This is distinct from the why-question "contrast-class" phenomenon, which does not involve a set of acceptable answers but rather a question component which an acceptable answer must address: for example, "Why is Susan's car blue (as opposed to green, red, etc.)?" does not request a member of the semantic field but an explanation of the car's particular color as opposed to other colors in the field. (In my exposition I am glossing over the distinction between semantic fields and what Grandy calls "contrast sets"; by way of excuse, see Grandy 1992, 109-110.)
21. Another psychological aspect of semantic fields is their relevance to practical negation. As Miller and Johnson-Laird (1976, 262) remark: "People frequently use negation in common speech to indicate that some customary or expected state of affairs is not the case...That is to say, people do not ordinarily go about uttering such denials as 'George Washington is not a

table' or 'Sealing wax is not a dog,' even though they are perfectly true...These denials seldom occur because their corresponding affirmations seldom occur. In short, the way negation is conventionally used in ordinary discourse [e.g. 'That's not a table, it's a chair'] limits attention to contrastive sets of terms..." This suggests that adverting to semantic fields for the determination of contrasts as in example 7 (anticipating the proposal below) is not such a departure from simply adverting to the negation of the topic. Specifically, in cases where the (internal) negation of the topic is a reasonable candidate for the contrast, another reasonable candidate is the semantic field "presupposed" by the negation (or, a hypothetical negator) in the way that Miller and Johnson-Laird suggest.

22. Grandy calls a semantic field not composed of monolexemes a "derived" set, and a field whose members contrast only relative to a context a "contextual" set (1987, 275), but doesn't discuss these much. Grandy raises and then puts aside the question of whether there is a "deep philosophical difference" between contextual sets and others, but there seems to be a fundamental difference which he doesn't mention: presumably knowing a "contextual" set is not a matter of linguistic competence.

23. Similar considerations apply to the semantics of stress generally. Jackendoff (1972, 243) remarks: "...the variable [for the focus contrasts] must be chosen in such a way that it defines a coherent class of possible contrasts with the focus, pieces of semantic information that could equally well have taken the place of the focus in the sentence, within bounds established by the language, the discourse, and the external situation." That is, the quantification over the variable must be restricted to enforce "coherence," in a way which depends on context. Jackendoff understates the possible effect of context, though. Noting that "Did the cop *arrest* Bill?—No, he only *leered* at him" seems a natural pair, he suggests that the variable should range over two-place predicates—in general, over items of common "functional semantic form"—and (in effect) that the predicates express "doing something nasty." But "Did the cop *arrest* Bill?—No, he only told him about the policeman's ball" is also natural, and "tell" is a 3-place predicate which is semantically unrelated to "arrest." Context may be such that no syntactic or semantic relation holds among the contrasts.

24. It sometimes happens that a contrast is an *answer* to a WDYM-question. To someone who said that Apple makes the best electronic computer, it would be natural to respond "What do you mean, 'electronic' computer?" if one thought that all computers are electronic. The speaker might happily use an abacus and consider it a computer, and so would answer: electronic as opposed to mechanical. This should be distinguished from the question's contrast: presumably, that so-and-so says that Apple makes the best computer.

25. This is the sister of the phenomenon illustrated by Quine's "Giorgionne was so-called because of his size," in which an unquoted expression is partly mentioned and partly used.

26. Note that my earlier discussion of focusing quotes and contrasts relates to hybrid quotes, not mention-quotes. The latter mandate a class of syntactic rather than semantic alternatives.

27. It is not clear to me whether van Fraassen would characterize a rejection as a denial of presupposition P3. At one point, he suggests that rejection implies there is no answer satisfying a given relevance relation which is also "telling" (131-132). However, elsewhere he suggests that rejection can be analyzed without an account of what makes an answer "telling" (146). There is a substantive difficulty here, not just a question of interpretation. For instance, van Fraassen remarks (citing Kuhn) that in the nineteenth century it was not required of chemical theories that they explain the surface qualities of compounds. So during that time the question of why such-and-such material is acidic, whose relevance relation pertains to the material's molecular structure, was rejected by the scientific community. One way to render this is as a denial that the requisite molecular structure exists, i.e. a denial of presupposition P3. But it seems also plausible to allow an admission of a molecular structure, coupled with a denial that the structure is a "telling" explanation of acidity, with "telling" analyzed independently of the relevance relation (e.g. in terms of how well "[an answer] *favors* the topic...as against the...members of the contrast-class"—146). The choice depends on how strongly one construes the relevance relation, i.e. in this case whether satisfaction of the relation entails any molecular structure, or more specifically a structure which on some evaluative measure indicates acidity. Van Fraassen does discuss this issue but without drawing a firm conclusion (144), suggesting that his construal of rejection is ambivalent.

28. There is a subtly different usage of "I meant what I said" to merely assert seriousness and sincerity—synonymously with "I meant it." "I meant what I said" in this idiomatic sense is neither direct nor corrective: to "What do you mean," one could not assert sincerity as a direct answer, since it answers how not what, or as a correction, since it does not deny any presupposition. In this respect I agree with Schiffer (1972) that "I meant it" represents a distinct sense of "meant." See also Davis (1992a, 224).

29. Irony also has to do in the first instance with how something is meant. Hence a WDYM-question cannot directly request whether irony was meant. But unlike illocutionary force, the attribution of irony permits inference of a propositional content which differs from what is said—the "opposite" of what is said, by convention. (But see Sperber and Wilson 1995, 237-243 for a dissenting view.) So a WDYM-question may indirectly serve to request ironical intent, via a request of content. A rejection may then indicate non-

irony. For example, to "What do you mean, 'That's great'?", the reply might be "I mean, 'That's great'," reiterating a belief and thus ruling out irony. A direct answer of "I meant that that's awful," on the other hand, would allow the inference of irony. I say irony has to do "in the first instance" with how rather than what because one can infer the content of the speaker's meaning from knowing that it is meant ironically. In contrast, metaphor also has to do with how something is meant but not in the first instance; notoriously, one cannot infer what is meant just from knowing that something is meant metaphorically.

30. Davis calls this "cogitative speaker's meaning," arguing that the notion is neglected but important—even proposing it as a substitute for Gricean speaker's meaning in the Gricean reductionist program.

31. It has been argued that van Fraassen's view of explanation is not a rival to traditional views; see Kitcher and Salmon (1987). But the argument has no bearing here, since they don't deny that explanations may be viewed as answers to why-questions, only that traditional problems in the study of explanation are solved on such a view. I have no commitment to the latter.

32. As Schiffer (1987, 242) puts it, Griceans seek to "define all public-language semantic notions in terms of propositional attitude concepts that themselves presuppose nothing about meaning in a public language." Vicious circularity should be distinguished from the "closed curve in space" that Schiffer earlier argued would not doom the Gricean program (1972, 14-15). He was referring to the possibility that propositional attitudes might turn out to be relations to sentences of a mental language, obviously not at issue here. It should also be distinguished from any circularity tolerable under Avramides' (1989) "reciprocal" construal of Gricean analysis, under which no primacy is claimed of psychological concepts over semantic. As she remarks, "even reciprocal analyses should beware of travelling in circles that are *too* small" (173).

33. Actually, there was no mismatch in the speaker's meaning locutions which Grice proposed to analyze in his original paper; they were in the same family as my type (1) WDYM-answer form. But Grice was taken to task for this, for example by Paul Ziff who noted that "Grice seems to have conflated and confused 'A meant something by uttering x'...with the quite different 'A meant something by x'..." (1967, 6). Later Grice explicitly recognized the distinction, and identified the "by uttering x" locution as his main topic of concern (1989, 91). But neither Ziff nor the later Grice note that "A meant something by uttering x," and "A meant that p by uttering x" represent metalinguistic notions and not everyday notions, which I suspect explains why these locutions didn't immediately occur to Grice in the first place. (Not all Griceans have followed the later Grice. For e.g. Davis 1992a, "by uttering x" and "by x" are equally apt for the Gricean notion, what he calls "cognitive speaker's meaning"; I don't agree.)

34. See for example Bach and Harnish (1979, 150), who distinguish between, among other things, speaker's meaning in the sense of a speaker using an expression in a certain way and speaker's meaning "proper," i.e. Gricean speaker's meaning. In one sense of "using an expression," the former is illustrated by my example 7. Schiffer has explicitly acknowledged the distinction, in personal correspondence.

35. Yu (1979, 281) makes the same point. Note that on the stipulative construal, the Gricean definition of speaker's meaning is not subject to any of the counterexamples that abound in the literature. Yu concludes that vacillation on the proper construal has had "momentous consequences" by leading critics to focus on the wrong facet of the Gricean program, i.e. Plank B instead of Plank A. I don't agree with this. Both planks need attention, and the counterexample-driven literature can be construed as addressing the intentions accompanying meaningful communication if not a conceptual analysis of speaker's meaning. But I agree that the vacillation has caused confusion, and would add that it was enabled by the absence of any systematic analysis of everyday speaker's meaning.

36. Chomsky (1975a, 67-69) is another who does not accept Plank A, arguing that the analysis of speaker's meaning inevitably must appeal to sentence meaning and hence is circular. Note that this entails that the theory, construed as Planks A and B, is defective—not that it is intralinguistic. That is, if Grice's notion of speaker's meaning really did presuppose meaning, then given his commitment to an account of meaning he would not then have a notion of everyday speaker's meaning, but just an incorrect theory. A modified theory rid of Plank A would not necessarily be incorrect since there would be no circularity (as Chomsky allows), but it would still not be intralinguistic.

37. A sample: Fodor (1977, 22-23), Putnam (1990, 298), Levinson (1983, 17; 2000, 381).

38. Wilson and Sperber (1986, 48) reach the contrary conclusion on the basis of this paper, i.e. that Grice took his technical notion of speaker's meaning to apply to implicature. I cannot see any justification for this conclusion.

39. The question arises why Grice refers here to "'even' what he meant." For what it's worth, my feeling is that despite his own indications of a distinction between his technical notion and the notion required for ordinary discourse (n. 33), Grice was not entirely comfortable with it. I suspect this was because of his not being entirely clear on its basis, namely the distinction between intralinguistic and metalinguistic; to my knowledge, he never pointed it out.

40. For discussion and further examples see Levinson (1983, 127-132), and Lycan (1984, 109-129), from whom I am taking the term "lexical presumption."

41. Analogous WDYM-questions can arise for those presumption-bearing items which are syntactically optional modifiers (e.g. "only"): in particular, the contrasts differ from the topic solely with respect to the absence of the word in question. But for other words there is another possibility, namely a perhaps restricted semantic field. For instance, in "Sal is a policeman, but he's honest" the presumption is that policemen are not usually honest. A policeman might respond "What do you mean, 'but'?", expressing a question whose contrasts evidently would correspond to those connectives which do not carry the same presumption as "but"—e.g. "and" and "also," but not "yet" and "nevertheless." Note it is not required that the presumption be disputed for such questions to be motivated; one might just be curious as to the justification.

42. Another example is the implicature that the speaker has good reason for believing that *p*, generated from an assertion that *p* and Grice's "maxim of quality." This is identical to a felicity condition for assertions; for a defense of the view that illocutionary preconditions are subsumable by quality implicatures see Levinson (1983, 105, 241). For the reverse subsumption, see Gazdar (1979, 45-48). On Gazdar's analysis, the non-applicability of speaker's meaning falls out of our earlier observation that WDYM-questions do not request illocutionary force, taken as including preconditions.

43. For an early attempt to further analyze this intention, see Walker (1975, 154-163), who modifies the analysis of metalinguistic speaker's meaning by among other things adding an intention that the implicature be calculated partly on the basis of the uttered sentence's meaning. Note that while this would make Grice's analysis of speaker's meaning partly relevant to ordinary discourse, it wouldn't blur the distinction between the Gricean concept and the intralinguistic. The assumption of meaning renders an adapted concept such as Walker's unsuitable for the reductionist program. Note moreover that the application of even an adapted Gricean analysis of communicative intentions to ordinary speaker's meaning is circumscribed: at issue is only speaker's meaning involved in implicature. Once again, I cannot see that any of this matters to the Gricean program.

44. Introduction rules sometimes appear to be needed in order to derive non-trivial implications, as in: $(P \vee Q) \rightarrow R$; P; $P \vee Q$ (by $\vee$-introduction); therefore R (by *modus ponens*). Sperber and Wilson point out however that in such cases substitution of a logically equivalent premise dispenses with the need for the introduction rule: $(P \rightarrow R)\&(Q \rightarrow R)$; $P \rightarrow R$ (by &-detachment); P; therefore R. They also argue that the resulting derivations are more psychologically realistic. For discussion see Gazdar and Good (1982, 89-90), Sperber and Wilson (1982, 101-102), and Sperber and Wilson (1987b, 740-742) and backward references therein.

45. The foregoing exposition has been drawn from Wilson and Sperber (1986) and Sperber and Wilson (1987a) in addition to Sperber and Wilson (1995). The latter is the second edition of their 1986 book, to which all the criticism referenced in this section is addressed. But the text is nearly identical. Substantive revision in the second edition is confined to a Postface, which as far as I can tell doesn't affect any of my conclusions; but see note 50.

46. See also Wilson (1994). For critical discussion see Cutler (1987), Pettit (1987), and Sperber and Wilson (1987b, 737, 747-748).

47. See Wilson and Sperber (1981); for criticism, see Davis (1998, 100-102).

48. See van Fraassen (1980, 146-151) for metrics in which an answer likewise figures. Sperber and Wilson similarly comment "Given an assumption about [what the communicator intended to communicate], it may be manifest that the communicator could have used a more relevant stimulus..." (164). It might be thought that my rendering of the counterfactual is too tidy. In the same passage Sperber and Wilson note that the hearer may not be able to identify the counterfactuals (164). But this is not a reason for modifying the metric as I've described it; it's just that the hearer can't apply the metric in this case. (How serious a difficulty this is for Sperber and Wilson's theory is another matter; see Walker 1989, 153-154.)

49. See 1987b, 742, and references therein. As Bach and Harnish (1987) put the criticism, "there is no requirement on the relevance of *what* is communicated" (711)—i.e. no criterion of relevance applied to the set *I* itself. For earlier discussion, see Gazdar and Good (1981, 97-98), and Sperber and Wilson's response (1982, 108-109).

50. Sperber and Wilson say that while capturing intuitive judgments of relevance may be "a starting point," "the value of our theoretical notion of relevance will ultimately depend upon the value of the psychological models which make use of it, and, in particular, on the value of the theory of verbal comprehension that it allows us to formulate. Intuitions of relevance are not the only kinds of intuition involved in comprehension" (119-120). But it won't do to try to capture an intuitive judgment and then upon failure say that it wasn't really important to capture. What's needed is some principled means of saying in advance which ones the theory is concerned with and which ones not, notwithstanding that capturing the former provides only limited support for the theory. I hope to have now provided such a means.

  In the Postface, Sperber and Wilson reformulate the PR (recast as the "second" principle of relevance), revising the first part of the "presumption of optimal relevance" as "The ostensive stimulus is relevant enough for it to be worth the addressee's effort to process it" (270). On the face of it, this affects my conclusions because there is no longer any mention of the assumptions *I* that the speaker intended to communicate. But as long as the "ostensive stimulus" in the case of verbal communication involves content that the speaker intended to communicate, my conclusions still apply. And I don't see why it wouldn't, because the rationale for their revision is based only on considerations of the hearer's effort; they do not explain why they drop out *I*. But I can't be sure about this, so I restrict attention to the PR as formulated in the main text.

51. See e.g. Sperber and Wilson (1987a, 706). Davis (1998, 62-113) argues that most implicatures fail Grice's calculability requirement, and offers this as one reason to give up on Grice's framework altogether as an explanation of implicature recovery; relevance theory, he argues, fares no better (98-106). His overall case is persuasive because, as he points out, it largely rests on an assembly of widely-accepted conclusions. From my perspective, the import of his case lies in the added support it gives to analyzing speaker's meaning as it pertains to metaphor and other conceptual indeterminacy in terms of a conceptual e-reason rather than a communicative p-reason. As I argue: the lower the calculability of some content, the greater the irrationality of an intention to communicate it by the utterance, and the less likely that a communicative p-reason is present.

52. A fallback position is that even if an implicature framework cannot explain the interpretation of metaphor, it may at least explain its recognition (see e.g. Levinson 1983, 156-161). This will be discussed in Chapter 5. Wilson and Sperber concluded in an earlier paper (1981, 159-164) that metaphors are not explicable as implicatures in Grice's framework; I'm suggesting that they are not explicable as implicatures in any framework.

53 For a sample of opposing views, see Suppes (1985), and Chomsky (1975a), chapter 2.

Notes to Chapter 3

1. Much of the research is within relevance theory; see Sperber and Wilson (1995, 176-193) and Carston (1988) for some of the basic thinking.

2. For discussion of "and," see Carston (1988, 1993), and Wilson and Sperber (1993). The Scope Principle originated with Cohen (1971), and has since been used by many others. It is not without difficulties, though. One must be sure that the logical operator is not operating "metalinguistically," as in an example of L. Horn: "Their victory was not an historic event; it was a historic event." Here it is not truth-conditions which are negated, but something about the way they are expressed. The Scope Principle assumes operation on truth-conditions (Recanati 1993, 269-274).

3. See Carston (1998) for a survey article. See Levinson (2000) for a detailed defense of the generalized conversational implicature approach, references, and a critical overview (194-198).

4.   In this vein see Wilson (1994, 38-39). It might be thought that my argument
      can be turned around: since the speaker *might* intend to communicate the
      enriched content, the relevance relation does not necessarily have to do with
      what the speaker wanted to say. The point, however, is that if the content is
      of an implicature, there would be no accounting for the WDYM-question's
      relevance relation in cases where neither speaker nor hearer expect the
      content to have been communicated. Whereas if the content is of what is said,
      one could account not only for such cases but also for the communicative
      case; after all, one might intend to communicate what one has said. (In the
      previous chapter, I made a similar argument for communicative intentions vis-
      à-vis conceptual reasons.) My intuition is that in the latter case, the relevance
      relation remains a p-reason in terms of what the speaker wanted to say. But
      in any case the current argument tells against an implicature analysis of
      enriched content. It also applies to Bach's "impliciture" analysis, which is
      also a matter of communicative intention (1994, 126).
5   It seems to me that in these cases the contrast is the trivial one, the negation
      of the topic.
6.   The distinction is not always clear, because it can depend upon semantic
      analysis. For example, Recanati (1989, 304-306) argues that "The park is
      some distance from the house" actually does not express a proposition, i.e.
      that there is some distance or other relating the park and the house—contrary
      to our earlier supposition (following Carston 1988, 164). Rather, there is a
      domain of quantification left unspecified, which a suitable enrichment must
      supply to enable a proposition. Further examples abound. Consider Kratzer's
      (1977) analysis of such sentences as:
           All Maori children must learn the names of their ancestors.
           The ancestors of the Maoris must have arrived from Tahiti.
           If you must sneeze, at least use your handkerchief.
           When Kahukura-nui died, the people of Kahungunu said: Rakaipaka
           must be our chief.
      There are different readings of "must" here: deontic (referring to a duty),
      epistemic, dispositional, and preferential, respectively. There are multiple
      possibilities under each category (e.g. many different kinds of duties) and
      additional possible categories, to the extent that it is implausible to posit
      ambiguity. Kratzer proposes instead that the possibilities are accounted for by
      a relativizing phrase, as in:
           In view of what their tribal duties are, the Maori children must learn the
           names of their ancestors.
           In view of what is known, the ancestors of the Maoris must have arrived
           from Tahiti.
           If in view of what your dispositions are you must sneeze, at least use
           your handkerchief.

> When Kahukura-nui died, the people of Kahungunu said: In view of
> what is good for us, Rakaipaka must be our chief.

On this proposal, instead of an absolute "must" we have "must in view of," the meaning of which is unitary but requires a contextually-supplied argument. So when "must" is unaccompanied by a relativizing phrase, there is not yet a proposition because this argument is missing. Alternatively, one could maintain that syntax is unaffected, and that the meaning of "must" can be accounted for by a level of semantic representation which is non-isomorphic to syntactic representation. The point here is the non-obviousness of either conclusion, owing to the dependence on semantic analysis. (For an overview and alternative approach to modals, see Papafragou 1998. For discussion of methodological issues, see e.g. Partee 1984 and Heim and Kratzer 1998, 45-49.)

7. For a precise formulation of the attributive approach, see Kamp (1975) (who argues against it on the grounds that it can't account for the semantics of comparative constructions); see also section 5. Attributive adjectives should be distinguished from "measure" adjectives, which depend for their denotation on a "comparison class." For instance, what counts as "tall" depends whether we are talking about men, women, or basketball players. As Siegel (1979) argues, this does not imply that "tall" requires a common noun phrase to denote, only that the denotation is sensitive to a contextually-determined class. She points out a heuristic for the distinction: whereas for measure adjectives, a "for a" paraphrase is appropriate—as in "She is tall for a woman—for attributive adjectives, an "as a" paraphrase is appropriate—as in "She is clever as a clown." The distinction isn't always clear. I've suggested "big" as an attributive adjective, but it may be a measure adjective for which the relevant measurement is unspecified.

8. I do not mean to imply that this constitutes a legitimate criticism of Ryle. For a discussion see Dennett (1978, 95).

9. This assessment will be revised in the next chapter.

10. Strictly speaking, homophonic disquotation requires not just that the speaker's language is English, but that his idiolect is the same as ours (the utilizers of the principle). This condition is not important for current purposes, but will be important later (Ch. 4, sec. 3).

11. Actually, not quite; for instance, two sentences of different languages might have the same character. But the alternative formulation is in the same spirit; see Chien (1985, 279-280).

12. See Block (1986, 621-622), for a statement of the dual content view as motivated by indexicals and natural kinds. For an example of the debate, see the exchange between Block and Fodor in Loewer and Rey (1991). Stalnaker (1999, 201) argues that character should not be assimilated to "narrow content" (relevant to explaining behavior), as Block and others do; if he is

right, my criticism to follow doesn't rule out a proper, character-less account of narrow content. But it is not clear to me that "accepted" sentences explain behavior on such an account.

13. And that the pure indexicals are also distinguished by their lack of bound-variable readings (Ch. 2, n. 11).

14. As earlier reviewed, there is another reading of "I meant what I said" on which it rejects a WDYM-question (Ch. 2, sec. 3, and n. 28). This can happen not only when the speaker's meaning has to do with a conceptual reason but also when it has to do with what is said. Take ellipsis resolution. I've argued that "By 'Tonight' Dad meant that he would take everyone for ice cream tonight" is explanatory in virtue of giving Dad's reason for saying "Tonight": to say that he would take everyone for ice cream tonight. The explanation is not alternatively given, even as an abbreviation, by "Dad meant what he said." Rather this rejects the request for explanation.

15. I'm reminded of an episode of an old television show:
    Chief: You're a disgrace. You're an incompetent, bumbling fool.
    Secret Agent (eyes narrowing): What are you getting at?

16. It might seem that there is some similarity to cases discussed by Stalnaker and others, where a proposition apparently could be "accepted" because it is "close" to true, but not believed. For example, an economist might for purposes of theory construction accept an idealized description of trade involving perfectly rational agents, without believing the description to be true. Likewise one might for practical purposes accept that a table is 6 feet long, while believing that it's 5.85 feet long. The interpretation of such cases bears upon a contested issue, whether or not acceptance entails belief. (See Stalnaker 1984, 93; Clarke 2000, 38-40; Engel 2000.) The current sort of example is actually more dissimilar than similar to these cases. For one thing, the "precise" belief can be subconscious, as just noted; one can express oneself with the "approximation" while not being aware that one believes something more precise. For another, one can believe both the "approximate" thing, that John is clever, and the "precise" thing, that John is clever in the sense of quick-witted (both that John is clever "overall" and in this particular sense). It does seem possible, though, to believe that John is clever in the sense that he is quick-witted while not believing but accepting that John is clever, on the basis of the belief in his quick-wittedness (where "accept" here should not be confused with Perry's sense of "accept"). This suggests that acceptance does not entail belief, but as this is a peripheral issue for me I will not explore it further.

17. This assumes that the reduced conjunction test is valid, a matter on which not everyone agrees. For criticism, see Zwicky and Sadock (1975); for defense, see Atlas (1989, 73-77).
    Parenthetically, nothing for me depends on Atlas' view that different

scope configurations do not determine different meanings. Atlas argues that "The king of France is not bald" is not ambiguous between predicate negation and sentence negation, i.e. between "There is a king of France, and he is not bald" (which is false if there is no king of France), and "It's not the case that the king of France is bald" (which is true if there is no king of France). Rather, the sentence has a univocal meaning which is not specified for scope. However this may be, the issue here is not ambiguity versus conceptual indeterminacy in my sense. While a speaker's meaning report may specify scope relations, as in "By 'Someone loves everyone' I meant a particular person, the Pope, loves everyone," what is addressed in such a case isn't conceptual indeterminacy, which cannot arise unless something has been said. I presume that what is said determines truth-conditions, which require that scope relations be specified. Whatever the phenomenon claimed by Atlas, it is thus resolved at this level. I'm not presently concerned with the issue of whether what is resolved is ambiguity or an unscoped content. (More generally, I have not been concerned with what Bach 1994 calls "structural underdetermination"; see 127-130.)

Atlas would not himself endorse this way of putting things. He concludes from scope-neutrality ("sense-generality") that truth-conditional semantics is misguided, since no logical form or truth-conditions can be assigned to a scope-neutral sentence. But he does not address the possibility of a level of "unscoped" logical form. While such forms do not support truth-conditions, they are precursors to forms that do, and fit within a general truth-conditional paradigm (e.g. Moran 1988). Similarly, Kaplan's notion of a "character" was proposed to accommodate sentences which can't be assigned truth-conditions without information from context. Atlas is aware of this, but argues that character won't help because "in *any* context a sense-general sentence can express any of its propositions...In any context, 'the F is not G' can express either negative proposition..." (133). But this surprising claim requires argument, and Atlas gives none. (The claim is perhaps convenient for him though: Burton-Roberts 1991 points out that if Atlas had to explain contextual inferability of a sense from a sense-general sentence, he could not appeal to the standard device, i.e. implicature, because it relies on "what is said" in a truth-conditional sense, the existence of which Atlas wishes to deny.) So it would seem that his alternative account of the readings of a sense-general sentence as "verifications" or "justification conditions" (63, 128, 134) needs more motivation. I would suggest that the data on "The F is not G," whatever they might be, are too narrow a consideration to decide the choice of an entire paradigm for semantic theory. I also think Atlas fails to appreciate the close connection between verification and the concept of truth (the dictionary meaning of "verify" being "establish the truth of"). If Atlas denies that "The F is not G" has truth-conditions, then he needs to explain the sense in which we can nonetheless "verify" it; but he does not.

18. See Kamp (1975, 123-127) and Partee (1995, 323-330). The treatment can also explain other examples of Cohen's such as "stone lion," wherein "lion" apparently refers not to lions but to a representation of a lion. Presumably any noun denoting a species of plant, animal, or artifact is capable of similar usage. But surely the usage does not have to be learned separately for each noun, as it would if the representational meaning were in each case listed in the lexicon. Rather, it can be grasped "on the fly," as the representational meaning is generated by the noun together with an appropriate modifier. So Cohen argues. But an "insulationist" semantics can equally account for the facts by rendering "stone" as a kind of "privative" attributive adjective like "former" or "fake." Just as a former senator is not a senator and a fake gun is not a gun, a stone lion is not a lion. The "representational" meaning is generated by the function for "stone" given the meaning of "lion." No extra listing in the lexicon is required; the meaning is instead generated by "interaction," just as Cohen would have it, but the underlying semantic theory is not "interactionist" (Partee, 340). I am not so concerned with this example, however, because even if Cohen were right it would be with respect to not a robust ambiguity but a limited one, which hence would not be a potential alternative explanation for conceptual indeterminacy. (Cohen gives other examples in this vein, such as the dispositional/occurrent ambiguity for "driver," "leader," etc., and the act/object ambiguity for "perception," "digging," etc.; see 227.)

19. I say this while recognizing Ross's (1981) work, which analyzes a broad range of purported word meanings related by analogy, in line with Cohen's notion of creative ambiguity. I don't mean to imply that this work is not of value (though for what it is worth I find that much of Ross's book could be more perspicuous), only that we can't expect too much progress in any theory without cooperative assault on problems by a community of researchers, as has been the case for the Tarski-based paradigms.

20. I think the same arguments weigh against taking "good" as an attributive adjective, as many do. A sense of "good" depends on elements other than the modified noun phrase. Thus the signification of "good" in "Mother Theresa is a good person" and "Ralph Nader is a good person" presumably differ, even though the same noun is modified in both; and different people might mean by "Mother Theresa is a good person," with some impressed by her charity, others by her stoicism. But "good" is not a source of conceptual indeterminacy in my sense. Certainly, there are any number of things that a speaker might mean by "That was a good thing Mike did": Mike did something that will be healthy for him, Mike did the morally right thing, etc. Further, a speaker's meaning would seem to involve content fixing in the sense that we have considered. Thus the speaker might believe that Mike did

a good thing just in the sense that he did something that will be healthy for him. We wouldn't expect her in that case to infer that Mike is a philanthropist, or to ask Mike if he will contribute to the homeless shelter. However, the constraints on speaker's meanings are not a matter of competence. If a speaker were to mean by "That was a good thing Mike did" that Mike did something that will be *un*healthy for him, it need not be because he had not acquired the word "good"; he may just be a malicious person. If there are constraints here, they are not of a linguistic nature. (I will not further consider purely normative terms in this book.)

21. This argument has been modified from section 3 in that I am now appealing to reasons for believing-true rather than reasons for belief. I take the argument to be no less sound. A speaker's reasons for believing-true a sentence largely correspond to his reasons for the corresponding belief (as the discussion of "counterfactual inductive strength" and "favoring" in the next two chapters will make clear).

22. Of course semantic theory would still require complex contextual mechanisms for anaphora resolution and other phenomena. A more thoroughgoing simplicity may be possible by regarding not just conceptual indeterminacy but also some aspects of what is said as a matter of the speaker's meaning. That is, suppose we take this aspect of context as one of the features relative to which the truth of a sentence is determined (Lewis 1972, 175-176). We posit the speaker's meaning as the sole determining factor for disambiguation, for instance, rather than worrying about the various contextual influences on disambiguation. Following the argument of section 2, this would properly distinguish the speaker's meaning from clues about the speaker's meaning, and take the former as what determines the proposition expressed. For example, in the case of "wheels" the correct reading would be determined by what the speaker means, at the leaf node (just as the reference of "I" would be resolved prior to composition, relative to the identity of the speaker construed as an element of the context). Then there is no problem for compositionality: a single meaning would get passed up the tree in standard fashion. On this approach the sentence subject does not determine the disambiguation: rather, it is a good but fallible indicator of what the speaker means. In "Unicycles have wheels" he might have the non-dependent reading in mind, in which case the sentence is simply false. Presumably he would be confused or dishonest, but the theory should not assume the responsibility of correcting him. In general, semantic theory should not be concerned with the problem of how hearers disambiguate; see Lycan (1984, 201-203), for one account of how great a weight this is.

23. Although the grammar would have to include some level of semantic representation which does not mirror the syntactic structure (n. 6).

24.   Recanati (1989) recognizes the constraint by calling this type of enrichment "strengthening." Carston (1998) speculates that the asymmetry between strengthening and "loosening" (as in "fake gun" or "stone lion"), whereby one but not the other may enter into what is said, may not be principled and needs to be rethought.

25.   The constraint is rendered as a constraint on answers in an obvious way: we require that the content of the propositional attitude specified in the answer logically imply the corresponding content of the topic. An answer indicating that the speaker said that Sheila looked at the bill "and" fainted in order to say that Sheila looked at the bill and as a result fainted meets the constraint since

   Sheila looked at the bill and as a result fainted

entails

   Sheila looked at the bill and fainted.

Note that we could not very well require an entailment between the speaker's saying these things. Alternatively, we could build the constraint into the relevance relation itself.

   Note that there must be at least one other constraint, preventing arbitrary strengthening. Carston (1988, 169-170) suggests the principle of relevance for this purpose.

Notes to Chapter 4

1.   Cavell (1964, 108), objecting to Mates' (1964) claim that "what an individual means by a word depends at least in part upon what he wants to mean by that word," remarks that "an individual's intentions or wishes can no more produce the general meaning for a word than they can produce horses for beggars, or home runs from pop flies, or successful poems out of unsuccessful poems." But this is not inconsistent with Mates' claim construed as applying to intralinguistic speaker's meaning, which does not supplant the "general meaning."

2.   With speaker's meaning as with language generally (not to mention music and art), constraints are the flip side of creativity; see Chomsky (1968, 100-114). But Chomsky objects to the notion of constraints known to all competent speakers; for him there is no "public language" in this sense. I will touch on this in section 4.

3.   Burge's view on the role of examples in concepts is part of his "anti-individualism," according to which the content of one's thought is determined by not just psychology but various social and environmental factors (see Burge 1979, 1982, 1986). Thus Burge (1979) concludes that a layman who thinks that arthritis can occur in his thigh is still thinking about arthritis, the same thing that a medical expert thinks about. But I will not be concerned with these issues, and need not be because Burge's anti-individualism does

not follow just from his view on the role of examples in concepts. To anticipate the exposition of Burge (1989) below, it would be possible to claim that even if a layman shares a concept with the expert despite having a different understanding of it, nonetheless the contents of their respective thoughts differ because the understanding rather than the concept itself determines this content. This would be consistent with the position I will be developing. So I can be neutral with regard to Burge's anti-individualism, and needn't defend it from objections (e.g. Bilgrami 1992, 22-56 and Marconi 1997, 115-121).

4.   It could be that the speaker knew about skilift chairs but had not accounted for them. In this case the stock does not actually grow, but the explication must still be adjusted. Burge comments: "my ability to come up with better explications by considering examples with which I am already familiar indicates that I have more to go on than my initial explications suggest. Perhaps I have 'tacitly cognized' more than what I give as my reflective explication, before I arrive consciously at a better explication" (183). But this does not mean that the explication adds nothing over and above what is known tacitly. The conscious dialectic between explication and examples may serve the purpose of putting together previously separate items of knowledge. It may be for instance that the speaker did not initially believe that there were legless chairs, even though he had the requisite experience of skilift chairs; the revised explication may be what triggers the appropriate revision of belief. Burge offers this as one reason why the notion that "our tacit conceptual explications exhaust our concepts" (183) is false. While not disagreeing, I think that the term "tacit conceptual explication" is unfortunate: as I understand it, this refers to the improved explication before the speaker articulates it. But Burge himself elsewhere characterizes an explication as not tacit but conscious. And his own point here is that the improved explication of "chair" need *not* be tacit all along, only the materials on which it builds.

5.   Experts may be required even if the essential nature is "accessible" in the sense of observable without special training. According to Wilson (1992, 56), "a species is a population whose members are able to interbreed freely under natural conditions." Despite exceptions and other difficulties (see Dupre 1981, 85-87), biologists accept surprising consequences of this notion of species. For example, there are perceptibly identical species of the giant silkworm moth which are distinguished by the hours of the day at which the female issues mating calls. The males respond only to the females of their species (Wilson, 57-58). The need for experts here is not so much a matter of being able to observe the ability to interbreed as it is to recognize its fruitfulness for scientific taxonomy.

6.   Burge does not emphasize this, but makes some relevant remarks in passing. He mentions "perceptual capacities that are modular and preconceptual" and enter into explications (183). Perhaps he would include projection tendencies here, though he does not elaborate. I will discuss below a later reference to "kind-forming abilities."

7.   Note that Burge's account is not of how concepts are acquired. No one would deny that examples play a role in learning. According to Locke, "there is nothing more evident" than that children first associate words with "ideas" which represent particular individuals in the immediate environment. As their experience grows, they encounter other things which in certain respects resemble these individuals. In then forming a "complex idea" they "make nothing new, but only leave out...that which is peculiar to each, and retain only what is common to them all" (Nidditch 1975, 411). Like Locke, Burge takes perceptually-based concepts to depend upon example referents, but his concern is with the *ongoing* role of examples: not in the developmental stages of concepts but in their "steady states." (As a separate issue, Burge is sympathetic to critiques of the Lockean view which point out the radical underdetermination of concepts by encountered examples; see 179. On this basis Fodor and Chomsky have argued that we are born with our concepts, such that experience with examples helps us not to learn them, but to label them with words. For discussion see Fodor 1975, 79-97, Putnam 1988, 4-18, and Chomsky 1992a.)

8.   For an attack on the traditional view from a different angle, see Fodor, Garrett, Walker and Parkes (1980). Notice properties of a shared nature may still be necessary and sufficient for term application. For instance, perhaps H_2O is necessary and sufficient for the application of "water." The point is that there are no necessary and sufficient conditions that need be apprehended by competent users. They needn't even be apprehended by experts. "Water" for instance had been in use before its chemical structure was understood, i.e. used in the same sense as today (Putnam 1975, 224).

9.   It is not generally true even for natural kind terms that reference is determined by a "real," scientifically discoverable nature. Dupre (1981) points out that the paradigm natural kind terms, those for biological kinds, often refer to no scientific taxon at all. For example, "lily" in ordinary usage refers to some of the flora biologists recognize as belonging to the lily family, but not to others such as onions and garlics. Many other kind terms do refer to a taxon, but at a level higher than the species; for instance, "beech" refers to a genera and "duck" to a family. Since it is only at the level of species that it is even tempting to posit a real kind, again the natural kind term does not "latch onto" a real kind even if we assume that there are such kinds.

10. See Burge (1986). He asks us to imagine someone who knows the linguistic practices with regard to the word "sofa," but thinks that they are mistaken. He has a sophisticated theory of how sofas are religious artifacts, and how this has escaped the attention of language users. Nonetheless his concept of sofas might be the same as ours; his concept is not determined by his odd theory, but the wider linguistic practice. The point of interest here is that the speaker is competent, notwithstanding his theory. So if Burge is right competence requires only knowledge *of* the stereotype, not necessarily belief that the ascriptions implied by the stereotypes (in this case, that a sofa is a kind of furniture made for sitting) are true. This subtlety will not however bear on anything that follows.

11. Burge (181) calls this the "translational meaning," which he explicitly contrasts with the conceptual explication—or strictly, with the "explicational meaning" (termed the "lexical" meaning in 1993, 316), which is "the semantical analog of the conceptual explication."

12. Constraints on projection should not be identified with "projectibility" in Goodman's (1965) sense. Goodman was concerned with confirmation. In his sense, projectibility of a predicate entails the confirmability of its generalized attribution given its attribution in instances. My concern is with the projection of perceived essential properties from instances, given that a certain term applies to them. In my sense projectibility need not involve an inference to unencountered instances; it has to do not with confirmational features but compatibility with the "meaning" of the term. Thus no one who had acquired the term "chair" would project chair-if-examined-jello-otherwise from examples, which is not projectible in Goodman's sense, but then neither would one project objecthood, which is (or rather, "object" is projectible in his sense).

13. See Quine (1969, 118) for an argument that kinds may be treated as sets. The assumption is only for simplicity; it's not that I care to deny with Quine that kinds are intensional.

14. And not just them, or just philosophers. Much psychological research (beginning with Eleanor Rosch's) suggests that for many concepts speakers have uniform judgments of the "typicality" of concept instances, such as that dogs are highly typical animals, spiders less typical, and bacteria least. Futhermore these judgments correlate with a range of other phenomena. For example, the greater the typicality of an instance, the sooner it tends to be recognized in childhood development, and the easier it is to categorize. Broadly speaking this research tends to suggest a special role for "prototypical" examples in understanding and reference. Care must be taken, though, since there is no widely agreed-upon theory to interpret the experimental results. It's commonly thought for instance that typicality judgments have been shown to determine the conditions for category

membership: the more typical, the greater the degree of membership. But as Kobes (1986, 365-380) among others argues, this is not so clear. It may on the contrary be that typicality can be judged only once membership in the category is already established. The interpretive models which are consistent with Putnam and Burge's perspective are those on which typicality judgments serve not to determine the reference of a concept, but rather to provide heuristics for identification. Consistently with this there may be distinct factors fixing reference and semantic relations between concepts. For further discussion, see Smith and Medin (1999) and Rey (1999).

15. To be sure, there is evidence which, as one prominent geneticist puts it, "shows quite convincingly that some traits of personality—aggressiveness, introversion, and so on—have a genetic component" (Jones 1993, 190). But note the "some." Note also that it is very probably not instances of any mentalistic term that have genetic explanation, but instances of some particular sense of a term. For example, one study suggests that a certain proneness to violence is linked to a gene relating to transmission of nerve impulses: "faced with circumstances which would not perturb most men, [the subjects of the study] fly into a rage" (192). This does not suggest a genetic nature of those who are violent, quite, but only of those who are violent in a certain sense; the study need not have anything to do with the sort of violent nature displayed by a hardened criminal, say. A notorious special case is "intelligent." As Stephen Jay Gould has reviewed, there are periodically arguments for a genetic nature shared by those who fall under the term, typically claimed to correlate with race. But the arguments have mostly been politically motivated, and are not nowadays taken seriously in the scientific community; for discussion, see Jones (1993, 194-196) and Gould (1996).

16. Fodor argues in a speculative way that general reasoning is not "encapsulated," by drawing an analogy between intelligence and theory confirmation in science (101-119). It seems to me that his argument is fallacious as a demonstration of the non-modularity of general reasoning, even though I think the conclusion is true; but I've given my reasons for this elsewhere (Chien 1995), and nothing I say here depends on them.

17. A function need not "use up" all the elements of the range: that is, some elements of the range may not be any function output. This is important because in positing a shared range for different speakers' projection functions, I am supposing that the range aggregates the speakers' varying projections on any given input. Thus for any property in the range there could be speakers who never project that property.

18. This would include Putnam's usage on which meaning determines reference (1975, 245-246; 1988, 9-11), and Burge's distinction between "lexical meaning" and "translational meaning" (1993, 312-318).

19. Idiolects aside, the sense in which "English" is a language is not actually of interest in linguistics because it involves political, geographical, and other extralinguistic factors (Chomsky 1992a, 101). In what follows, "language" should strictly speaking be taken in the sense of "dialect." That is, the issue will be idiolectical variation within a dialect.

20. While I take it to be a standard notion that an idiolect is relatively stable over time, it is not universal. As George (1990) describes a differing view, "idiolects so vary with the present moment, audience and speaker that no two people are likely to share an idiolect and even that at no two times is an individual likely to have the same idiolect" (277). But the view, at least as based upon Davidson's (1986) argument from malapropism, does not seem to be well-founded; see George, 277-283, and note 22. I will attempt to show that in any case idiolects do not vary on account of conceptual reasons.

21. Note that the example here is not of a clever individual, but of clever behavior. I am assuming that "clever" is not thereby ambiguous, but rather can have referents of both sorts. In any case I take it that one may reasonably guess at a sense of "clever" from an example of behavior.

22. A separate issue is what the existence of usage which violates constraints implies about idiolectical variation. In "A Nice Derangement of Epitaphs," Davidson suggests radical variation based on considerations of malapropism, as when Mrs. Malaprop means "epithet" by "epitaph." Davidson takes malapropisms to threaten "the distinction between speaker's meaning and literal meaning...since here the intended meaning seems to take over from the standard meaning. I take for granted, however, that nothing should be allowed to obliterate or even blur the distinction between speaker's meaning and literal meaning. In order to preserve the distinction we must, I shall argue, modify certain commonly accepted views about what it is to 'know a language'" (1986, 434). The argument that follows seems to me poorly motivated, because I take it that in "By 'epitaph' Mrs. Malaprop means 'epithet'" the speaker's meaning does not "take over" in any sense which threatens the distinction that Davidson wants to preserve. I've argued that speaker's meaning does not compete with meaning (what Davidson here calls "first meaning"). Typically the meaning is presupposed when inquiring into the speaker's meaning. In general, the speaker's meaning "takes over" only in the uninteresting sense that it is of greater relevance to understanding the speaker, as opposed to what he said, than the "standard meaning." Far from blurring the distinction with meaning, this is just the nature of speaker's meaning.

To be sure, malapropism is a special case. In the kind of malapropism where the speaker inadvertently misspeaks, as in "Lead the way and we'll precede," the speaker's meaning report expresses not a direct but a corrective answer to a WDYM-question. If the speaker is ignorant of the meaning, as in

Mrs. Malaprop's case, then the report expresses a direct answer which violates other constraints. In the first case, what is corrected is not the presupposition of what is said, based partly on the meanings of the speaker's words, but the presupposition that this is what is believed; so there is no "taking over" from meaning. In the second case, the violation of constraints associated with Mrs. Malaprop's idiolectical concept does not entail that they are not relevant on this occasion: they apply, but are not met. In either case a hearer might be able to spontaneously infer an answer to the WDYM-question for himself, as Davidson emphasizes (though not in these terms), enabling communication—with the meaning of "precede" and the violation of constraints on "epitaph" enabling the inference in each case. So nothing follows about the "commonly accepted views about what it is to know a language," because meaning and public constraints as recognized in the "commonly accepted views" remain operative. Similar conclusions can be drawn for other sorts of circumstance reviewed by Davidson, including intentional misspeaking and made-up words.

23. Taking some further examples, Burge (1979) posits shared content on the basis of social norms; Bilgrami (1992) allows semantic norms as a kind of recommendation for communicative success; and Marconi (1997) appeals to a notion of "convergence" among individual competences to account for "normativity" (as distinct from norms). None of these pertains to the intraspeaker aspect of projection constraints. Their pertaining to the interspeaker aspect is not ruled out in advance, but I have no commitment to Burge's account (n. 3), or to Bilgrami's because it is based on communication. And convergence in Marconi's sense has to do with a degree of overlap in realms of application and beliefs about referents (1997, 120), not what projection constraints have to do with. My meaning quick-witted by "clever" and your meaning good at numbers both fall within projection constraints, but display little if any such overlap.

24. The earlier analysis must be slightly adjusted, since the contrasts now involve sentences rather than propositions. Whereas we took the contrasts to be the propositions expressed by substitutions into a schema, now the substitutions suffice. How multiple contrasts figure in a further constraint is discussed below (n. 27).

25. See Chapter 2, note 27, on the tradeoff between accounting for a constraint by appropriate construal of the relevance relation and accounting for it by a distinct metric.

26. One of the thorny issues involved here relates to a concern expressed by (among others) Barbara Partee. Commenting on Schiffer's (1987) argument that compositionality is not in fact required to explain how language users can understand an infinity of potential sentences, Partee (1988) suggests (following earlier work) that the motivation is mistaken to begin with: "the

real argument for compositional truth-conditional semantics is not that a language user can *understand* indefinitely many novel utterances, but rather that there are indefinitely many *semantic facts* to be explained, indefinitely many pieces of basic data about truth-conditions and entailment relations among sentences of any given natural language" (49, Partee's emphasis). If she is right, then the explanation for the understanding of language users will presumably have to come from somewhere other than compositionality. And I surmise that the grasping of projection constraints would be especially difficult to explain. Either the "piggybacking" would have to be of projection constraints which have to do with understanding on top of "meanings" which do not, or else the piggybacking idea would have to be abandoned.

27.   Van Fraassen's measure can be regarded as combining two independently noted features of inductive strength. The first is that if probability is to be the measure, one cannot simply consider the conditional probability of the conclusion given the premise. The probability that Fred will not get pregnant, given that he has eaten lunch, is high; but there is no inductive strength here because his having eaten lunch has nothing to do with it. The premise must be relevant, a notion that has to do with the comparison between the conditional probability and the "prior" probability, i.e. of the conclusion without assuming the premise. Here these probabilities are equal; that is, Fred's having eaten lunch doesn't raise the probability that Fred will not get pregnant. (See Salmon 1975.)

The second feature is dependence on a contrast. Taking an example of Dretske (1972, 429-430), the evidence for thinking that Clyde robbed the grocery store, as opposed to someone else, might include Clyde's fingerprints on the cash register. But this would not be evidence for thinking that Clyde robbed the store, as opposed to simply having handled the cash register. See also Lipton (1991), who makes the point with respect for explanation, not justification; but while he (like van Fraassen) denies that explanation in general consists of providing a reason for believing in the truth of the explanandum, he does not deny that it often does (26).

Recall that my assumption of a single contrast is only for simplicity. "Favoring" in the current sense takes multiple contrasts into account. Van Fraassen remarks: "Two facts matter: the minimum odds of [the answer] against [the contrasts] and the number of alternatives [among the contrasts] to which [the answer] bears these minimum odds. The first should increase, the second decrease" (148). In the "clever" example, this presumably happens with regard to multiple contrasts as generated by the members of a semantic field for "clever" (Point 2 above). The first "fact," because John's quick-wittedness tends to confirm his cleverness; the second, because John's quick-wittedness tends to disconfirm those contrasts corresponding to members of the field which are not synonyms, such as that John is dull.

Another simplifying assumption is that all probabilities are conditional on a corpus of background information which includes the assumption that x is rational. For notice that it is not really the probabilities of John's being clever and John's being dull that are at issue, but the probabilities of x's believing these things. On the assumption of rationality, though, there is minimal difference—none, if the rationality is ideal. (Alternatively, one could formulate the metric in terms of the contents of the relevant beliefs.) Note that application of the favoring measure requires general knowledge and reasoning, in virtue of the background corpus and probability measures (construed as "subjective" probabilities).

28   A similar notion is natural for why-questions. Here is a further excerpt from Bill Moyers' interview with physicist Steven Weinberg.

> If you ask any ordinary question about everyday things—"Why is the sky blue?" or "Why is water wet?"—we actually know the answer. For example, a question about why the sky is blue would be answered in terms of the properties of dust grains and light and air transmitting light. And then if you ask "Why are those things true? Why does light behave the way it does? Why are light waves of one wavelength scattered differently than light waves of a different wavelength?"—you can answer those things, too, in terms of a more fundamental description using atoms and quantum mechanics. Then we ask, "Why are those the way they are?" We've come a long way here, too. We now have a theory of elementary particles, which is more fundamental than the ordinary quantum mechanics of atoms and radiation...I want to help to trace these chains of "why" down to their roots.

29   I am not assuming that answering is a transitive relation, i.e. that whenever b answers a and c answers b, then c answers a. If it were, then we could just say that the propositions deeper than a are the propositions that answer it. One problem with demonstrating transitivity is the contrast; see Chien (1987, 108-112).

30. See e.g. Davidson (1984), especially 141-144. Not everyone would pose the problem this way; see Lewis (1974b, 331-334). For more recent discussion and pointers to the literature, see Fodor and Lepore (1994) and Davidson's (1994) reply.

31. Consistently with the foregoing it is still possible to doubt that there is more than one true speaker's meaning, for the same reason one could doubt that there is *any* true speaker's meaning: it might be doubted that attribution of any belief is something that is true or false. But so far as I can see, I am not forced to any particular position on "intentional realism." To be sure, I am using the word "true," begging the question on the issue; but this is for simplicity. Anyone sympathetic to an instrumentalist view of belief attribution

can substitute an instrumentalist rendering of "true," provided a multiplicity of speaker's meanings is still recognized (not a problem, presumably).

Notes to Chapter 5

1. I am not talking here about "dead" metaphor—"fork in the road," "fiery temper," etc.—wherein an originally novel usage has lost its metaphorical character over time through general use. Following the standard view I take the result to be a new lexicon entry, making for additional ambiguity. (I don't mean to imply that dead metaphor is uninteresting; see Lakoff and Johnson 1980, on "conventional" metaphor.)

2. The writers I have in mind are Lakoff and Johnson (1980, 201-202), who quote the remarks of Davidson above to support their contention that "the objectivist account of truth [and] meaning...[excludes] all subjective elements—that is anything peculiar to a particular context, culture, or mode of understanding," and Kittay (1987, 100-113), who argues that "literal language is no more context-free than metaphor is," an argument she presents as counterpoint to Davidson who according to her claims that "meaning in language is context-free" (97). Lakoff and Johnson's careless use of Davidson's remarks comes amidst an attack on not only "objectivism" but "Western philosophy"; more on this below. Kittay does register an objection which is not beside the point, namely that word meanings are productive and limitless (107-108). If she were right about this then Davidson does mischaracterize meanings, since then a word meaning could be produced in a context of utterance, not having been established in advance; and it would not be ruled out for metaphor to reside in word meanings (as Kittay herself holds). But I don't think she is right about this, inasmuch as she follows Cohen whose brand of robust ambiguity I argued against previously (Ch. 3, sec. 5). Kittay does recognize that metaphorical senses of a word are not in the lexicon (121), hence that they are not word meanings in the usual sense.

3. See e.g. Henle (1981, 84-85), Beardsley (1981, 110-111), and Elgin (1983, Chapter 4). (The first two are reprints of work that appeared before the time Black was writing.) Black himself argues in an earlier paper that "metaphor" sometimes applies to words without consideration of users: "We recognize that to call a man a 'cesspool' is to use a metaphor, without needing to know who uses the expression, or on what occasions, or with what intention. The rules of our language determine that some expressions must count as metaphors; and a speaker can no more change this than he can legislate that 'cow' shall mean the same as 'sheep'" (1981, 66). To be sure, Black goes on to remark that "We must also recognize that the established rules of language leave wide latitude for individual variation, initiative, and creation" (66-67), which is more in line with the criticism here of Davidson; the characterization

of his theory as "semantic" (by himself and others) is puzzling. But the point here is that the consensus suggested by Black does not seem to exist.

4.   Searle for example proposes a number of interpretive rules without claiming more than that they enable determination of "possible values of R" (1981, 275), i.e. possible speaker's meanings in his sense.

5.   In contrast, analyzing it as her conceptual reason is general because it then is present whether or not a communicative intention is also (Ch. 2, sec. 2.1, Ch. 3, n. 4).

6.   The argument just reviewed is part of what Cooper calls the "indeterminacy objection," i.e. that the "standard view" cannot explain the fact that sometimes a metaphor "admits of more than one interpretation, none of which can be demonstrated as uniquely correct" (70). His argument is that indeterminacy cannot be explained as uncertainty as to the speaker's meaning since the speaker's meaning may be completely indeterminate while interpretation is only partly so, and conversely the speaker's meaning may be known while the interpretation remains indeterminate. He argues that it also cannot be explained as either indeterminacy of the speaker's meaning itself, or indeterminacy as to what possible speakers might mean. I cannot make sense of any of this, because it seems to me that there is no unique fact of indeterminacy to be explained but rather various indeterminacies. (The latter two are similar in spirit to what I've called psychological indeterminacy and conceptual indeterminacy.) Indeed Cooper's survey begins to sort them out; meanwhile he takes as the unique fact to be explained a particular sort of indeterminacy, having to do with interpretive discretion. So his objection amounts to the claim that various other sorts of indeterminacy cannot account for Cooper's favored sort, which seems neither surprising nor significant.

7.   These points apply to other writers as well. Kittay argues that meaningfulness, in metaphor and in general, does not depend on inferring a speaker's intention; rather it depends on semantic and pragmatic rules on the basis of which we infer an intention (48-49). (See also Beardsley 1981, 111, arguing similarly for metaphoricity.) Her notion of speaker's meaning is Gricean, in the sense not only of a particular analysis of communicative intention but also a reductionist analysis of meaning. But even taking the spirit of the objection as applying to intralinguistic speaker's meaning, it is hard to see what the issue is. If rules for interpretation are utilized in attempts to infer the speaker's meaning, why conclude that speaker's meaning is "not pertinent to metaphor" (44)? The only answer I can see is that Kittay is implicitly taking "metaphor" to mean just that which is derivable from the "rules"; of course the actual speaker's meaning is then not pertinent to the derivation, or else the account of interpretation would be circular. That's fine, but just a terminological choice for "metaphor."

8. The content of the usage in this case ("promissory" content) will be discussed in section 6. For a recent alternative account of these issues, see Nogales (1999, 100-164).

9. See Vanderveken (1991) for an analysis of ironical speech acts. He moreover proposes a general framework for "non-literal speech acts" including metaphor.

10. Not including the empty set. A set of n elements has 2^n subsets, including the empty set. (A subset is defined by a "decision" of either in or out for each element; thus, these two possibilities multiplied n times.)

11. Cohen mentions Searle (1981) as facing difficulty; but Searle does not think of speaker's meaning as a speech act, and his analysis of metaphor does not posit metaphorical speech acts.

12. The respect of similarity is explicit in the case of the construction "is as...as," e.g. "He is as free as a bird."

13. "In a sense" may be combined with the other modifiers to the same effect, as in "similar in a sense" and "like in a sense." Thus just as a sense in which Sid is a policeman is a respect in which Sid is weakly similar to policemen, so a sense in which Sid is *like* a policeman is such a respect. The presence of both modifiers doesn't make for "extra-weak" similarity.

14. Similarly for multi-place predicates. Miller suggests that in the interpretation of "The rich perform leisure," the values of y and y' in

   perform (the rich, leisure) $\Rightarrow (\exists F)(\exists y, y')[F$(the rich, leisure) is similar to perform$(y, y')]$.

   are instrumental. Two likely choices are "poor" and "duties," respectively, or "actors" and "play," which would seem to determine two distinct interpretations. But it seems to me that we can account for the interpretations just by different possible values for F. Thus one might mean that the rich labor in service of their leisure, or that the rich pretend to enjoy their leisure, where values for y and y' are irrelevant.

15. Tversky's explanation of asymmetry is not however along these elementary lines. He proposes that the similarity between a and b is a linear combination of the positive contribution of shared properties and the negative contribution of distinctive properties, i.e. properties that a has but b does not and properties that b has but a does not:

   $$S(a,b) = \theta f(A \cap B) - \alpha f(A - B) - \beta f(B - A).$$

   ("—" denotes set difference.) Here A is the set of properties of a and B the set of properties of b; f is a measure of the salience of a set of properties, reflective of e.g. "intensity, frequency, familiarity, good form, and informational content" (332); and θ, α and β are weighting parameters. Asymmetry follows from inequality of a and b, desirable because

   > Similarity judgments can be regarded as extensions of similarity statements, that is, statements of the form "a is like b." Such a

statement is directional; it has a subject, *a*, and a referent, *b*, and
it is not equivalent in general to the converse similarity statement
"*b* is like *a*." In fact, the choice of subject and referent depends, at
least in part, on the relative salience of the objects. We tend to
select the more salient stimulus, or the prototype, as a referent, and
the less salient stimulus, or the variant, as a subject. We say "the
portrait resembles the person" rather than "the person resembles
the portrait." We say "the son resembles the father" rather than
"the father resembles the son" (328).

He adds, "one naturally focuses on the subject of the comparison. Hence the
features of the subject are weighted more heavily than the features of the
referent (i.e. $\alpha > \beta$). Consequently, similarity is reduced more by the
distinctive features of the subject than by the distinctive features of the
referent (333)."

   Tversky has been influential, but I do not myself think that this is a good
account of similarity as it is linguistically expressed, which he acknowledges
to be his topic of concern. Predication attributes to the subject properties
associated with the predicate. In the case of a simile, the properties may be
regarded as respects of similarity. Whether the predication is true depends
upon whether the subject possesses the associated properties; the possession
of other properties is irrelevant. Thus common properties of the subject and
"referent" (predicate reference) should count toward the truth of the simile
only if they are associated with the predicate. Keeping in mind that similes
assert weak similarity, Sid's having a badge, carrying a gun, or being
authoritative all count toward the truth of "Sid is like a policeman" (given an
implicature analysis of the implication that Sid is not a policeman). On the
other hand, properties which Sid shares with policemen and which are not
associated with "policeman," such as being an adult human, do not count. But
on Tversky's metric, it is not the shared properties associated with
"policeman" that count positively, but all the shared properties—i.e. the
intersection of Sid's properties with the properties that all policemen happen
to have. So the metric incorrectly entails that Sid's being authoritative does
not count positively, while his being an adult human does.

   Distinctive properties of the "referent" should likewise count against the
truth of the simile only if they are associated with the predicate. Suppose all
policemen have natural hearts. Then if Sid is a recipient of an artificial heart,
he would lack a property of policemen. This should not count against the truth
of "Sid is like a policeman," but on Tversky's metric it would. Any distinctive
properties of either the subject or "referent" count negatively, because the
properties of the latter up for consideration are not those associated with
"policemen" but those which all policemen happen to have. The problem with
respect to all three terms on the right side of his formula is that the assigned

polarity of the contribution to similarity is valid only for properties associated with the predicate; all others are irrelevant. The salience measure f does not affect this. If it were construed as a function from a set of properties to another set, then in principle it could for each term pick out just the relevant properties; but on Tversky's conception it is rather a function from properties to numbers (332, 338). Anyway salience is not the distinguishing factor: Sid's artificial heart, for instance, is presumably quite salient given its rarity.

So while what is expressed by a simile is indeed an asymmetric relation, the reason for this is not Tversky's. The reason is rather that the relevant respects of similarity derive from the predicate, not the subject. The basic point has to do with predication, not even similes in particular.

16. I'm not pronouncing on the empirical question of what thought processes attend the comprehension of metaphor, raised by Miller (242-244); thus I have been characterizing the result of interpretation as opposed to a psychological process. But note Miller himself is not arguing from psychological evidence. His structures are presumably supposed to have a certain prior plausibility, making them worth putting to empirical test. What I am suggesting is that they are not obviously needed in a conceptual account of metaphorical usage. I take it that their prior plausibility is less insofar as this is true; but this doesn't rule out the possibility of their eventually being proven psychologically real.

17. It might be claimed that there is no similarity if properties are not shared. Searle (1981) for instance argues that temperature metaphors for emotions are not girded by any similarities. Coldness and hostility, for example, are psychologically associated but not similar (267-268). (See also Beardsley 1958, 138, and Richards 1981, 59.) If this were right, then it would constitute a more serious criticism than mine of Miller's or any theory according to which metaphor involves similarity: not just that it is awkward and unilluminating, but that it is false. I am not myself making this claim because I am not sure whether similarity requires shared properties; I am not sure whether coldness and hostility have properties in common, or if they do not, whether they are nonetheless similar. But nothing of present concern hinges on this. If the stronger criticism is correct, so much the better for my downplay of similarity.

18. Alternatively, we might take them to be "endomorphic" operators, which attach to expressions of a category to form new expressions of the same category. On this approach "In a sense man is a wolf" is elliptical for "Man is a wolf in a sense," wherein "wolf in a sense" is a common noun phrase; similarly under syntactic analysis the main verb phrase of "In a sense their marriage suddenly vaporized" is "vaporized in a sense." Likewise for "in the sense that" (although it would be replaced where appropriate by "in the sense of," as in "Man is a wolf in the sense of fierce"). But the point would remain

that the operators attach to syntactic constructions with greater versatility than "like" does.

19. Goodman is more explicit on this in his "Seven Strictures on Similarity"; see especially his "fifth stricture" (1964, 440). I think that the strictures have retained their power, and that this has not been sufficiently appreciated. For instance I take the problems with Tversky's influential account (n. 15) to imply partial vindication of Goodman.

20. Note that the mapping is a partial function; that is, not all elements of the domain of war are mapped to a counterpart in the domain of a government campaign. For many further qualifications and refinements on the homomorphism theme, see Indurkhya (1987).

21. See e.g. Cooper (1986, 201-202), Davidson (1981, 213), and Elgin (1983, 68). Tellingly, these claims are made in passing and cite no evidence.

22. I think one enabler of the patent falsity view is too much attention paid to a single form: nominative predication, wherein two noun phrases with disparate referents make for patent falsity. For proper perspective see Brooke-Rose (1958), the classic survey of syntactic variety in metaphor. One form she examines in depth is what she calls "the genitive": e.g. "the hostel of my heart," "the roses of her cheeks," "the fire of love." Though such constructions have received scant attention in the philosophical literature (but see Miller, 230-231), ironically Brooke-Rose complains that they are too often taken as canonical among rhetoricians: "One is astonished at the way [this form] turns up to illustrate sweeping statements about metaphor in general" (149).

A good recent example of overgeneralizing from the nominative case is Nogales, who claims in passing that most metaphors are of this form (1999, 189). For her the point is especially important because her analysis of metaphor, and specifically metaphoricity, is based on nominative metaphors while claiming to be general. What makes a metaphor, she says, is what she calls "reconceptualization": "In the case of nominative metaphors, such as an utterance of 'Steve is a sheep dog', the grammatical form of the utterance dictates that the audience assign the subject of the sentence (and the metaphor) to the class represented by the metaphor vehicle...the audience must reconceptualize the metaphor vehicle to determine the intended class" (18). What about non-nominative metaphors? She claims that "while the surface form is different, the underlying processes (involving the selection of the relevant systems, the construction of a new class in terms of the role the metaphor vehicle plays in the relevant system, and the reconceptualization of the metaphor vehicle and subject) are the same," and briefly illustrates with two other forms. Supposing these illustrations to be valid, still Nogales omits discussion of predicative and sentential metaphors (Miller's M1 and M2), and for the latter especially it is not at all obvious how a class-inclusion story is supposed to work. Also "reconceptualization" in Nogales' sense does not seem to apply to "systematic" metaphors in the sense previously discussed, and as recognized in the literature. Consideration of these further issues requires us to either recognize a variety of underlying structures (or "processes," as Nogales prefers), or else choose a more general mechanism than class inclusion—such as homomorphism, which subsumes the nominative case.

It is possible to interpret Nogales' offhand claim that most metaphors are nominative as justification for the emphasis she places on "reconceptualization" in her class-inclusion sense. But evidence is required for this claim, as is an argument that special importance would attach to nominative metaphors even if the claim happened by statistical accident to be true, but Nogales provides neither. Brooke-Rose's observation should be sobering in this regard.

23 In section 2 I argued that a condition of Bergmann's for metaphorical assertion, that its content be successfully inferred by a hearer, entails arbitrary divisions and incorrect normative assessments of metaphorical use. I now add that another of her proposed conditions, that an utterance be successfully identified as metaphorical, wrongly takes identification to be independent of interpretation.

24. I have in mind Lakoff and Johnson (1980, especially Chapter 24), who go further than Black originally did, claiming that consideration of metaphor refutes "objectivism," i.e. the view that "the world is made up of distinct objects, with inherent properties and fixed relations among them at any instant." In the case of "This relationship isn't going anywhere" or "There was a magnetism between us," "the objectivist must not only bear the burden of claiming that love has inherent properties similar to the inherent properties of journeys, electromagnetic phenomena, and sick people; he must also claim that love is sufficiently clearly defined in terms of these inherent properties so that those similarities will exist." However, "the similarities arise as a result of conceptual metaphors and thus must be considered similarities of interactional, rather than inherent, properties. But the admission of interactional properties is inconsistent with the basic premise of objectivist philosophy" (215). The argument is apparently that for a given metaphor a realist metaphysics is committed to the existence of a similarity relation which is independent of the metaphor; since such relations do not exist, realism is false.

This argument is very bad. Most relevant here is that the second premise is false. The notion that similarity "arises as a result of" the metaphor can be deflated in the way just outlined above; what arises is only a novel content. The reason that "love," say, is not "well-defined" is not that any similarity between love and physical forces involves "interactional" properties, but simply that many different contents are possible. Once a content has been determined, one can then judge its truth by looking to relations in the world (though this might be difficult, as is often the case outside of metaphor). Anyone who denies this has the burden of explaining how a metaphor comparing love to a magnetic force can being distinguished from, say, one comparing love to a repellent force or to lack of a force.

Not that it is clear why the admission of "interactional" properties is incompatible with realism ("objectivist philosophy"). But then, Lakoff and Johnson's "objectivist" is a stupid creature, incapable of introducing the slightest subtlety to his position. So not only is "the objectivist" unable to conceive of another account of similarity in metaphor, he is also too ignorant to consider a Lockean distinction between an object's primary and secondary qualities. He is also decisively refuted by the mundane observation that the truth of a sentence is relative to what the sentence expresses in context. That is because his notion is of what Lakoff and Johnson, in an attempt to make fun of the concept of truth, variously call "objective truth," "absolute truth," "objective, absolute truth," "objective (absolute and unconditional) truth," and the view that "truth is always absolute truth." So "the objectivist" is not for instance aware of truth-conditional models of context as proposed in, say, Davidson and Harman's 1972 volume *Semantics of Natural Language*—to which Lakoff contributed, curiously enough. (See e.g. Lewis's essay—which Lakoff and Johnson even cite—175-176, 213-216, and Lewis 1980. See also Lycan 1984, 200-201.) Further, Lakoff and Johnson take "the objectivist" to represent most all of Western philosophy, even adding moral overtones (159).

In fairness I should consider a more careful account. Acknowledging the paradoxical air of the thesis that metaphor can create similarity, Black (1979) attempts to dispel it in two ways. First, similarity is not an "objective" relation but rather a "variegated set of relations," with an indispensable subjective component (38). Second, there are on the face of it various "things in the world" with subjective components for which it is plausible to say that their existence depends upon being perceived. Surely the slow-motion appearance of a horse did not exist before the invention of cinematography, for instance. Black thinks that at least some metaphors are "cognitive instruments" which, analogously, are "indispensable for perceiving connections that, once perceived, are then truly present...When I first thought of Nixon as 'an image surrounding a vacuum,' the verbal formulation was necessary to my seeing him in this way" (39).

The problem here is that the mere existence of a subjective component, *in addition to* an "objective" one, is not sufficient to make the case. To say that metaphor "creates similarity" is at best misleading unless the objective component is denied, which Black does not do. Consider that Black presumably would not consider "Nixon is an image surrounding a solid rock" to express an equally apt metaphor. It is difficult to see how he could account for this in any way other than by appealing to the original metaphor's somehow involving a better fit with reality. But then it seems he would have to concede that the metaphor does not create the relevant reality, any more than the unapt metaphor does.

As for similarity being a "variegated set of relations," the problem does not imply any special power of metaphor, because many literal statements may with equal justification be regarded as expressive of similarity relations. The problem is simply the incongruity of the notion of similarity, as Goodman and others have long argued.

25. The reducibility thesis as characterized by Black likewise allows that cognitive effects may get lost in a paraphrase, but for a different reason: it allows for differences between a content expressed metaphorically and the same content expressed literally (1981, 70). The current point has to do with cognitive differences between different contents.

26. Challenging the claim that metaphor entails false assertion, MacCormac comments that "Constable's assertion that 'Painting is a science...of which pictures are but experiments' seems to produce an insight that the hearer on first encounter takes to be a true assertion *in some sense*" (1985, 207, my emphasis). But the problem is that the hearer does not thereby apprehend any metaphor or insight. I'm suggesting that it's typical to make MacCormac's mistake with the "in some sense" implicit.

27. One can reach the same conclusion by taking seriously the comparison between conversational metaphor and scientific models, a comparison that Black himself has made (1962, 236-238). It is not controversial that a good model's function is to explain, e.g. that modeling gas molecules as billiard balls helped to explain certain macroscopic behavior of gases. (The nature of the explanation is another matter; for one account, see Hesse 1966, 157-176.) That explanation in turn is enabled not by the model in and of itself, but by an explanation of the model in terms of what properties of gases are illuminated. The latter explanation is thus expressible literally, i.e. in terms appropriate to gas molecules rather than billiard balls. This doesn't devalue the model: on the contrary, the model is what enables the explanation.

28. One linguist who has attempted to account for perceptual content is Jackendoff (1990, 32-34 and Chapter 10), who proposes a theory of how three-dimensional visual models are represented in the lexicon.

BIBLIOGRAPHY

Alston, W. 1971: "How Does One Tell Whether a Word Has One, Several or Many Senses?" In *Semantics*, ed. D. Steinberg and L. Jakobovits. Cambridge: Cambridge University Press.

Atlas, J. 1989: *Philosophy without Ambiguity*. Oxford: Clarendon Press.

Aune, B. 1972: "On an Analytic-Synthetic Distinction." *American Philosophical Quarterly* 9, 235-242.

Austin, J. L. 1962: *How to Do Things with Words*. New York: Oxford University Press.

Avramides, A. 1989: *Meaning and Mind*. Cambridge: MIT Press.

Bach, K., and Harnish, R. 1979: *Linguistic Communication and Speech Acts*. Cambridge: MIT Press.

_____1987: "Relevant Questions." *Behavioral and Brain Sciences* 10, 711-712.

Bach, K. 1987: *Thought and Reference*. Oxford: Oxford University Press.

_____1994: "Conversational Impliciture." *Mind and Language* 9, 124-162.

Baker, C. 1989: *English Syntax*. Cambridge: MIT Press.

Barsalou, L. 1992: "Frames, Concepts, and Conceptual Fields." In Lehrer and Kittay.

Beardsley, M. 1958: *Aesthetics*. New York: Harcourt Brace.

Beaver, D. 2001: *Presupposition and Assertion in Dynamic Semantics*. Stanford: CSLI Publications.

Bennett, J. 1976: *Linguistic Behavior*. Cambridge: Cambridge University Press.

Bergmann, M. 1991: "Metaphorical Assertions." In Davis.

Bilgrami, A. 1992: *Belief and Meaning*. Oxford: Basil Blackwell.

Binkley, T. 1981: "On the Truth and Probity of Metaphor." In Johnson.

Black, M. 1962: *Models and Metaphors*. Ithaca: Cornell University Press.

_____1978: "How Metaphors Work: A Reply to Donald Davidson." In *On Metaphor*, ed. S. Sacks. Chicago: University of Chicago Press.

_____1981: "Metaphor." In Johnson.

Block, N. 1986: "Advertisement for a Semantics for Psychology." In *Midwest Studies in Philosophy*, Vol. 10, ed. P. French, T. Uehling, and H. Wettstein. Minneapolis: University of Minnesota Press.

____1991: "What Narrow Content is Not." In Loewer and Rey.

Brooke-Rose, C. 1958: *A Grammar of Metaphor*. London: Seeker and Warburg.

Burge, T. 1979: "Individualism and the Mental." In *Midwest Studies in Philosophy*, Vol. 16, ed. P. French, T. Uehling, and H. Wettstein. Minneapolis: University of Minnesota Press.

____1982: "Other Bodies." In *Thought and Object*, ed. A. Woodfield. Oxford: Oxford University Press.

____1986: "Intellectual Norms and Foundations of Mind." *Journal of Philosophy* 83, 697-720.

____1989: "Wherein is Language Social?" In *Reflections on Chomsky*, ed. A. George. Oxford: Basil Blackwell.

____1993: "Concepts, Definitions, and Meaning." *Metaphilosophy* 24, 309-325.

Burton-Roberts, N. 1991: "Review of J. D. Atlas' *Philosophy Without Ambiguity*." *Mind and Language* 6, 161-176.

Carston, R. 1988: "Implicature, Explicature and Truth-Theoretic Semantics." In *Mental Representations*, ed. R. Kempson. Cambridge: Cambridge University Press.

____1993: "Conjuction, Explanation, and Relevance." *Lingua* 90, 27-49.

____1998: "1995 Postscript to 'Implicature, Explicature and Truth-Theoretic Semantics." In *Pragmatics: Critical Concepts*, Vol. IV, ed. A. Kasher. New York: Routledge.

Cavell, S. 1964: "Must We Mean What We Say?" In Chappell.

Chappell, V., ed. 1964: *Ordinary Language*. New York: Dover.

Chien, A. 1985: "Demonstratives and Belief States." *Philosophical Studies* 47, 271-289.

____1987: *On Vagueness*. Doctoral dissertation, University of Massachusetts at Amherst. Ann Arbor: University Microfilms.

____1996: "Why the Mind May Not be Modular." *Minds and Machines* 6, 1-32.

Chomsky, N. 1968: *Language and Mind*. New York: Harcourt Brace Jovanovich.

____1975a: *Reflections on Language*. New York: Pantheon.

____1975b: "Questions of Form and Interpretation." In *The Scope of American Linguistics*, ed. R. Austerlitz. Lisse: Peter de Ridder Press.

____1992a: "Language and Interpretation: Philosophical Reflections and Empirical Inquiry." In *Inference, Explanation and Other Frustrations*, ed. J. Earman. Berkeley: University of California Press.

____1992b: "Explaining Language Use." *Philosophical Topics* 20, 205-231.

Clarke, D. 2000: "The Possibility of Acceptance Without Belief." In Engel.

Cohen, L. J. 1971: "Some Remarks on Grice's Views about the Logical Particles of Natural Language." In *Pragmatics of Natural Language*, ed. Y. Bar-Hillel. Dordrecht: D. Reidel.

____1979: "The Semantics of Metaphor." In Ortony.

____1986: "How is Conceptual Innovation Possible?" *Erkenntnis* 25, 221-238.

Cohen, T. 1981: "Figurative Speech and Figurative Acts." In Johnson.

Cooper, D. 1986: *Metaphor*. Oxford: Basil Blackwell.

Cutler, A. 1987: "The Task of the Speaker and the Task of the Hearer." *Behavioral and Brain Sciences* 10, 715-716.

Dascal, M. 1979: "Conversational Relevance." In *Meaning and Use*, ed. A. Margalit. Dordrecht: D. Reidel.

Davidson, D. 1968: "Actions, Reasons, and Causes." In *The Philosophy of Action*, ed. A. White. Oxford: Oxford University Press.

____1981: "What Metaphors Mean." In Johnson.

____1984: *Inquiries into Truth and Interpretation*. Oxford: Clarendon Press.

____1986: "A Nice Derangement of Epitaphs." In Lepore.

____1991: "James Joyce and Humpty Dumpty." In *Midwest Studies in Philosophy*, Vol. 16, ed. P. French, T. Uehling, and H. Wettstein. Notre Dame: University of Notre Dame Press.

____1994: "Radical Interpretation Interpreted." In Tomberlin.

Davidson, D., and Harman, G., ed. 1972: *Semantics of Natural Language*. Dordrecht: D. Reidel.

Davis, S., ed. 1991: *Pragmatics*. Oxford: Oxford University Press.

Davis, W. 1992a: "Speaker Meaning." *Linguistics and Philosophy* 15, 223-253.

____1992b: "Cogitative and Cognitive Speaker Meaning." *Philosophical Studies* 67, 71-88.

____1998: *Implicature*. New York: Cambridge University Press.

Dennett, D. 1978: *Brainstorms*. Cambridge: MIT Press.

DeMey, S. 1981: "The Dependent Plural and the Analysis of Tense." In *Proceedings of the NELS XI*, ed. V. Burke and J. Pustoevsky. Amherst: University of Massachusetts.

Donnellan, K. 1966: "Reference and Definite Descriptions." *Philosophical Review* 75, 281-304.

Dowty, D., Wall, R., and Peters, S. 1981: *Introduction to Montague Semantics*. Dordrecht: D. Reidel.

Dretske, F. 1972: "Contrastive Statements." *Philosophical Review* 81, 411-437.

Dupre, J. 1981: "Natural Kinds and Biological Taxa." *Philosophical Review* 110, 66-90.

Elgin, C. 1983: *With Reference to Reference*. Indianapolis: Hackett.

Engel, P., ed. 2000: *Believing and Accepting*. Dordrecht: Kluwer.

Field, H. 1978: "Logic, Meaning, and Conceptual Role." *Journal of Philosophy* 74, 379-409.

Fodor, J. 1977: *Semantics*. Cambridge: Harvard University Press.

Fodor, J. A. 1975: *The Language of Thought*. Cambridge: Harvard University Press.

____1981: *Representations*. Cambridge: MIT Press.

____1983: *Modularity of Mind*. Cambridge: MIT Press.

____1991: "Replies." In Loewer and Rey.

Fodor, J. A., Garrett, M., Walker, E., and Parkes, C. 1980: "Against Definitions." *Cognition* 8, 263-367.

Fodor, J. A., and Lepore, E. 1994: "Is Radical Interpretation Possible?" In Tomberlin.

Fogelin, R. 1988: *Figuratively Speaking*. New Haven: Yale University Press.

Garman, M. 1991: *Psycholinguistics*. Cambridge: Cambridge University Press.

Gazdar, G. 1979: *Pragmatics*. New York: Academic Press.

Gazdar, G., and Good, D. 1982: "On a Notion of Relevance." In Smith.

George, A. 1990: "Whose Language is it Anyway? Some Notes on Idiolects." *The Philosophical Quarterly* 40, 275-298.

Goodman, N. 1964: *Problems and Projects*. New York: Bobbs-Merrill.

____1965: *Fact, Fiction, and Forecast*. New York: Bobbs-Merrill.

____1981: "Languages of Art." In Johnson.

Gould, S. 1996: *The Mismeasure of Man*. New York: Norton.

Grandy, R. 1987: "In Defense of Semantic Fields." In Lepore.

____ 1992: "Semantics Fields, Prototypes, and the Lexicon." In Lehrer and Kittay.

Grice, H. P. 1957: "Meaning." *Philosophical Review* 66, 377-388.

____1969: "Utterer's Meaning and Intentions." *Philosophical Review* 78, 147-177.

____1989: *Studies in the Way of Words*. Cambridge: Harvard University Press.

Harman, G. 1973: *Thought*. Princeton: Princeton University Press.

____1974: "Meaning and Semantics." In *Semantics and Philosophy*, ed. M. Munitz and P. Unger. New York: New York University Press.

____1986: *Change in View*. Cambridge: MIT Press.

____1987: "(Nonsolipsistic) Conceptual Role Semantics." In Lepore 1987.

Hartshorne, C., and Weiss, P., ed. 1934: *Collected Papers of Charles Sanders Peirce*, Vol. 5. Cambridge: Harvard University Press.

Heim, I., and Kratzer, A. 1998: *Semantics in Generative Grammar*. Oxford: Basil Blackwell.

Henle, P. 1981: "Metaphor." In Johnson.

Hesse, M. 1966: *Models and Analogies in Science*. Notre Dame: University of Notre Dame Press.

Higginbotham, J. 1986: "Linguistic Theory and Davidson's Program in Semantics." In Lepore.

Indurkhya, B. 1987: "Approximate Semantic Transference: A Computational Theory of Metaphors and Analogies." *Cognitive Science* 11, 445-480.

Jackendoff, R. 1972: *Semantic Interpretation in Generative Grammar*. Cambridge: MIT Press.

____1990: *Semantic Structures*. Cambridge: MIT Press.

Johnson, M. 1981: *Philosophical Perspectives on Metaphor*. Minneapolis: University of Minnesota Press.

Jones, S. 1993: *The Language of Genes*. New York: Doubleday.

Kamp, H. 1975: "Two Theories about Adjectives." In *Formal Semantics of Natural Language*, ed. E. Keenan. Cambridge: Cambridge University Press.

Kaplan, D. 1989: "Demonstratives." In *Themes From Kaplan*, ed. J. Almog. Oxford: Oxford University Press.

Kitcher, P., and Salmon, W. 1987: "Van Fraassen on Explanation." *Journal of Philosophy* 84, 315-330.

Kittay, E. 1987: *Metaphor*. Oxford: Clarendon Press.

Kobes, B. 1986: *Individualism and the Cognitive Sciences*. Doctoral dissertation, University of California Los Angeles. Ann Arbor: University Microfilms.

Kratzer, A. 1977: "What 'Must' and 'Can' Must and Can Mean." *Linguistics and Philosophy* 1, 337-355.

Kripke, S. 1979: "A Puzzle About Belief." In *Meaning and Use*, ed. A. Margalit. Dordrecht: D. Reidel.

____1984: *Wittgenstein on Rules and Private Language*. Cambridge: Harvard University Press.

Lakoff, G. 1972: "Linguistics and Natural Logic." In Davidson and Harman.

____1987: *Women, Fire, and Dangerous Things*. Chicago: University of Chicago Press.

____1993: "The Contemporary Theory of Metaphor." In Ortony.

Lakoff, G., and Johnson, M. 1980: *Metaphors We Live By*. Chicago: University of Chicago Press.

Larson, R., and Segal, G. 1995: *Knowledge of Meaning*. Cambridge: MIT Press.

Lehrer, A., and Kittay, E., ed. 1992: *Frames, Fields, and Contrasts*. Hillsdale: Lawrence Erlbaum Associates.

Lepore, E, ed. 1986: *Truth and Interpretation*. Oxford: Basil Blackwell.

____1987: *New Directions in Semantics*. London: Academic Press.

Levinson, S. C. 1983: *Pragmatics*. Cambridge: Cambridge University Press.

____2000: *Presumptive Meanings*. Cambridge: MIT Press.

Lewis, D. 1972: "General Semantics." In Davidson and Harman.

____1974a: "Languages and Language." In *Minnesota Studies in the Philosophy of Science*, Vol. 8, ed. K. Gunderson. Minneapolis: University of Minnesota Press.

____1974b: "Radical Interpretation." *Synthese* 23, 331-334.

____1980: "Index, Context, and Content." In *Philosophy and Grammar*, ed. S. Kanger and S. Ohmann. Dordrecht: D.Reidel.

Lipton, P. 1991: *Inference to the Best Explanation*. New York: Routledge.

Loewer, B., and Rey, G., ed. 1991: *Meaning in Mind*. Oxford: Basil Blackwell.
Lycan, W. 1984: *Logical Form in Natural Language*. Cambridge: MIT Press.
_____1991: "Review of Avramides." *Mind and Language* 6, 83-86.
Lyons, J. 1995: *Linguistic Semantics*. Cambridge: Cambridge University Press.
MacCormac, E. 1985: *A Cognitive Theory of Metaphor*. Cambridge: MIT Press.
Marconi, D. 1997: *Lexical Competence*. Cambridge: MIT Press.
Margolis, E., and Laurence, S. 1999: *Concepts: Core Readings*. Cambridge: MIT Press.
Martinich, A. 1991: "A Theory for Metaphor." In Davis.
Mates, B. 1964: "On the Verification of Statements About Ordinary Language." In Chappell.
Miller, G. 1979: "Images and Models, Similes and Metaphors." In Ortony.
Miller, G., and Johnson-Laird, P. 1976: *Language and Perception*. Cambridge: Harvard University Press.
Moran, D. 1988: "Quantifier Scoping in the SRI Core Language Engine." In *Proceedings of the 26th Annual Meeting of the Association for Computational Linguistics*. Morristown: Association for Computational Linguistics.
Nidditch, P., ed. 1975: Locke's *An Essay Concerning Human Understanding*. Oxford: Oxford University Press.
Nogales, P. 1999: *Metaphorically Speaking*. Stanford: CSLI Publications.
Ortony, A., ed. 1979: *Metaphor and Thought*. Cambridge: Cambridge University Press.
_____1993: *Metaphor and Thought*. Second edition. Cambridge: Cambridge University Press.
Papafragou, A. 1998: "Modality and Semantic Underdeterminacy." In *Current Issues in Relevance Theory*, ed. V. Rouchota and A. Jucker. Amsterdam: John Benjamins.
Partee, B. 1984: "Compositionality." In *Varieties of Formal Semantics*, ed. F. Landman and F. Veltman. Foris: Dordrecht.
_____1988: "Semantic Facts and Psychological Facts." *Mind and Language* 3, 43-52.
_____1995: "Lexical Semantics and Compositionality." In *An Invitation to Cognitive Science, Vol. 1*, ed. L. Gleitman and M. Liberman. Cambridge: MIT Press.
Perry, J. 1979: "The Problem of the Essential Indexical." *Nous* 13, 3-21.
_____1980: "Belief and Acceptance." In *Midwest Studies in Philosophy*, Vol. 5, ed. P. French, T. Uehling, and H. Wettstein. Minneapolis: University of Minnesota Press.
Pettit, P. 1987: "Inference and Information." *Behavioral and Brain Sciences* 10, 727-729.
Putnam, H. 1975: *Mind, Language and Reality*. Cambridge: Cambridge University Press.

____1988: *Representation and Reality*. Cambridge: MIT Press.

____1990: *Realism with a Human Face*. Cambridge: Harvard University Press.

Quine, W. V. 1969: *Ontological Relativity and Other Essays*. New York: Columbia University Press.

____1991: "Two Dogmas in Retrospect." *Canadian Journal of Philosophy* 21, 265-274.

Recanati, F. 1988: "The Pragmatics of What is Said." *Mind and Language* 4, 295-329.

____1993: *Direct Reference*. Oxford: Oxford University Press.

Rey, G. 1999: "Concepts and Stereotypes." In Margolis and Laurence.

Richards, I. A. 1981: "The Philosophy of Rhetoric." In Johnson.

Rooth, M. 1985: *Association with Focus*. Doctoral dissertation, University of Massachusetts at Amherst. Ann Arbor: University Microfilms.

Ross, J. 1981: *Portraying Analogy*. Cambridge: Cambridge University Press.

Russell, B. 1945: *A History of Western Philosophy*. New York: Simon and Schuster.

____1991: *Autobiography*. New York: Routledge.

Ryle, G. 1949: *The Concept of Mind*. New York: Barnes and Noble.

Salmon, W. 1975: "Confirmation and Relevance." In *Induction, Probability, and Confirmation*, ed. G. Maxwell and R. Anderson. Minneapolis: University of Minnesota Press.

Schiffer, S. 1972: *Meaning*. Oxford: Oxford University Press.

____1982: "Intention-Based Semantics." *Notre Dame Journal of Formal Logic* 23, 119-56.

____1987: *Remnants of Meaning*. Cambridge: MIT Press.

____1991: "Does Mentalese Have a Compositional Semantics?" In Loewer and Rey.

Searle, J. 1969: *Speech Acts*. London: Cambridge University Press.

____1979: *Expression and Meaning*. London: Cambridge University Press.

____1981: "Metaphor." In Johnson.

Siegel, M. 1979: "Measure Adjectives in Montague Grammar." In *Linguistics, Philosophy, and Montague Grammar*, ed. S. Davis and M. Mithun. Austin: University of Texas.

Smith, E., and Medin, D. 1999: "The Exemplar View." In Margolis and Laurence.

Smith, E., Osherson, D., Rips, L., and Keane, M. 1988: "Combining Prototypes: A Selective Modification Model." *Cognitive Science* 12, 485-527.

Smith, N., ed. 1982: *Mutual Knowledge*. New York: Academic Press.

Sperber, D., and Wilson, D. 1982: "Reply to Gazdar and Good." In Smith.

____1987a: "Precis of *Relevance: Communication and Cognition*." *Behavioral and Brain Sciences* 10, 697-710.

____1987b: "Authors' Response." *Behavioral and Brain Sciences* 10, 736-751.

____1995: *Relevance*. Second edition. Oxford: Basil Blackwell.

Stalnaker, R. 1984: *Inquiry*. Cambridge: MIT Press.

____1999: *Context and Content*. Oxford: Oxford University Press.

Suppes, P. 1985: "The Primacy of Utterer's Meaning." In *Philosophical Grounds of Rationality: Intentions, Categories, Ends*, ed. R. Grandy and R. Warner. Oxford, Clarendon Press.

Tomberlin, J., ed. 1994: *Philosophical Perspectives*, Vol. 8. Atascadero: Ridgeview.

Tversky, A. 1977: "Features of Similarity." *Psychological Review* 84, 327-352.

Vanderveken, D. 1991: "Non-Literal Speech Acts and Conversational Maxims." In *John Searle and His Critics*, ed. E. Lepore and R. Van Gulick. Oxford: Basil Blackwell.

Van Fraassen, B. 1980: *The Scientific Image*. Oxford: Clarendon Press.

Walker, R. 1975: "Conversational Implicatures." In *Meaning, Reference, and Necessity*, ed. S. Blackburn, 133-181. Cambridge: Cambridge University Press.

____1989: "Review of *Relevance*." *Mind and Language* 4, 151-159.

Wilson, D. 1994: "Relevance and Understanding." In *Language and Understanding*, ed. G. Brown, K. Malmkjaer, A. Pollitt, and J. Williams. Oxford: Oxford University Press.

Wilson, D., and Sperber, D. 1981: "On Grice's Theory of Conversation." In *Conversation and Discourse*, ed. P. Werth. London: Croom Helm.

____1986: "Inference and Implicature." In *Meaning and Interpretation*, ed. C. Travis. Oxford: Basil Blackwell.

____1993: "Linguistic Form and Relevance." *Lingua* 90, 1-25.

Wilson, E. 1992: *The Diversity of Life*. Cambridge: Harvard University Press.

Wittgenstein, L. 1953: *Philosophical Investigations*. New York: Macmillan.

Yu, P. 1979: "On the Gricean Program About Meaning." *Linguistics and Philosophy* 3, 273-288.

Ziff, P. 1967: "On H. P. Grice's Account of Meaning." *Analysis* 28, 1-8.

Zwicky, A., and Sadock, J. 1975: "Ambiguity Tests and How to Fail Them." In *Syntax and Semantics* 4, ed. J. Kimball. New York: Academic Press.

INDEX